Advance Praise for
Big Little Breakthroughs

"As a seasoned entrepreneur and investor, Josh Linkner knows that innovation rarely happens in a blinding flash of inspiration. With engaging stories and rich examples, he shows how ordinary ideas can fuel extraordinary results."

—**Adam Grant,** *New York Times* bestselling author of *Think Again* and *Originals*, and host of the chart-topping TED podcast *WorkLife*

"*Big Little Breakthroughs* sets the new standard for using creativity in everyday life. Inspiring stories, fascinating research, and a practical guide that shows how all of us can be everyday innovators."

—**Mel Robbins,** *New York Times* bestselling author of *The 5 Second Rule* and star of *The Mel Robbins Show*

"*Big Little Breakthroughs* provides a clear path to help you build an army of everyday innovators, and turn ideas into action."

—**Steve Case,** CEO, Revolution; co-founder and former CEO, AOL

"*Big Little Breakthroughs* is a work of creative genius. Josh Linkner unlocks the techniques behind some of the world's most remarkable innovations and shows how those techniques are there for the taking—accessible to anyone curious enough to set aside old ways and find out just how creative they can be."

—**Eric Schurenberg,** CEO, Fast Company & Inc.

"Here's a secret that the top business schools don't want you to know: everyone has the ability to be an innovator. With the tools and practices found in *Big Little Breakthroughs*, you'll learn how to unleash your inner creativity and apply it to everything you do. With never-before-told stories of everyday innovators from across the globe, Josh Linkner inspires us to contribute to our communities through our creativity."

—**Vijay Govindarajan,** *New York Times* bestselling author of *The Three-Box Solution* and the Coxe Distinguished Professor at Dartmouth College's Tuck School of Business

"Building a culture of innovation in large companies is critically important, and there's no better way to learn than with a trusted roadmap of tools and real-life examples. *Big Little Breakthroughs* illustrates how innovative thinking is possible for every employee and business leader, so we can all unlock our full creative potential."

—**Mike Kaufmann,** CEO, Cardinal Health

"This is a terrific book. It could change the way you approach your creative practice. Don't hesitate, it's worth your time."

—**Seth Godin,** *New York Times* bestselling author

"This is a masterclass on creativity from one of the most creative people I've ever met. The stories are compelling, the steps are clear, and the advice is hard fought from thirty years of building up companies and individuals. Josh Linkner continues to shine when it comes to creating actionable advice for people like you and me."

—**Jon Acuff,** *New York Times* bestselling author of *Do Over, Finish,* and *Soundtracks*

"A true breakthrough in the study and practice of innovation. Josh Linkner makes human creativity accessible in a practical way for leaders who are driven to accelerate growth despite breathtaking change."

—**Mark C. Thompson,** world's #1 CEO coach and *New York Times* bestselling author

"I've had the pleasure of sharing the stage with Josh Linkner and he's the real deal. This book is littered with bright light bulb ideas that will inspire a-ha moments!"

—**Johnny Cupcakes,** top innovator in retail, keynote speaker, and CEO of the world's first T-shirt bakery

"Josh has created a roadmap for injecting innovation into everyday life and everyday business. He brings you actionable advice, inspiring stories, and even some laugh-out-loud moments. If you want to unlock your inner creative, this book is for you!"

—**Peter McGraw,** Ph.D., director of the Humor Research Lab at University of Colorado and author of *Shtick to Business*

"*Big Little Breakthroughs* provides a blueprint to a culture of innovation and achievement. When teams get more creative, they perform better and enjoy far better outcomes. In our highly competitive world, this book delivers the edge we're all looking for."

—**John Foley,** former lead Blue Angels pilot
and *New York Times* bestselling author

"Organizations that equip every single team member to become innovators are the ones that win over the long term. *Big Little Breakthroughs* delivers a powerful framework that will unlock hidden creativity in order to drive growth, innovation, and sustainable success. It will undoubtedly become the new standard for everyday innovation."

—**Duncan Wardle,** former head of innovation and creativity, Disney

"An adventure worth taking. *Big Little Breakthroughs* shows us how to inject innovation into our daily lives through captivating stories, surprising research, and practical tools that are easy to implement. It's my new field guide for creativity."

—**Alison Levine,** team captain of the first American Women's Everest Expedition, *New York Times* bestselling author, and professor at United States Military Academy, West Point

"*Big Little Breakthroughs* is the ideal mix of academic rigor and practical application. The book provides a systematic framework to harness and maximize both individual and organization creativity in order to boost results. Inspiring stories reinforce the point that we can all be innovators, regardless of our background or job function."

—**David Brophy, Ph.D.,** professor of finance, University of Michigan Ross School of Business; founding director, Center for Venture Capital and Private Equity Finance

"Josh is a wonderfully engaging storyteller who masterfully folds entrepreneurial tales into little meringue-like peaks of inspiration. *Big Little Breakthroughs* is a perfect potion for those I-can't-do-it blues."

—**Neil Pasricha,** *New York Times* bestselling author of *The Happiness Equation* and *You Are Awesome*

"Beginning with a single microscopic idea, each of us has the power to create the change we seek. *Big Little Breakthroughs* flips innovation on its head with POWERFUL and practical advice for anyone looking to up their everyday innovation."

—**Tiffani Bova,** global growth and innovation evangelist, Salesforce; *WSJ* bestselling author of *Growth IQ*

"*Big Little Breakthroughs* provides an insightful framework for innovation and creativity by demonstrating how small is big and humble is bold."

—**Dr. Kent Fuchs,** president, University of Florida

BIG
LITTLE
BREAKTHROUGHS

HOW SMALL, EVERYDAY INNOVATIONS
DRIVE OVERSIZED RESULTS

JOSH LINKNER

Post Hill
PRESS

Post Hill Press
New York • Nashville
posthillpress.com

Published in the United States of America
1 2 3 4 5 6 7 8 9 10

To my two grandmothers,
whom I miss dearly.

Mickey, for teaching me
the love of language.

And Ronnie, for teaching me
that anything's possible.

"Great things are done by
a series of small things brought together."

—VINCENT VAN GOGH

Contents

Introduction

As the hurried shopkeeper navigated the crowded London sidewalk, his right hand began the habitual sequence of flicking his nearly finished cigarette butt onto the cobblestone street. But just before launching the smoldering projectile, a bright yellow object caught his eye. Clutching his fast-fading cigarette, he was drawn toward the edge of the sidewalk on Villiers Street to discover a glowing yellow container mounted at eye level on an aluminum post.

In large black letters on the lemon-yellow box, a question was posed: "Who's your favorite superhero, Batman or Superman?" To vote his allegiance to the Man of Steel, the storekeeper inserted his cigarette butt into the small opening under his hero's name. He watched his nicotine-stained filter fall into the receptacle, behind the glass front, and land atop a mound of others, piling high on one side of the bin. Realizing that his hero was, in fact, in the lead over the Caped Crusader, a nearly undetectable smile rose in the corner of his tightly closed jaw. The merchant rushed off to open his store, barely realizing that he'd broken his morning routine of littering in the crowded streets.

While each butt is less than an inch long, cigarette remnants are the single biggest litter problem in the UK. In central London alone, the annual cost to clean up and properly dispose of cigarette butts is over $1.4 million. Worldwide, an estimated 4.5 billion cigarette butts are thrown on the ground each year, releasing harmful toxins and creating a serious hazard for children or wildlife that may ingest them. They are the largest source of marine litter, outranking both plastic straws and plastic bags.

Enter Trewin Restorick, an environmental activist who uses his creativity to help the planet. With a dry British wit, he reminds me of a slightly disheveled James Bond who traded in his overpriced tuxedo for a pair of faded jeans. He's the kind of guy you'd love to spend a couple of hours with at a neighborhood pub, savoring his stories as much as the cold pints and warm chips (or as Londoners prefer, warm pints and cold chips). He's neither a world-famous inventor nor an artistic luminary.

Trewin, in fact, is one of us. Just like you and me.

Staring down the cigarette litter problem with the intensity of a pistol duel, he just knew the problem could be solved. Lacking an aristocratic trust fund or benevolent benefactor, Trewin tapped into the universal resource that we all share: the great equalizer of human creativity. His invention—the Ballot Bin—challenged people to "vote with their butts."

The fluorescent-yellow Ballot Bins are made from powder-coated steel with a bonded glass front and can be mounted on a pole, wall, or railing. The funky ashtrays are customizable, allowing for any two-answer question such as "Brexit, yes or no?", "Would you rather watch the Grand Prix or the US Open?", "Favorite food, pizza or hamburgers?", or "Trump's hair, real or fake?" Smokers then vote by putting their cigarette butts in the slot beneath their preference, immediately seeing a tally of which option is in the lead.

While other efforts to decrease cigarette pollution have largely been ineffective, the Ballot Bin reduces litter by up to 80 percent on city streets. A video of the first receptacle on London's Villiers Street reached more than six million people in just forty-five days. Today, the inventive ashtrays are used in twenty-seven countries, making a significant impact on the global environment.

The Ballot Bin didn't take years to develop or millions to fund. It wasn't designed by a team of lab coat–wearing super geniuses or Silicon Valley tech wizards. In fact, Trewin's Ballot Bin is a *Big Little Breakthrough*.

Big Little Breakthroughs are small creative acts that unlock massive rewards over time. They are the sparks that fuse into a raging fire. Sometimes microscopic and invisible to the naked eye, they are the molecules that bind together to solve our trickiest problems and unlock our biggest opportunities. *Big Little Breakthroughs* are the unsung heroes that, in the aggregate, drive far more progress than their elusive change-the-world counterparts.

Throughout this book, we'll travel the globe to explore the stories of everyday innovators like Trewin Restorick. We'll examine cutting-edge research, dispel common myths, and bust down barriers that seem impenetrable. We'll also study the habits of well-known creative luminaries such as Lady Gaga, Steven Spielberg, and the mysterious artist Banksy to decode their habits and borrow from their approaches. We'll explore the dramatic ups and downs of celebrity entrepreneurs, leaders of iconic global brands, and mad-scientist inventors.

To discover surprising truths, we'll go behind the scenes of a high-tech chemistry lab in Santa Barbara, a punk rock concert in Berlin, a greasy burger joint in Manhattan, and a disaster-relief effort in Nepal. We'll even visit a Texas prison and New

Zealand yacht racing team. All to uncover a practical approach to unleashing your own creative potential.

But this book isn't only about stories and science. For me, this book is personal.

From an early age, I always felt a bit odd. If there were twenty kids in the room, I felt like the outcast misfit. To be clear, I didn't feel superior. Quite the opposite, I was filled with self-doubt and insecurity. I just felt weird most of the time, and still do.

Yet developing creative skill became my salvation. It powered my successes and helped me bounce back from my many defeats. Creativity is who I am, not because I was born with creative chops but because I deliberately developed them over time. You may still be skeptical, but together we'll see how creativity can be learned, just like math or tennis or Jazzercise.

I discovered the *Big Little Breakthroughs* framework through nearly thirty years of research and practical experience. I've personally used these principles to start and sell tech companies, launch a venture capital fund, perform as a working jazz musician around the world, and raise four beautiful and quirky kids. The ideas we'll explore together are simple, practical, and accessible. Take it from a kid who was born in the city of Detroit…these concepts can absolutely work for you.

Like me, Trewin Restorick was no creative prodigy. "I was definitely not one of their best students," he tells me about his university days as we sat down to chat over a pot of extra-dark coffee. Trewin grew up in a working-class family and didn't demonstrate exceptional promise as a kid. After barely graduating college and carrying a mountain of student debt, he returned to his home of Plymouth, a shipyard town in southwest England. He landed a gig with the local municipality, helping to train unskilled workers to find new jobs during a period of particularly high unemployment. He lived a pretty normal life by all accounts, just trying to pay the bills and make it through the week.

But there was a little flicker inside him, an instinct that his life could be something more. Perhaps you recognize that feeling and have a similar spark of your own right now. For Trewin, he'd been drawn toward environmental causes from a very young age. He had a deep love for nature and felt somehow compelled to help make a difference in our increasingly polluted world.

Although he lacked any training or experience in the environmental sector, Trewin began doing volunteer work to help clean up his hometown. The more he got involved, the more he wanted to make activism his new career. He decided to take the plunge in 2013 when he founded a small nonprofit called Hubbub. "We had no money but had massive ambition," he reminisces. "I was determined to make it work."

Trewin's primary asset was human creativity, a resource that we all share but too often remains dormant. Instead of dealing in monetary donations to tackle complex environmental challenges, imagination was Trewin's primary currency. "Our mission is to make everybody an environmentalist, whether he or she knows it or not," he explained.

To move his mission forward, Trewin carefully studied traditional environmental charities and quickly found the flaws. Typical programs use guilt in an attempt to compel supporters to cough up donations. The causes often feel too abstract, a key reason why most efforts fall flat. In contrast, Trewin saw an opportunity to make activism fun, accessible, and easy. The Ballot Bin was lighthearted and simple, which is why the pint-sized idea drove such an oversized result.

Through a series of *Big Little Breakthroughs*, Trewin's Hubbub gained momentum. One time, they installed small speakers inside public garbage cans in a busy town square to encourage people on the street to properly dispose of their trash. Would you litter when you can put your empty coffee cup into a trash can that thanks you in a funny voice or burps after you deposit your no-longer-needed shopping bag?

Today, Hubbub has nearly one hundred full-time employees, thousands of volunteers, and major corporate backing and is making a significant environmental impact in thirty countries around the world. But we can't forget that it began just a few years ago in a small seaport town by a normal guy with a big dream.

Funny enough, Trewin didn't originally think of himself as especially creative. "I guess in my mind, a creative person was somebody who was a brilliant artist or maybe someone who could act. I felt the creative people were all in creative industries, and I knew that definitely wasn't me." Yet his success only materialized when he expanded his definition of what it meant to be creative, unlocking his imagination in order to achieve.

Big Little Breakthroughs aren't just for propeller-head inventors, fancy pants CEOs, or hoodie-donning tech billionaires. Instead, they enable every one of us to become an artist in our own way. Whether you're old or young, a Stanford MBA or high school dropout, *Big Little Breakthroughs* can help you grow into the person you're meant to become, in the same way they enabled Trewin to realize his vision.

In our time together, we'll dispel the myth that innovation is only for C-suite execs, senior-level R&D leaders, and marketing savants. Instead, we'll see how a healthy dose of creativity can be injected into every functional area, pesky problem, and box on the org chart.

The approaches we'll discover aren't just for prodigies with multiple Ivy League degrees and celebrity connections. Quite the opposite. In fact, the *Big Little Breakthroughs* framework is innovation *for the rest of us*.

It's for Trewin Restorick.

It's for the customer service rep who wants to contribute more and get a promotion.

It's for the lawyer who wants to win more cases.

It's for the startup that's looking to take on industry giants.

It's for the dentist who wants to grow her practice and serve more patients.

It's for the multinational corporation trying to gain competitive advantage against other industry giants.

It's for the family-owned business hoping to lock in a path to sustainable success.

It's for the new college grad trying to stand out in a competitive workforce.

It's for the small business owner who wants to break into the next category of growth.

It's for the leader of a company in a developing country that's trying to compete in the global markets.

It's for the architect trying to boost his practice by producing more inventive designs.

It's for the church leader seeking to drive change in his community.

It's for the achievement junkie looking to take her game to the next level.

It's for the factory foreman who seeks creative ways to drive efficiency and boost safety in the manufacturing process.

It's for the high school basketball coach trying to discover new tactics for her team to win a state championship.

It's for the playwright hoping to get her show funded on Broadway.

It's for the ad agency trying to land that big new account.

It's for high-potential up-and-comers.

It's for senior leaders and middle managers.

It's for entrepreneurs.

It's for dreamers and doers.

It's for us all.

Dots and Circles

In 1884, the now-legendary artists Georges Seurat and Paul Signac broke free from their conservative counterparts to pioneer a new painting technique called pointillism. Unlike the popular impressionist artists of the day who mixed their paints into thousands of individual hues before applying the paint in elegant brushstrokes onto the canvas, Seurat and Signac used small precise dots of pure, unmixed color as the basis of their revolutionary technique. Neither the paint mixture nor the application technique was remarkable at all, but when combined in a creative way, the small dots became the stunning masterpieces that have been studied and revered ever since.

The neo-impressionist movement of pointillism is a good way to think about *Big Little Breakthroughs*. Just like the cover of this book, each individual dot of color is actually pretty basic. You, me, or any self-respecting seven-year-old could easily produce a purple or yellow dot with ease. Yet as one dot fuses with the next, they coalesce into a work of art that has texture, depth, and meaning. The masterpiece, therefore, is the assembly of lots and lots of small creative pokes, not a singular imposing work of divine inspiration.

Together, we'll explore how to generate an abundance of microscopic creative flourishes that can add up to gigantic outcomes. We'll learn how to reverse-engineer the biggest breakthroughs imaginable, deconstructing them into their requisite bite-sized components. And by the end of our conversation, you'll be generating your own *Big Little Breakthroughs* with ease.

From Georges Seurat's *The River Seine at La Grande-Jatte* (oil on canvas, 1888) to Henri-Edmond Cross's *The Lake in the Bois de Boulogne* (oil on canvas, 1899), many of the most famous pointillism works depict the still waters of ponds and lakes. If you've ever been on a summer picnic, you'll recall what happens if you toss a small rock into the resting water. As the pebble breaks the water's surface, ripples emanate from the point of impact. A rock no bigger than a gumball can send circular swells all the way to the still shores in the distance.

As we learned in middle school, the ripple effect is the notion that a small disturbance can cascade into large-scale, pervasive impact. Seemingly small acts throughout history—such as Rosa Parks's refusal to give up her seat on an Alabama bus—have set into motion revolutionary movements and wide-sweeping transformation. As the rings of change radiate from their source, the littlest acts can lead to the largest achievements.

Think of a *Big Little Breakthrough* as that stone cast into a sleeping pond causing a chain of events to unfold on a distant shore. Beginning with a single microscopic idea, each of us has the power to create the change we seek. Throughout this book, we'll explore how remarkable successes were once nothing more than a small pebble colliding with a tranquil lake.

Not Giving Up My Shot

The thunderous applause was deafening. I could feel my heart pounding through my chest as I leapt to my feet alongside 2,192 other wide-eyed fans. I had chills.

It was the fall of 2015 and I knew I'd just witnessed history. The standing ovation continued for so long that my hands became numb from clapping so much. The scene was the historic Richard Rodgers Theatre in New York City where my wife, Tia, and I had just experienced *Hamilton*.

A breathtaking performance of the Founding Fathers engaged in an epic battle of right and wrong, punctuated by hip-hop music, expressive modern dance, and nonwhite historical figures, instantly propelled the musical to become one of the most successful Broadway shows of all time.

Hamilton racked up eleven Tony Awards, a Pulitzer Prize, a Grammy, and a Billboard Music Award. *Rolling Stone* and *Billboard* both featured the music in their Best Albums of 2015 issues, and the *New Yorker* labeled the show as "an achievement of historical and cultural reimagining." It broke the single-week Broadway box office record in November 2016 with $3.3 million earned in just eight performances. By January 2020, total box office sales eclipsed $625 million, making it the seventh most successful Broadway show in history. In July 2020, Disney anteed up $75 million to broadcast the musical on its Disney+ streaming service.

Getting tickets to *Hamilton* was about as easy as catching a barehanded fly ball from the bleachers at a Yankees game. And if you were lucky enough to score a seat, you'd shell out as much as $2,500 for the privilege.

Hamilton wasn't created by Broadway royalty such as Andrew Lloyd Webber or Stephen Sondheim. Instead, it's the work of Lin-Manuel Miranda, who was just thirty-five years old when the show opened to sold-out crowds. He wrote his first Broadway hit, *In the Heights*, before he was old enough to order a beer.

With such remarkable success at such a young age, it's easy to think of Miranda as a natural-born legend. The one-in-a-million virtuoso who won the creative lotto at birth. The Beethoven of his day. We conclude his otherworldly talents were imbued by the gods and that his angelic gift is completely out of reach for us mere mortals.

Yet his story is nothing like you'd imagine. In fact, Lin-Manuel Miranda is surprisingly more like Trewin Restorick than you may think.

Miranda was born to immigrant parents and grew up in Inwood, a working-class Hispanic neighborhood of New York City. He was an awkward kid, often unsure of himself and frequently an outcast. He had pimples. He was bullied. His girlfriend dumped him. He didn't get picked first (or even third) for the football team. He didn't attend the Juilliard School.

In fact, Lin-Manuel was just like you and me in so many ways. And he still is.

"Anytime you write something, you go through so many phases. You go through the 'I'm a fraud' phase. You go through the 'I'll never finish' phase," said Miranda in 2018, long after his extraordinary rise. "Sometimes the writing doesn't happen as fast as I'd like it to. I have a hard time finding the balance between not beating myself up and not wasting time while I wait for it to happen."

That's right. This legendary creative force struggles, just like we all do.

It took Miranda a long time to find his voice. He worked at his craft, bit by bit, in the same way a welder learns her trade. He composed lousy music. He wrote stories that were awful. He had hundreds of ideas that fell flat. He has bad days and good days, and then more bad days. He was plagued by doubt and uncertainty, anxiety and fear. He wasn't conceived a creative genius; he *grew to become one.*

And if he could grow into it, *what if we all could?*

Having studied many of the most celebrated inventors, entrepreneurs, musicians, and artists, I learned that breakthrough creativity is more like a magic trick than wizardry. The wizard has innate powers, allowing him to cast spells and live for a thousand years (not to mention, grow one hell of a beard). A magician, on the other hand, *appears* to create magic but actually has no inherent special powers. David Blaine is an illusionist—not a wizard—enthralling his audiences with seemingly impossible feats, all while possessing no actual magical capabilities. In fact, he learned and practiced a skill that, when performed at high levels, appears magical.

That's exactly how human creativity works. It's a universal skill that can be learned rather than a biological advantage only bestowed upon a select few. From Beyoncé to Jimi Hendrix, Henry Ford to Elon Musk, Pablo Picasso to Georgia O'Keeffe, master creators are people who develop and practice their crafts. While they may possess some natural talent, their achievements are far more the result of their habits than their DNA.

Imagine how tragic it would be if Lin-Manuel never cultivated his talents and shared his creativity with the world. No *Hamilton*, no Academy Award, no *In the Heights*, no soundtrack to *Moana*. Not only would the world miss his incredible music, but think what a waste it would be if he'd never pursued his calling. Imagine how unfulfilled he'd be had he taken a menial job just to pay the bills. Thankfully, Lin-Manuel refused to give up his shot, just like immigrant-turned-Founding-Father Alexander Hamilton refused to give up his own.

The Surprising Power of Little Ideas

The pressure to generate big ideas can feel overwhelming. We know that bold innovations are critical in these disruptive and competitive times, but when it comes to breakthrough thinking, we often freeze up.

Instead of shooting for a $10 billion IPO or a Nobel Prize, the most effective innovators focus instead on something much smaller. According to Harvard University professor Stefan Thomke, 77 percent of economic growth is attributed to small creative advances, not radical innovations. While change-the-world transformations are sexy, it's the understated *Big Little Breakthroughs* that drive our economy.

Our fifth-grade Little League coach demanded that we swing for the fences, which is the exact opposite approach we should take if we want to become more innovative. (Incidentally, I achieved the game-losing strikeout using this strategy on the last game of the season, officially ending my pursuit of baseball glory.) Instead, developing a daily habit of creativity is the ideal, albeit counterintuitive, route. Small creative acts not only drive a high volume of little wins, but daily practice is the fastest route to discover the massive breakthroughs we seek.

The *Big Little Breakthroughs* framework provides a specific and practical approach to unlocking dormant creative capacity. Instead of wild, risky, and expensive moonshots, you'll learn how to unleash little, daily creative sparks that drive gigantic results over time. You'll see how cultivating high volumes of micro-innovations builds the much-needed skills that lead to colossal transformations and the creative confidence to take responsible risks.

In **Part One**, we'll examine human creativity under the microscope. We'll dissect and demystify the creative process, learning from neuroscientists, billionaires, nerdy researchers, and even a convicted felon. We'll dive into the need for creative problem solving and inventive thinking in all roles and walks of life. We'll also explore how to build creative muscle mass, one small step at a time.

By the end of Part One, the foundation will be set. You'll understand how creativity works, where innovation comes from, and how to develop your own skills. The myths will be busted, the blockers will be removed, and the poisonous voices of complacency will be silenced. You'll be energized and may even feel a little punch-drunk, ready to rocket your abilities to the next level.

Part Two delivers a systematic framework for inventive thinking and creative problem solving. We'll explore the *Eight Obsessions of Everyday Innovators* through the stories of legends and misfits, heroes and troublemakers. We'll reveal their mindsets, learn their secrets, and steal...er...I mean...*borrow* their tactics.

Simply put, Part Two will give you all the tools you need to blast off. You'll be inspired, entertained, and equipped with a new tool kit to harness and deploy *Big Little Breakthroughs* as a powerful competitive advantage. You'll laugh, you'll be surprised, and you'll even snag some fresh material to try out at cocktail parties.

You can also access a trove of bonus material at BigLittle-Breakthroughs.com/toolkit. This online tool kit includes a Quick Start guide, a summary of key points by chapter, downloadable worksheets, reference material, team exercises, and a *Big Little Breakthroughs* cheat sheet.

In our time together, I'm hoping you'll consider an upgrade. Upgrades are pervasive in our lives, from the new mobile phone with a 117-megapixel camera to that must-have liquefying blender. We upgrade our laptops, minivans, and lawnmowers. At work, we upgrade our manufacturing equipment, office furniture, and the food for the annual summer picnic. In our personal lives, we work hard to upgrade our relationships, health, and neighborhoods. And as we explore the power of *Big Little Breakthroughs*, let's set our sights on a Creativity Upgrade.

For starters, I don't recommend trying to leap too quickly from rigid-rule-follower to raucous-and-racy-Rembrandt. Instead, consider a *5 percent Creativity Upgrade*—a growth spurt that is completely accessible to us all. Expanding your creative capacity by just 5 percent can translate into a disproportionally massive boost in your overall performance. Your *5 percent Creativity Upgrade* will not only help you earn more, it will help you get more out of all the areas of life that matter most. And a 5 percent upgrade is completely within your grasp.

Together, let's dispel the myths, unpack the science, and embrace the inventive mindset. Let's unleash a torrent of *Big Little Breakthroughs* to fuel the progress we seek. And let's have some fun along the way.

So, grab your double espresso, and let's dive in.

PART ONE

LIGHTNING IN A BOTTLE

CHAPTER 1

Decoding the A-HA

After completing her intense daily workout, Caron Proschan craved something refreshing. Coming off the high of her exercise routine, she gulped down some purified water and then reached for her trusty pack of gum. But something just didn't add up.

Caron was passionate about living a healthy lifestyle, eating organic foods, and caring for the environment. Pulling the crumpled, stale gum package from her musky gym bag, she felt perplexed. Why was her favorite gum so synthetic that it could survive a direct hit from a 41,000-pound nuclear warhead? As Caron looked down at the glowing neon package of gum in her athletic hand, the disconnect was jarring. Alien blue is not a shade generally found in nature, after all.

As someone who valued clean living, Caron was frustrated. Why must something that's supposed to be refreshing have the nutritional value of a half-eaten Twinkie? Racing up the stairs of her Brooklyn apartment, she couldn't wait to search online for a healthier alternative. If there were organic, non-GMO, free-range, grass-fed, all-natural, ethically raised pomegranate seeds, there just *had* to be a healthy gum option.

Shocked at what she found—well, more like what she didn't find—Caron had a big idea. What if she started a healthy gum company to make a product with all-natural ingredients that would satisfy the tastes and preferences of those who prefer wheatgrass shots and acai bowls over vodka shots and three-bean chili? From the colors to the ingredients to the eco-hazardous packaging, there's nothing natural about most elements of the $26 billion global chewing gum industry, so Caron decided to change all that.

A dream—and a startup—was born. It was simply called: Simply Gum.

Over the years, I've been fascinated with the mythical a-ha moment—those magical instants that change the world. Where do these ideas come from? Why do some people generate more a-has than others? Do breathtaking ideas only come from super-genius savants and protégé artists? Is there a way for everyday people like you and me to generate more and better ideas?

In this chapter, we're going to put the idea-creation process under the microscope. We'll explore how the human brain forms new ideas so we can understand the psychology of ideation and learn how creative conception actually occurs. Together, let's decode the human a-ha.

Back to that moment in Caron's tiny kitchen when her newborn idea took its first breath of life, the initial spark alone could have easily been extinguished like so many others that appear on the high-def technicolor screens of our minds. It could have been one of those flashes that was quickly discarded, considering Caron had zero industry experience, capital, manufacturing know-how, or distribution contacts.

But because it was protected, nurtured, and developed, the idea took root. First, Caron had to learn all she could about the gum industry. She learned that 60 percent of the entire global market is controlled by two multinational giants, Wrigley and Cadbury. She learned that the US Food and Drug Administration (FDA) allows manufacturers to list "gum base" as a catch-all ingredient, but upon further exploration it turns out this vague description covers more than eighty synthetic ingredients, including plastic. The more she learned about gum, the more she agreed with the old adage of never swallowing a piece.

She had a cause: healthy gum. She had an enemy: the gum industry oligopoly. Now she just needed...um....a product, a brand, a process, a team, capital, a manufacturing facility, distribution, packaging, inventory, equipment, and enough profit to buy a couple batches of cold pressed kale-lemon-celery-carrot juice to keep her moving. She had to walk, chew gum, and get extremely creative all at the same time.

With no formal training or fancy equipment, Caron began to experiment in her kitchen, which wasn't much bigger than the packs of gum she was hoping to produce. The idea for a healthy gum came quickly, but figuring out how to actually make the stuff took her over a year of green tea–fueled late nights. She undertook thousands of experiments using every natural ingredient you can imagine.

To ditch the plastic and still offer the right chew and elasticity, constant tinkering led her to an alternative approach using chicle, the milky sap from the Central American sapodilla tree. In order to produce an end product that had the right texture with a delicious flavor while lasting long enough to compete with other gums, the a-ha of her initial idea became more complicated than inventing a new procedure to treat chronic rheumatoid arthritis.

"I don't have a chemistry background; I can barely even cook. It definitely was a leap for me to decide to just make it on my own in my kitchen," Caron told me as we sat down over sparkling mineral water. "I just started tinkering and experimenting, and it was very tedious. I had no idea what I was doing, but sure enough, one year later, I finally was able to create a formula that tasted like real gum."

The gum was biodegradable, a claim that no major competitor could make. It had no artificial flavors or ingredients, polluting neither the body nor the environment. In an industry that had seen little innovation in decades, Caron had set out to reinvent gum the way the Wright brothers set out to reinvent transportation.

Realizing that she could finally make the gum itself, her challenges were far from over. So often, the process of innovation is like the game of whack-a-mole: knock down one obstacle, and three new hurdles pop right up. Gum foundation conquered; now on to flavor.

Most gums offer the obvious and predicable flavor options such as cool mint or cotton candy. Simply Gum, instead, offers natural flavors such as Ginger, Maple, and Fennel. Caron even invented her own flavor combos such as Cleanse (grapefruit, prickly pear, cayenne, and sea salt), Boost (lemongrass, turmeric, and cayenne), and Revive (lime, chili, and sea salt).

Great gum, fun flavors…but you can only make so much gum on a two-burner stovetop in a walk-up kitchen. The obvious solution would be to outsource manufacturing, considering the high costs of machinery, labor, and real estate. Manufacturing is a messy business full of safety hazards and equipment malfunctions. Naturally Caron rejected tradition, opting instead to build her own manufacturing facility in Brooklyn.

"I didn't have any manufacturing experience and so it was a steep learning curve," Caron told me. "But making the gum is such an important part of what we do, and no one else can make it the way that we do. Even now, people ask if we could train someone else to do it. That would certainly be easier, but having our own manufacturing plant gives us a level of control, it gives us a level of flexibility that we wouldn't have if we used a co-manufacturer or a third party. I'm very glad that we're doing it ourselves. It's proving to be a competitive advantage."

At this point, she could actually make a decent product. But Caron didn't set out just to produce gum; she was determined to actually create a company, requiring many more ideas to launch and thrive. The raw material for her gum base may have been from a sapodilla tree, but the raw material for her fledgling businesses was imagination. Lots of it. Next up on the innovation docket: packaging.

Wanting a highly differentiated, modern, inviting, and upscale look, she decided to design the packaging herself, despite the fact that she had no design training or experience. "I think the best thing we did was to not use any sort of agency that does CPG [consumer packaged goods] products because they most likely would have just come up with another version of what was already out there," she told me with a beaming smile. "I think that by looking at it as an outsider and thinking about it totally out of the box, I was able to come up with a product and package that didn't look like what was already available, which served us really well. My inspiration was Apple and the fact that their packaging was almost universal in its appeal, equally appealing to both males and females, to every kind of age group and demographic."

After hundreds of concepts, failures, and missteps, the final package is worthy of display at the Museum of Modern Art. With its gorgeous, clean matte white box with photographic images of raw ingredients, you won't confuse Simply Gum for a pack of Bubble Yum. The label includes every single all-natural ingredient in the gum rather than hiding behind the cloak of an FDA term that was likely developed over expensive dinners in wood-paneled steakhouses hosted by pinstripe-suit-clad lobbyists. "There are some innovations in the packaging as well," Caron explains. "There are little wrapping papers that are tucked into the back of the package for quick and clean disposal when you're done chewing. People love them. Because how many times have you been in a situation where you need to dispose of your gum but can't find a napkin?"

But a tasty natural gum and sleek packaging still wasn't enough. How does a solo-preneur with no industry contacts get her gum on store shelves? Caron explains, "I didn't have relationships at Target or Kroger. I knew that we weren't going to start that way. It was really going to be hustling, going door to door and starting at the smallest local level. I went to the Whole Foods in Columbus Circle here in New York and at that time, local stores were allowed to make individual buying decisions. It took another seven or eight months for me to convince the buyer in that single store to stock the product."

After two hard years of hustle, rejection, and too many nights in sketchy motels, Caron started to build meaningful distribution.

Once Simply Gum was stocked in the obvious places, Caron continued to break free of conventional thinking, seeking out nontraditional locations to sell her gum unlike her clunky giant competitors. Simply Gum is now the only gum offered in specialty stores like Urban Outfitters, Cost Plus, and Anthropologie. She also sells the gum direct-to-consumer from the Simply Gum website, a practice that was historically taboo in the gum industry.

Always bucking the trend and looking for creative approaches to grow her business, she embraced the dual strategy of selling both direct and through retailers. If there's a new way to get this natural gum in customers' hands, Caron is going to find it. Her product is now one of the top-selling gums on Amazon, for example, with a recent Prime Day boosting her sales by 1,327 percent in a single afternoon.

In 2017, Caron expanded into mints. Mints have a similar function—a refreshing way to boost your breath—so it made for the ideal extension. Just like gum, she had to once again figure out the product, packaging, flavors, manufacturing, and distribution. And once again, through a mix of creativity and grit, she nailed it.

Today, Simply Gum is simply thriving. The company's products are now on shelves in more than ten thousand retail stores, and it's the number one selling product in the natural gum category, which has since attracted a slew of copycats. Even fighting against deeply entrenched multibillion-dollar competitors, Caron figured out a way to launch, scale, and win.

Simply Gum wasn't just a solitary idea followed by mindless execution. Caron's success was based on hundreds of *Big Little Breakthroughs*. There was the initial idea for a healthy gum, followed by the idea to research and dissect the gum industry. The idea to use tree sap instead of plastic, followed by the idea of having coffee bean–flavored gum instead of Outrageous Orange. And the big idea to keep manufacturing internal along with the thousands of micro-innovations that enabled that to actually happen. The idea to sell both direct and through retailers; the idea and hustle to find a way into Whole Foods. The idea for upscale, gorgeous packaging and then to expand into mints.

With so many interconnected *Big Little Breakthroughs*, we envision Caron as a gifted creative prodigy. As a toddler, she was probably sitting at her highchair painting stunning seascapes out of pureed carrots while fluently speaking the Romance language she learned the prior Thursday.

Yet even after her incredible success, Caron still didn't consider herself a creative person when I complimented her ingenuity. "It's funny that you say that. I actually still to this day don't necessarily think of myself as creative, but I suppose I am. I was not traditionally creative growing up. I didn't really have any creative hobbies. No music, no painting, no art. I think that it's manifested itself in this other way, which is to make gum. And that's really, I guess, how I've expressed my creativity. And you are right: designing a company, designing organizations, designing teams, all of that is actually a creative endeavor. I think that it's really only now that I've kind of come into that and realized that."

Caron's story is fascinating to me on so many levels. She built a wildly successful company in a highly competitive industry, with no experience, capital, or formal training. She wasn't handed anything and had to figure it out for herself, against overwhelmingly difficult odds. Her achievement was not only based on a single idea but by innovating in every aspect of her business. And her ability to win at the highest levels was driven by dozens of smaller creative feats, all while she didn't consider herself to be an especially creative person.

Caron Proschan's epic quest for gum supremacy will serve as the backdrop for our exploration into how ideas are actually formed and how we can master the process of creating them.

Your Brain, On Creativity

When we hear stories about business builders like Simply Gum's Caron Proschan, or widely celebrated virtuosos like Lin-Manuel

Miranda for that matter, we immediately think these people must have some special gift that we normal folk are missing. As if the skies opened for a brief moment and the gods anointed a chosen few with heavenly powers. We're led to believe that we're either creative or we're not, and there's very little we can do about it.

This is what we've been told our whole lives. And it's dead wrong.

Over the last decade, neuroscientists have made massive leaps forward in understanding the human brain. Much of this bold discovery has been the result of advanced technology such as fMRI machines, providing history-making clarity and unlocking century-old mysteries about how the brain functions.

A key finding is the concept of *neuroplasticity*, now widely accepted in the scientific community. Until recently, the prevailing belief was that your brain was fixed. It was wired the way it was wired, and that was that. You've probably heard myths such as brain cells can't regenerate or that cognition is the result of a piece of static equipment, incapable of adapting or growing.

If your brain was the lawnmower you bought at a garage sale, there was nothing you could really do to upgrade it shy of replacing it entirely by shelling out $1,900 for a brand-new John Deere E120 42 in., 20 hp, V-twin Gas Hydrostatic Riding Mower (try discount code: *neuroplasticity*).

It turns out, the brain isn't at all like the old lawnmower that can't be rebuilt. It's more like the lawn itself. Your lawn is malleable, responding to changes in environment, fertilizer, pesticides, new seeds, and your neighbor's yappy brown poodle. If you never water your lawn, it turns to scorched earth. Leave it unprotected and it becomes a hideous weed field. But if you add new seeds, fertilizer, and irrigation, trimming—if you protect and care for it—your emerald-green lawn can become the envy of the subdivision. A lawn is something that responds to change; it can be grown or killed, thickened or depleted, beautified or polluted. With the right care, it can quickly bounce back from previous neglect, once again growing and thriving.

That is the essence of the incredible breakthrough of neuro-plasticity: your brain isn't fixed...it can change, adapt, and grow. One of the least-technical definitions I found was from a 2017 article in the painfully dry scientific journal *Frontiers in Psychology: Auditory Cognitive Neuroscience*: "Neuroplasticity can be viewed as a general umbrella term that refers to the brain's ability to modify, change, and adapt both structure and function throughout life and in response to experience." (Pro tip: reading technical neuroscience research is an excellent cure for insomnia.)

What made bespectacled research scientists want to stand up from their lab desks to dance in a conga line? It was the proof that our brains can form new pathways, synapses, and connec-tions. We're not just talking learning; we're talking actual changes in brain chemistry and composition. Just as coal can transform into diamonds and snotty teenagers can eventually transform into tolerable human beings, your brain is something that can be shaped and developed.

Relating to your creativity, I'm taking a big leap here and coining a new phrase: *INNOplasticity*. (Should I disappear unex-pectedly, please notify the authorities to investigate the evil geniuses behind *Frontiers in Psychology: Auditory Cognitive Neuroscience*.)

Building on its big brother neuroplasticity, innoplasticity is the notion that your creativity is expandable just like your brain. Swapping out a few words from the above definition, think of innoplasticity as "a general umbrella term that refers to one's ability to modify, adapt, and grow creative capacity throughout life and in response to training, development, and experience."

Innoplasticity is a fancy way of saying that your creative potential is far greater than the creativity you had at birth, in eleventh grade, or even now. All of us can cultivate and improve our imagination, the same way brains—and front lawns—can transform for the better. Caron Proschan did it, and you can too. And these changes can happen much faster than you might think.

Awesome, Dude

Most of us have experienced that chills-down-your spine feeling of awe. The texture of handmade al dente pasta at La Darsena, an outdoor café in the lakefront town of Como, Italy. The dangerous acrobatics of a Cirque du Soleil performance during a hot Montreal summer. For me, seeing my newborn twins—Avi and Tallia—make it through 104 days in neonatal intensive care after being born fourteen weeks premature and each weighing only two pounds. (Today they are both happy, healthy, and hilarious four-year-olds.)

Moments of true awe are inspiring. It turns out, they also boost creativity.

In the Lombardy region of Italy, just seventy-four minutes by car from the aforementioned pasta, researchers conducted a study to gauge the impact of awe on creativity. Participants volunteered for the 2018 study, which was a joint effort between Università Cattolica del Sacro Cuore and Webster University Geneva.

Each participant was given a virtual reality headset and asked to watch a short film. Split into two randomly selected groups, half the participants were shown an awe-inspiring video that depicted stunning nature scenes—majestic redwood trees, dramatic cliffs descending into crashing waves in the ocean below, a rainbow of iridescent fish circling a coral reef. The less-lucky control group tried to stay awake while being shown an incredibly dull video of hens wandering the grass.

Immediately after viewing the videos, participants were asked to complete parts of the Torrance Test of Creative Thinking, widely considered to be the gold standard test for measuring creativity. The participants were an equal number of men and women, all from the same geographic region with similar educational backgrounds and work experience, so you'd expect each group to perform identically. Yet the simple step of experiencing awe or dullness had a massive impact on creative output. In fact, participants who first experienced awe crushed the other group with the ferocity that an NFL Pro Bowl team would smoke a group of high school freshmen.

The Torrance Test measures four components of creativity: fluency, flexibility, elaboration, and originality. In the experiment, the awe-inspired group outperformed the dullness group by 70 percent on fluency, 69 percent on flexibility, 79 percent on elaboration, and a whopping 114 percent on originality. When averaged together, the group that was nearly identical going in outperformed their peers by 83 percent simply by having an inspiring experience before attempting a creative task.

Whether or not a subject viewed themselves as creative before arriving, simply injecting a little awe into their consciousness boosted their creative performance by a country mile. How can such a small change to environment play such a gigantic role in output? The key insight: we already have an enormous reservoir of dormant creativity waiting to be unlocked. The high percentage increase indicates that the participants' ability was already there, since a new skill can't be learned and mastered so quickly. Instead, those abilities were hidden away, just waiting for someone to unlock the vault and let them out to play.

Researchers at Stanford University conducted a similar experiment back in 2014, inspired by one of their local heroes: Steve Jobs. Jobs wasn't only known for his business temper tantrums; most people who had a meeting with Steve found themselves walking instead of sitting. Accordingly, the Stanford team wondered if creativity was enhanced by going for a walk. Could a simple stroll be one of the keys to Jobs's brilliance?

The study of 176 students and adults tested how walking impacted creative output. Various walking experiments were conducted to explore how duration, scenery, weather, and companionship affected creativity. Immediately following the walks, participants were given divergent thinking tests, which involve coming up with a nonobvious use for an item. For example, after being shown a picture of a tire, a subject might suggest it could be used as a pinky ring for the Jolly Green Giant.

Researchers isolated walking from all other factors to determine the impact of strolling on creativity. The results: creative output increased by an average of 60 percent when the person was walking compared to sitting. Not .6 percent, not 6 percent, but *60 percent.*

In addition to getting people in a fresh environment and allowing them to zoom out during their walk, a likely factor of the creative boost is something called Brain Derived Neurotrophic Factor, or BDNF for short.

Harvard's Dr. John Ratey refers to BDNF as "Miracle-Gro for the brain." A family of proteins that gets released in the brain after exercise, BDNF binds to brain cells to keep them fresh and energized. Targeting the hippocampus region of the brain (a key area for creativity), the BDNF proteins stimulate neurogenesis. Said plainly, moving your body triggers BDNF production, which in turn stimulates a key part of the brain for imagination while playing a role in actually growing new brain cells.

Remember, Caron Proschan's initial a-ha moment emerged immediately following a workout. Accordingly, her BDNF rush may deserve some credit in Simply Gum's juicy success.

The Italy study of awe and the Stanford study of walking both demonstrate that a person's creativity is not fixed but instead can be influenced by external factors. And there are dozens of similar studies that show, one after the next, that levels of creativity are like your weight, not your height. I'm not likely to sprout eleven inches taller at the age of fifty, but my weight can expand or contract, based on the number of Krispy Kreme raspberry jelly doughnuts I wolf down per sitting.

Hey...Don't Steal My Imagination

Positive external factors can clearly boost creativity, but as you might expect, negative external factors can be depletive. Unfortunately, we are subjected to a seemingly endless stream of these negative factors, resulting in highly underutilized creativity muscles in most adults.

Back in 1968, Dr. George Land conducted a now famous experiment. After devising a creativity test for NASA to help select innovative scientists and engineers, he gave the same test to 1,600 children, ages three to five. He then retested the same kids at age ten and age fifteen. The test was designed to measure a subject's level of creativity over time, through the influence of external factors. The results were jaw-dropping:

Average test scores for three- to five-year-olds: 98 percent

Average test scores for ten-year-olds: 30 percent

Average test scores for fifteen-year-olds: 12 percent

Same test given to 280,000 adults: 2 percent

"What we have concluded," wrote Land, "is that non-creative behavior is learned." In the same way our minds can expand and learn to be more creative, most of us suffer the opposite phenomenon. Unfortunately, instead of growing *into* our creative ability, too many of us grow *out* of it. It's been said that we enter kindergarten with a full set of colorful crayons and tragically graduate high school with a single blue ballpoint pen.

Seeing stats like these are infuriating. In a world that needs our full creativity more than ever, we're allowing it to be suppressed. Examining why this occurs, it's really a combination of factors. Well-intentioned parents trying to look out for us rather than let us explore, a school system that was designed in an era when doctors smoked cigarettes during checkup exams, and bosses who are too busy protecting their positions in the hierarchy to create something new. Diving into the root causes of society's creative decay is a discussion for another day, but these factors are hard at work trying to find your imagination's power-off switch. It's up to each of us to fight back.

The ABCs of BLBs (Big Little Breakthroughs)

There's more confusion around the meaning of words like "innovation" than the chaos at the airline ticket counter after a cancelled flight. At this point, I think it makes sense for us all to be on the same page to make the most of our time together.

Let's start with *imagination*. Imagination is the raw material that can be formed into creativity and innovation. Think of imagination as our ability to envision anything new. Imagining the world's biggest skyscraper floating sideways in the Suez Cancel and covered in a 1980s pastel argyle pattern or an oddly shaped goat that can perform graduate-level trigonometry calculations are both examples of imagination. As far as I know, neither of these things exist in the actual world, so the fact that I'm describing them requires me to imagine them.

You'll notice that neither my skyscraper nor goat idea possesses even a shred of utility or value. While both are novel ideas, neither one will win me a Peabody Award. For imagination to move up the food chain into creativity, it has to have some inherent value.

When Avi (my four-year-old) pounds on my piano with the force of a sumo wrestler, he is doing something imaginative but not all that creative. He may play the same number of notes per minute as the legendary jazz pianist Herbie Hancock, but I'm afraid that Avi is not yet threatening Herbie for a gig at Carnegie Hall.

Next, we can define *creativity* as something that's imaginative (novel, fresh, new) and also has some inherent value. Herbie Hancock carefully selects which notes to play and how to play them, following a specific set of musical guidelines. He also decides what not to play, so his reasoning and judgment are involved as he creates music that will be appealing to others. Avi is more likely to color on the piano with a Sharpie or to explore how his PB&J sandwich may fit nicely between the keys. That's imaginative but not creative.

When creativity graduates to *innovation*, the element of "utility" enters the picture. In other words, does the creative act produce something useful? If I dump five buckets of neon paint on my wife Tia's car, that is imagination. But raw imagination without value or utility translates to me sleeping on the couch for six months. Now, if she always wanted a racing stripe on her car and I carefully painted flaming stripes in her favorite color, her desire for novelty combined with my shaky painting skills may qualify as something creative. Here, creativity is in the eye of the beholder. Tia would likely find her newly painted car to be an eyesore, while I may appreciate its artistic value. Creativity is subjective, to be sure, as is the case with music, sculpture, spoken-word poetry, and all other forms of art.

Following this one step forward, if I were able to invent a new paint compound that could change colors based on an electrical current, enabling car owners to choose their paint color each morning with a button on their dashboards, that would qualify as innovation. It would be useful, and the profits could help me fund some much-needed painting lessons.

Let's recap:

Imagination = *any new idea*
Creativity = *a new idea that has some value,*
   artistic or otherwise
Innovation = *a creative idea that has utility*

Does Size Matter?

For some reason, we've been taught that for creativity and innovation to count they need to have a magnitude the size of the 1989 San Francisco earthquake.

As you may recall, earthquakes are measured on something called the Richter scale. According to the *American Heritage*

Scientific Dictionary, the Richter scale is "a numerical scale for expressing the magnitude of an earthquake on the basis of seismograph oscillations." Simply put, the higher the number the more damage it does. The San Francisco earthquake was a monster, coming in at 6.9 on the Richter scale. But does that mean that the magnitude 5.8 earthquake that hit Puerto Rico in January 2020 didn't count? Whether a quake is a magnitude 9.0 (total devastation) or a magnitude 2.4 (barely felt), an earthquake is still an earthquake.

The same is true for innovation and creativity. Inventing a life-saving drug therapy is a bigger innovation than inventing a new doorbell that tells knock-knock jokes, but both are still considered to be innovative. My most recent jazz composition pales in artistic quality compared to Miles Davis's historic *Kind of Blue* album, but both are, in fact, creative.

Creativity researchers Dr. James C. Kaufman and Dr. Ronald Beghetto developed a clever structure called the 4C model. Think of it as the Richter scale of creativity. Their model begins with "mini-c," which are the baby steps of creativity. When my four-year-old Tallia shows me what she just made with finger paint, we can all agree this isn't going to be featured in the Louvre. This mini-c was still made with care, but it lacks the objective artistic value of a work by Joan Miró. That said, if Tallia is to become a famous artist, she'll develop her skills one mini-c at a time.

Next up is "little-c," Kaufman and Beghetto explain. Here, a creative work has perceived value beyond its creator. Three years from now, if Tallia's paintings are featured in the school newspaper and subsequently win a local award, she'll have graduated to little-c status. At this point, her work won't fetch $175,000 at auction, but hey…it's progress.

Moving on, we land on "Pro-c." Imagine Tallia earns her master's degree in artistic composition and, with a little commercial success, is able to stop waiting tables and pursue her art full-time. Clearly, the quality and value of her work has crossed into a professional level since she can now afford her 550-square-foot studio apartment and an occasional two-topping pizza.

Finally, we reach "Big-C," which is history-making. Rembrandt, Kahlo, Picasso. The artistic works that are the stuff of legends. The vast majority of highly talented professionals never reach this point, but it doesn't mean their work lacks value. Tallia could earn a wonderful living and have a meaningful artistic career despite never painting a Big-C masterpiece. Big-Cs are spectacular, to be sure, but too often this is the bar we set to consider something creative or not. If the reference point is the master work of Vincent van Gogh, no wonder most of us don't feel like we're creative.

The thing is, Georgia O'Keefe and Paul Cezanne didn't pop out of the womb as the masters they became. They ascended to Big-C in the same way every other artist, inventor, and musician did: they started with mini-c and worked their way up through practice. Da Vinci's first painting wasn't the *Mona Lisa*; da Vinci first had to learn to paint. The fact that every artist progresses from step to step should feel liberating. We can each grow into our full creative potential, one bad painting at a time.

The word "innovation" is even more loaded than creativity. If Henry Ford's invention of the assembly line is what it takes to be innovative, your new idea to save eleven seconds in the lunch line may feel awfully puny. Truth is, both ideas are innovative, just like any magnitude earthquake is still a seismic event.

I like to think of innovation in three flavors: INNOVATION (all caps), Innovation (capital I), and innovation (lower case).

INNOVATION in all caps is the big stuff. Inventing the electric guitar was an INNOVATION. Digging the Panama Canal, INNOVATION. The combustion engine? Yep. INNOVATION.

INNOVATION in all caps is much like Big-C creativity. We're talking life-altering, history-making legendary innovation. Movable type. Penicillin. Wireless communications.

But again, something doesn't need to reshape history to be innovative. One double-click beneath INNOVATION is Innovation (capital I). These are important innovations that each of us may discover once or twice a year, not once in one hundred lifetimes. Maybe it's a new product offering that helps boost revenue 28 percent in just six months. Or a new production process that creates a 13 percent cost savings. Capital I innovations are juicy and meaningful even though they may not have books written about them by future generations.

And then there's the often-bullied innovation (all lower case). Just like little-c creativity, lowercase innovation can be dismissed as not valuable enough. A lowercase innovation might be reimagining the way you conduct a job interview, refining the process to submit an expense report, or discovering a faster route to work. These are, in fact, *Big Little Breakthroughs*. Yet too often, small-minded people discriminate against small-sized innovations.

But just as the case with creativity, there is magic and power in bite-size sparks. As the most overlooked and underutilized of the innovation family, these babies are the pound-for-pound champions. They are less risky, easier to discover, and faster to implement. They cost less and are accessible to us all. And in the same way artistic legends advance from one stage of creativity to the next, if you really want to develop an all-caps INNOVATION, the best way to get there is to hone your skills through practice on a large number of lowercase innovations.

Let's stop thinking of ourselves as lacking innovation simply because we haven't patented 193 inventions or launched a billion-dollar company. And let's not fall into the trap of thinking we aren't creative because our first attempt at art didn't rival Frida Kahlo or Salvador Dalí. Instead, let's celebrate all levels of creativity and innovation, realizing that the more we practice, the greater the magnitude will become.

The Anatomy of an Idea

Caron Proschan built Simply Gum into a wildly successful business despite being dramatically outgunned by her competition. She did this with an intricate cocktail of imagination, creativity, and innovation, mixing the four varieties of creativity and the three flavors of innovation to find the perfect balance. But as we look deeper, the magic trick is less *magic* and more *trick* than we might think. Like a magic trick, what if the act of an invention could be dissected into its core components in order to better understand it and then replicate it?

Getting scientific for a moment, think about an atom. We imagine an atom as a single thing, but there are mission-critical subatomic particles (protons, neutrons, electrons) that allow the atom to exist in the first place. Just like atoms, several components need to fuse together to form an actual idea. The five molecular elements of an idea are *inputs*, *sparks*, *auditions*, *refinements*, and *slingshots*.

1. **Inputs.** Long before a fresh idea peeks into the sun for the first time, its DNA can be traced to its parents, which we'll call *inputs*. Inputs are the foundations of any idea and consist of previous experiences, context, research, point of

view, and external factors such as location. Caron's obsession with organic food and healthy living, combined with her love of chewing gum, both played a wildly important role in the idea of creating a healthy gum. Her previous involvement in another startup helped uncover the idea to start her own company. Generally speaking, if you want to improve your ideas (both quantity and quality), expand your input base. The more ingredients you have on the kitchen table, the more creative your soufflé will become.

2. **Sparks.** Often confused with the full idea itself, *sparks* are more like tadpoles. They are the early beginnings of an idea but not a fully developed version. Sparks are those raw, initial half-baked concepts that eventually form into something of value. Once Caron started working on the main formula for her gum, it took a full year of sparking. The idea for a healthy gum only came to life through hundreds of little idea sparks, most of which failed to see the light of day.

3. **Auditions.** After a spark is generated, it must be *auditioned*. Auditioning is the step that determines if a spark should be kicked off the bus or if it merits further exploration. When Caron was working on a healthy gum base, she tested and discarded dozens of sparks for every one that made it to her short list.

4. **Refinements.** Sparks that make it through the audition phase are now subject to further polish. The *refinement* step is where an idea is tweaked, improved, and sanded to perfection. Caron didn't rush to market with the first spark that passed a single audition. Instead, she refined her formula for taste and consistency. She made sure the flavor lasted long

enough through a series of tweaks and adaptations. She got feedback from dozens of test-chewers and then modified her approach based on their reactions. Throughout this step, she also refined for other factors such as environmental impact, production costs, and health benefits.

5. **Slingshots.** In the same way inputs are needed before an initial spark, *slingshots* are the required step to get an idea out of the lab and into reality. They are not detailed execution plans but rather provide a directional guide as to where the idea needs to go next. Once Caron's gum base was perfected, the next logical step was to add flavor. Once the flavors were locked down, it was clear that an efficient production process was required. Slingshots are the fasteners from one idea to the next in the same way one piece of a Sunday afternoon puzzle fits nicely into its neighbor. In fact, slingshots from one concept are often the inputs of the next in a sequence of interconnected creative ideas.

Breaking down the mythical idea into its respective components makes the ideation process much less overwhelming. Through this step-by-step approach, we can direct our creative energies with the precision of a pit crew during a Formula One race. In fact, each of Caron's breakthroughs came by way of this same idea sequencing.

Wanting cool packaging that stood out from the competition, Caron's *inputs* included her own tastes and preferences (she loved Apple's design, for example), a knowledge of competitive products, and her desire for something biodegradable. After hundreds of early *sparks*, she narrowed down a short list of possible winners in the *audition* phase. She tweaked and *refined* the concepts, ultimately selecting her favorite and landing on the *slingshot* to her next step, getting the product on shelves.

To get into retailers, Caron's *inputs* included the killer packaging (slingshot from prior idea), understanding of how retail decisions are made, and a list of stores to target. She tried many *sparks* that failed, but a few—such as getting into Whole Foods—made it through the audition phase. *Refinements* took several months, adjusting her approach to finally convince a single store to stock her gum, which became the *slingshot* to her next idea cycle of expanding distribution to more stores.

Think of your own ideas, the ones that worked best for you in the past. As an experiment, see if you can dissect what originally seemed like a single a-ha into the five molecules of an idea. By sequencing the idea genome, it turns out that stunning creativity can be surprisingly formulaic.

A Guitar Legend, a Jazz Musician, and a Neuroscientist Walk Into a Bar...

As his white electric guitar howled with feedback and distortion, he rocked a psychedelic version of the US national anthem to four hundred thousand captivated souls on that blistering hot August day. Perhaps the most revered performance at Woodstock, Jimi Hendrix's rendition of the sacred piece broke every rule and certainly ruffled some feathers. Bending strings so far they nearly broke, the intensity and drama of his performance represented the disenfranchised voice of a new generation of Americans. Fifty years later, the brash and largely improvised performance is still regularly cited as a creative masterpiece.

As a guitarist myself, I consider Hendrix one of my personal heroes. He combined instrumental mastery with a total disregard for musical convention. He made the instrument sing, cry, scream, and howl in a way that had never been done before. It's as if his tattered guitar cable were plugged directly into his soul, releasing and amplifying his raw emotions. I'm such a fan of Jimi Hendrix that when my friend Scott and his wife Chanel's newborn baby boy arrived, I suggested they name him Hendrix. They must love the famed musician too, since their son's birth certificate reads FIRST NAME: HENDRIX.

Deeply curious about how the creative brain operates, I wish we could have put Jimi Hendrix into an fMRI machine and watched the magic happen on that sweaty day in Bethel, New York. While we obviously can't conduct live research on an artist who's been gone for decades, Hendrix did leave us some clues that confirm new scientific discovery.

It turns out that Jimi Hendrix was mixed-handed, playing his guitar left-handed but eating and writing with his right. Could this have played a role in his bold creative legacy?

The long-standing belief is that the right hemisphere of the human brain is the party-going wild one, responsible for all the abstract, nonlinear, creative stuff, while the left brain is the logical, organized, detail-loving, straitlaced, suit-and-tie wearing bore. Yet new evidence reveals something quite different: creativity is, in fact, more tied to the *integration* of several parts of the brain as opposed to originating only in one place.

University of Toledo psychologist Stephen Christman studies mixed-handedness and the human brain and was curious about the connection of Hendrix's well-integrated brain with his extraordinary level of creativity. In an article published in the journal *Laterality* about his years of research into this question, Christman writes that Hendrix's mixed-handedness "enabled him to integrate the actions of his left and right hands while playing guitar, to integrate the lyrics and melodies of his songs, and perhaps even to integrate the older blues and R&B tradition with the emerging folk, rock and psychedelic sounds of the '60s."

Bob Dylan is another mixed-handed musician who has demonstrated extraordinary creativity, even winning the coveted 2016 Nobel Prize in Literature "for having created new poetic expressions."

Dylan's and Hendrix's masterful creativity supports what neuroscience has recently uncovered—that creativity comes through the integration of multiple brain regions, not through one single area that happens to be naturally gifted. Hendrix's and Dylan's mixed-handedness gave them a creative edge, but it turns out we don't need to be ambidextrous to develop this interconnected ability.

Dr. Roger Beaty, a Penn State professor who studies the cognitive neuroscience of creativity, led a 2018 study in which 163 participants performed creative tasks while inside an fMRI machine. The results disproved the typical left/right brain myth once and for all, revealing instead that three distinct brain networks interact to generate creativity.

Summarizing the research, author Rich Haridy writes, "The results found that three distinct brain networks were key to creative thinking. These are known as the Default Network (related to brainstorming and daydreaming), the Executive Control Network (which activates when a person needs to focus) and the Salience Network (known for detecting environmental stimuli and switching between executive and default brain networks)."

Dr. Beaty concluded, "It's the synchrony between these systems that seems to be important for creativity. People who think more flexibly and come up with more creative ideas are better able to simultaneously engage these networks."

The more we understand about the creative brain, the more we realize that we all have the required hardware to become wildly inventive. It isn't that Jimi Hendrix was born with special circuitry in his right hemisphere or Bob Dylan's success was based on some unique intercranial DNA. In fact, the evidence points to the fluidity of the brain, a situation that can be shaped and adapted toward higher levels of creative output. It isn't that we need a different brain but rather we need to develop the ability for three core elements of our brains to work in concert with one another. Through the notion of innoplasticity, our creative abilities can be expanded.

Dr. Elizabeth Hellmuth Margulis leads the Music Cognition Lab at Princeton University. She's not only a professor but also a highly accomplished pianist, earning her undergraduate degree in piano performance from the Peabody Institute, the conservatory of music and dance at Johns Hopkins University. With her passion for both music and neuroscience, she set out to discover how world-class musicians actually became so skilled. "There are lots of studies showing that musicians' brains have different networks than those of people who haven't had formal musical training," Margulis said. "But is this due to a genetic predisposition or to the effect of practicing an instrument for so long? We are still married to antiquated, nineteenth-century notions of genius and creativity."

Margulis conducted a study around the belief that "the de-freakification of musical talent could be very powerful." A group of professional-level violinists and flutists were placed in fMRI machines to examine their brain activity while listening to music. Both groups listened to a series of musical pieces, some featuring violin and others featuring flute, as the eager scientists watched their subjects' brains light up on high-definition monitors.

Margulis and her team were carefully monitoring the part of the brain responsible for producing music. If these talented musicians were born with a special-edition music brain, the brain region would light up equally regardless of which instrument was featured in the subject's headphones. But if the brain changed through practice, a violin player may show a different response when hearing her own instrument compared to a flute.

When a flutist heard his own instrument, the area of the brain in question lit up like a tacky Christmas tree. But when he heard violin music, the area was surprisingly quiet. The same was true in reverse, as violin players listened to their own instrument compared to the flute. "Violinists' brains, when they listen to violin music, look like flutists' brains when they listen to flute music. That extensive experience with their own instrument resulted in the recruitment of this special network," Margulis explained.

"This adds further support to the notion that it is training rather than genetic predisposition that makes a musician," Margulis concluded. "People can get the impression that musicians are alien beings whose brains are wired differently. But our study suggests it's a matter of the experience you have had in your life. It's practice, not magic."

Unlike classical violin and flute music, the art form of jazz is largely improvised. As someone who loves jazz and who's been playing for more than forty years, I've always wondered what happens inside the brain of an improvising jazz musician. Dr. Charles Limb, a neuroscientist, surgeon, professor, and musician, also wondered the same thing. And he decided to find out.

"Spontaneous artistic creativity is often considered one of the most mysterious forms of creative behavior, frequently described as occurring in an altered state of mind beyond conscious awareness or control while its neurophysiological basis remains obscure," said Limb. He set out to "examine musical improvisation as a prototypical form of spontaneous creative behavior, with the assumption that the process is neither mysterious nor obscure but is instead predicated on novel combinations of ordinary mental processes."

Conducting a study at the National Institutes of Health in Washington, DC, Limb spent nearly two years outfitting an fMRI machine so that it could accommodate an improvising musician. He then recruited professional jazz musicians and asked them to play a number of different things, some memorized and some improvised, over a seventy-five-minute testing period. His goal? To find out what in the heck is going on inside the brain during raw creative expression.

As expected, the medial prefrontal cortex lit up during improvisation. This is the area of the brain that houses the Default Network mentioned earlier, which is responsible for new ideas, daydreaming, and memory. What was fascinating, however, was the *deactivation* of the dorsolateral prefrontal cortex, the self-censoring area of the brain. The part of your brain that would be embarrassed if you showed up at a job interview wearing two different color socks shut down completely.

"That's a very unique combination," said Limb. "You don't typically see, in this part of the brain, one part going up and one part going down. What makes it really intriguing is the broad expanse of deactivation in the area that is the source of your inhibitors, your censors—all those inhibitory behaviors. They're turned off, I think, to encourage the flow of new ideas. You're not analyzing or judging what's coming out. You're just letting it flow."

In other words, we jazz musicians have trained our brains to operate in a very specific way by firing up the area for original thought while shutting down the area of inhibitions. It isn't that jazz musicians were born more creative than anyone else; we've just developed the ability to turn off our filters. (By the way, I'm pretty sure Tia wishes I'd turn my filter back on more often.)

It's the years of practice that allow jazz cats to bring down the house with breathtaking improvisation. The jazz musician brain is developed one fifteen-minute practice session at a time, not as an act of divine intervention.

You're More Creative Than You Think

Neuroscientist Allan Snyder came to a similar conclusion when researching creativity as a result of turning off one part of the brain. In an experiment he led at the University of Sydney in Australia, he gave 128 volunteers a puzzle to solve that can only be conquered with creativity. The subjects were asked to connect nine dots, arranged in three rows of three, using just four straight lines and without lifting their pens. This is a classic creativity test, since solving it literally requires a person to think outside the box. (Fun fact: this test is the origin of the phrase "think outside the box.") The only way to complete the puzzle is to draw lines far outside the three-by-three dot pattern, dramatically swooping in and out of the box of dots.

Unsolved puzzle   Solved puzzle

In the first trial, all 128 subjects failed the test. Snyder then used a transcranial direct current stimulation (tDCS) to temporarily immobilize the same area of the brain that jazz musicians shut down naturally. The result? More than 40 percent of the participants were able to solve the problem correctly within minutes after the electrical current deactivated the part of the brain that controls self-regulation, fear, and impulse control.

It's a tragedy that most adults don't feel all that creative. We equate job title or training with levels of creativity, thinking that sculptors are creative but accountants are not. Perhaps it's the lingering voice of a parent, teacher, or boss whispering in your ears that you're just not a creative person. While the Sydney study demonstrates that neuroscience proves otherwise, most of us still reach the incorrect conclusion that we just aren't very creative.

A 2020 Israeli study shows how deeply the anti-creative bias runs. Researchers asked sixty-one Israeli undergraduate students to participate in a series of divergent thinking tests and then self-rank their creative abilities. The originality of the students' ideas was evaluated separately by a panel of experts and then compared to the scores the participants gave themselves. The study found "a strong and statistically significant bias towards an underestimation of the originality of one's own ideas. This shows how strongly we tend to underestimate our own creativity." A series of follow-up experiments were performed with the same conclusion reached: "participants severely underestimated the creativity of their own ideas."

The fact that we don't feel creative has nothing to do with our brains or our capacity to expand our creative skills. The science is clear that the powerful force of human creativity is inside each of us; it's our job to unlock it, develop it, use it, and enjoy it.

If you're interested in gauging where your creativity sits today and what areas could use a boost, visit BigLittleBreakthroughs.

com to take a free online creativity assessment. You'll also discover reference material, links to many of the studies covered in this chapter, recommended further readings, and a roundup of inspiring quotations on creativity and innovation.

A Jolting Discovery

The surge of pain was like nothing he'd ever experienced before. When Derek Amato dove headfirst into the pool, he was hoping to catch the football tossed by one of his closest buddies. Instead, as his head slammed into the pool's concrete floor, he caught something far more unexpected.

It was 2006 when the thirty-nine-year-old sales trainer from Colorado sustained his injury. The drive to the emergency room seemed to last forever as his ears rang loudly and his head pounded with excruciating pain. His friends feared the worst, as Derek drifted in and out of consciousness and was decidedly confused. Remarkably, the forceful head injury that could have been fatal turned out to be less grave than his pals had feared. Instead of ending up in a wheelchair, Derek was thankfully only left with a severe concussion, slight memory loss, headaches, and 35 percent hearing loss in one ear. But the most significant change was still undetected.

Just four days after the accident, Derek was visiting one of his buddies from the accident who happened to be an amateur musician. Derek approached his friend's electric piano as if he were called to the instrument by a higher force. He began to play beautiful music, rich with haunting melodies and complex harmonic structures, playing for six hours straight without a single break. His masterful touch graced the instrument as music flowed effortlessly from his hands, in the same way a world-renowned pianist might play after a lifetime of practice.

But the odd thing in Derek's case—*he had never played piano before his accident.* He'd never even taken a music lesson.

"My hands took off like fire," said Derek. "It was like I'd been playing my entire life." After the shock wore off, Derek set out to find some answers. Bouncing from one expert to the next in an exhausting stream of internet searches, he discovered Dr. Darold Treffert from the University of Wisconsin School of Medicine.

Dr. Treffert devoted his fifty-year career to studying savants, people who possessed superhuman abilities in a single skill such as mathematics, music, memory, or art. Treffert consulted on the 1988 movie *Rain Man*, in which Dustin Hoffman played the character Raymond Babbitt, who was an autistic savant who struggled with normal life but could perform mathematical calculations as if his mind were a supercomputer.

Treffert's diagnosis of Derek Amato? *Acquired savant syndrome.*

While most savants can trace their gifts back to birth, acquiring extraordinary talents by way of brain injury is rare. There was the case of Orlando Serrell, who awoke from a baseball injury at the age of ten possessing a photographic memory and the ability to instantly compute complex numerical problems in his head. In another case, a high schooler who was brutally beaten in a mugging became the only known living person able to hand-draw the complex geometric patterns called fractals.

Dr. Bruce Miller, who leads the UCSF Memory and Aging Center in San Francisco, studies how brain trauma can lead to sudden gift-edness. In addition to acquired savant syndrome, he studies stroke victims who learn to paint beautifully and Alzheimer patients who "magically" begin to sculpt. He suggests that creative genius is already present in us all and that it can be unlocked. According to Miller, these talents "emerge because the areas ravaged by disease—those associated with logic, verbal communication, and comprehension—have actually been inhibiting latent artistic abilities present in those people all along. The skills do not emerge as a result of newly acquired brain power; they emerge because for the first time, the areas of the brain associated with creativity can operate unchecked."

What Derek Amato's case proves is that we all have untapped creative potential, hidden in our brains and waiting to be released. The notion that Beyoncé, George Lucas, or Snapchat founder Evan Spiegel were just born creative geniuses oversimplifies what it takes to become an innovative legend. While each of these three may have possessed some inclination or propensity toward achievement in their respective fields, their successes came as a direct result of their obsessive focus and years of pursuit. Their victories didn't come by way of birthright; rather their brains grew to support their artistic endeavors.

It took a traumatic brain injury to unlock Derek Amato's full creative potential. But for the rest of us, we can unshackle dormant creative capacity without a serious head injury. One *Big Little Breakthrough* at a time, we too can learn to invent like Caron Proschan or compose like Lin-Manuel Miranda.

Now that we've decoded the a-ha, explored the various degrees of creativity and innovation, dissected the idea, and absorbed the latest discoveries in neuroscience, it's time to explore how this powerful gift that we all share can be used to conquer our most pesky challenges and seize our full potential.

Chapter 2

The Great Equalizer

A poverty-stricken kid from New York becomes a drug kingpin and then loses everything after a betrayal from his best friend. Following a grueling prison sentence, he starts over with nothing and rises to become a wildly successful fitness entrepreneur.

A middle class white guy from the suburbs of Philly uses his bar mitzvah money to fund an amateur rap video. He's gone on to record with Snoop Dogg, Ariana Grande, and Justin Bieber, has over 1.5 billion YouTube views, and now stars in a TV show about his own life.

A young man from Detroit with dreams of being a basketball player joins a fledgling eleven-person company instead of pursuing sports. Seventeen years later, he owns 100 percent of the company, which has 6,300 employees and $5 billion in revenue, making this former jock a billionaire.

The fighter, the jokester, and the underdog. Now that they're über-successful, these three are considered creative geniuses. Yet each came from modest beginnings, faced tremendous disadvantages, and had to tackle seemingly insurmountable obstacles.

These were three ordinary people—just like you and me—who were able to conquer their challenges and achieve greatness. How did these outsiders break into guarded industries and win in such dramatic fashion? What creative steps did they take to level the playing field?

We'll meet Coss Marte, who grew up on the Lower East Side of New York. Raised by a single mom and struggling just to survive, he dropped out of school at age eleven to pursue a life of crime.

We'll get to know Dave Burd, a dorky and awkward kid from an ordinary family in suburbia. He took a vanilla office gig after college and appeared destined to a bland and unremarkable life.

We'll also meet Mat Ishbia, a regular guy from Detroit who just wanted to shoot hoops. In his early twenties, he decided to leave sports behind to take a desk job at a small mortgage company. As he sat making cold calls and processing paperwork in an uninspiring environment, it would be easy to imagine him sitting in the same cramped office forty years later. Coss, Dave, and Mat weren't born into great wealth. They weren't child prodigies. In fact, by all accounts, they were rather average. They didn't have insider access or family connections. They each appeared destined for a life just like their parents, repeating the generational cycle. But eventually, each unlocked their imagination and built deep creative skills that fueled their rise to greatness.

Through the ups and downs of their stories, we'll discover how each of us can use *Big Little Breakthroughs* to not only level the playing field but gain an edge in our own lives. We'll dispel the myth of overnight successes, reveal how oppositional thinking can drive results, and discover an often overlooked area where creativity can generate massive wins.

Why do underdogs win and how can we apply the same creative approach to achieve next-level results? Let's find out together.

The Fighter

There were nearly one hundred law enforcement officers on the scene when Coss Marte was forcefully slammed onto the hood of a police car, handcuffed tightly, and taken into custody. The coordinated sting was the grand finale of a yearlong investigation, culminating in the arrest of the drug kingpin himself.

On the surface, Coss doesn't seem like a sympathetic character. It's hard to have compassion for a convicted drug lord. Yet just like most things in life, Coss's story is far more complicated than it appears.

Born to an immigrant single mother on the Lower East Side of New York City, Coss was at-risk before he could crawl, as the gang-infested slums where he lived were a breeding ground of poverty and violence. "I grew up seeing stuff that no kid should ever see," Coss told me in a pained, quiet voice as we began our conversation. His crisp white fitness tee clung to his muscular physique as we sat together to discuss the remarkable peaks and valleys he'd experienced.

"My mom immigrated from the Dominican Republic when she was six months' pregnant with me, leaving my two sisters behind so I could become the first American-born citizen in our family. We both slept on my aunt's couch for several years...our life was a real struggle. She worked in factories, held odd jobs, sold beauty products on the subway. She did everything she could so we could just survive." At an early age, Coss felt the sting of poverty and decided to do whatever it took to have a better life.

With terrible peer influences, failing schools, and a difficult home environment, Coss followed an all too familiar path. He tried drugs for the first time at age nine. By the age of eleven, he was selling them. "The only people making real money in my neighborhood were dealing. That was the only way I knew to get ahead."

Coss started peddling drugs on the corner to junkies—first weed, then cocaine. But as the neighborhood started to gentrify, a new customer base emerged. Coss saw the profit potential of drunk lawyers and stoned business execs, so he took a creative approach to building his business. He ditched the baggy jeans for a suit and tie, leaving his spot on the street corner in favor of a new model: a high-end delivery service. "I was like Uber Eats, before Uber Eats," laughed Coss.

"It was just a crazy time. The cell phones back then only held 1,500 to 2,500 contact numbers, so I continuously had to get more phones. At one point, I had seven phones because my customer base was so big."

The business expanded and the money flowed. What started as a solo operation grew into a twenty-four-hour dispatch service with two-dozen delivery vehicles on the road. "I didn't think I was going to get caught because I was not serving the same clientele I had on the street."

"I gave a top dispatcher job to one of my best friends from back in the neighborhood. I gave him a salary. I bought him a condo on the Upper West Side. Gave him a car. He was living large...all he had to do was just sit in his apartment and pick up the phones. But eventually, he got greedy and started his own phone line on the side," Coss told me with disgust. "One of my old clients who had my personal phone number was like, 'Hey, I'm getting different product. What's going on?' He's also like, 'Do you have a new number? Somebody gave me a new card with a different number on it.' I was like, 'What? What are you talking about?' So, I got that phone number, called it up...and sure enough, my own dispatcher answered."

Coss's friend betrayed him, making off with $70,000 in cash and many times more than that in drugs, never to be seen again. Thinking the rip-off was behind him, the always-enterprising Coss Marte took over the traitor's drug line. "I kept operating with that number not knowing that my friend gave his card to a federal agent and that his phone was being tapped."

At the time of his arrest, Coss was making more than $2 million a year. He was twenty-three years old.

I asked him about that moment and what was going through his mind. "I think the first thing I thought about was my son," he told me with sadness in his voice. "My son was a year and a half, and he didn't deserve for this to happen to him. So that was the worst thing that I felt—that my son wouldn't grow up with his dad. I was going to be facing a long time in lockup."

When the judge read the sentence out loud in that crowded courtroom, sweat drenched through the white polyester dress shirt that Coss wore as he stood to hear his fate. He was sentenced to seven years in prison.

By the time he landed in his cell, Coss was in failing health. Based on his weight and high cholesterol at the time, a prison doctor told Coss that he would likely have a heart attack within five years. He looked in the mirror and decided this would be the last time he'd be repulsed by what he saw. Thinking of his young son, Coss swore to himself he wasn't going to die in jail and decided to take a different path once and for all.

He started exercising two to three hours a day, running around the yard with garbage bags under his clothes to sweat more. When he wasn't working out, he was reading about exercise and nutrition in the prison library. He became obsessed with fitness, which turned out to be his physical, emotional, and spiritual salvation.

Through trial and error and a mountain of persistence, Coss lost seventy pounds over the next six months.

When the other inmates saw his transformation, they asked for advice on their own workouts. Before long, Coss had a purpose: to help other inmates build self-control and discipline while getting in shape. With each prisoner he helped, his training system improved and his resolve strengthened.

Eventually, Coss had paid his debt to society and was released from lockup. He completed his prison term and wanted to pursue a legitimate future, a life of purpose. "I had 100 percent focus on never having my family go through that pain again. Not having my son experience seeing me in shackles, having him cry in visiting rooms, which just was one of the toughest things I had to witness in my life."

While that sounds good, Coss found it almost impossible to get a job as a convicted felon. He slept on his mom's couch for months and was rejected from every opportunity he pursued. He applied to dozens of menial jobs, never receiving a single callback. Running out of time and running out of options, Coss reflected back on his time in prison and the joy he felt from helping others get in shape. Maybe he could start his own gym, he thought.

He was broke. He had no formal education or industry experience. But could it be any harder than overseeing a complex drug organization or serving hard time? Fittingly, Coss decided to open up his own fitness studio.

Starting a gym was a flowery dream, but what landlord would give a former drug kingpin the key to a building? After dozens of rejections, Coss finally found a landlord to give him a shot. Ironically, it was at the same corner in Lower Manhattan where he got his start dealing drugs.

Now that he had his space, how could he possibly compete with the mega-gyms like Lifetime Fitness, Equinox, and LA Fitness? In another creative moment, Coss had an idea. Instead of opening up the world's 637th look-alike gym, what if he opened up the world's first gym of its kind. His idea: *a prison-themed fitness studio.*

Welcome to CONBODY. The slogan: "do the time."

The $27 billion fitness industry was nearly as brutal as Coss's prison life, and he had to do plenty of creative heavy lifting to stand out. When you walk into CONBODY, the cement block interior has a distinctive Alcatraz vibe. Continuing through a heavy steel-barred prison gate, you now enter the training room known as the "yard." Barbed-wire walls and no fancy equipment, you'll get a killer workout using the same exercises Coss developed while incarcerated. Just past the yard is a mug shot wall, perfect for posting workout pics on social media. As you might expect, members of the gym aren't called members—instead, they're known as "inmates."

Everything about the gym is nontraditional, even the workforce. Instead of hiring people from the fitness industry, every employee—from the front desk greeters to the personal trainers—was previously incarcerated. "My mission was to hire people coming out of the prison system, to give them a second chance," Coss beamed.

In an industry that typically displays about as much creativity as a dumbbell, CONBODY stood out from the pack. It is fun and creative, unique and authentic, compelling and different. Before long, Coss launched a series of fitness videos and line of merchandise and even opened a satellite gym inside Saks Fifth Avenue's flagship location. Today, CONBODY serves twenty-five thousand paying "inmates" in New York City and delivers classes online to customers in twenty-two countries outside the US.

For Coss, building the CONBODY empire wasn't just about money. For him, it was about redemption. And impact. "There was one moment when I'm in the gym after a class," he recalled to me. "This girl who was coming three or four times a week starts crying because it was her last visit before moving to LA. She told me CONBODY was her home and it changed her life and that she'd lost a hundred pounds with us. Her story brought tears to my eyes. To realize for a second, most of the time you just keep your head down and you just keep running and running and running. You don't really stop until moments like that happen. Like, wow, that's really creating an impact."

Coss used his creativity and hustle to build and grow his company in one of the most fiercely competitive industries. He's forging ahead in his own creative way, unwilling to be intimidated by overbearing competitors. "With their empty promises of overnight results...*they're* the biggest cons. *They* should be called CONBODY!" he laughs.

A few things really struck me as I spoke with Coss. While many of his peers ended up dead, incarcerated, or repeating the cycle of poverty, Coss was able to reframe the hustle he learned from the streets into a positive approach that changed his life. It was a series of imaginative ideas at each step of his ascent—not a single light-bulb moment—that drove his success. And Coss proved that neither gangs nor guns are a match for an indomitable creative spirit.

Why Only Playing Offense Is Offensive

In addition to the notion that innovation is only for the elite, one of the most common misconceptions is that it only applies when playing offense. After all, the most celebrated innovations are bold new product breakthroughs that upend traditional industries. In other words, we think of innovation primarily as a mechanism to drive growth. If you invent the next device to make the perfect hard-boiled egg and then sell eleven million of them on QVC, you have just innovated in the classic sense. Yet the wonders of innovation go far beyond product development.

Let's classify innovation into two camps: offense and defense. *Offense-focused innovation* is how most of us generally view the topic. Here, we use inventive thinking to seize new opportunities and fuel growth. These innovations take the form of marketing campaigns, new product breakthroughs, fresh business models, and inspired growth strategies. Just like a football team, offense-focused innovation is there to put points on the board. And just like most football teams, the offense generally overshadows the critical work of the defensive lineup.

Coss deployed several offense-focused innovations in building CONBODY. The idea for a prison-themed gym, streaming courses online, partnering with Saks, and his specific exercise routines are all examples of inventive thinking in action. But without a strong defensive game, he could never have grown his company.

Defense-focused innovation may not get all the glory, but it can be a powerful weapon in your arsenal. Here, we're using the same core ingredient of imagination to fight back against adversity, boost efficiency, overcome challenges, streamline operations, improve safety, solve pesky problems, and fend off competitors. Defensive innovation isn't usually as sexy, but this often overlooked domain can be the difference between raging success and crushing defeat.

On the defensive front, Coss used creative problem solving to finally earn a landlord's trust. He solved the industry's labor shortage by hiring from a new talent pool (ex-cons). I spoke to Coss during the COVID-19 pandemic, and he had already shifted to digital delivery of all his fitness classes, keeping customers happy and revenue high. In fact, his original idea was rooted in a defensive move after receiving a grim diagnosis from the prison doctor.

It took me years to realize that inventive thinking (offense-focused innovation) and creative problem solving (defense-focused innovation) are two sides of the same coin. It's such a liberating concept—that we can use our imagination to drive growth *and* overcome challenges. Which is exactly what a dorky kid from a Philadelphia suburb did to shatter the odds and become a rap legend.

The Jokester

There are few pursuits more difficult than breaking into the music business. With the promise of fame and fortune, tens of thousands vie for the very few top spots in the field. Programs like *The Voice* and *American Idol* show us just how exciting—and brutally competitive—the industry can be.

It's hard to make it in any genre, but achieving breakthrough success in rap is especially tough. Emanating from the struggles of poverty and oppression, this expressive art form has lifted people with troubled pasts to superstardom. Snoop Dogg, Jay Z, and Dr. Dre are the modern equivalent of Mozart, Bach, and Beethoven to a disenfranchised generation.

Rap legends tend to follow a certain pattern: African American young men and women with terrific dance moves boast about their endless supply of money, sex, and confidence. Often oppressed by a failing system and pervasive racism, they share their outrage in a raw and unapologetic manner. They represent the dream of unimaginable success to many who are just trying to make it through the day.

That's why David Burd may be the single most unlikely person to become a famous rapper.

Dave is a lanky kid from an upper-middle-class Jewish family in the suburbs of Philadelphia. A mop of untamed curly hair on his head and a poorly trimmed beard on his face, he looks more like a philosophy major than a rapper. He didn't go to juvenile detention; he went to summer camp. He can't dance, has no body art, and generally lacks style. Instead of exuding unshakable confidence, Dave has the insecure, neurotic vibe of a young Woody Allen. While most heavyweight rappers acquired their skills on the streets, Dave graduated near the top of his class at the University of Richmond.

After school, he moved to San Francisco and got a job at the ad agency Goodby, Silverstein & Partners where he performed menial and administrative tasks. To break the monotony of delivering a tiresome client report to management, Dave fashioned the report in the form of a homemade rap video. His colleagues were in tears with laughter, which is the feeling he cherished most.

Dave absolutely loved making people laugh. As a fan of rap music, with its intricate language and rhythms, he started to develop a dream in which humor was his differentiator. Humor combined with cartoons allowed *The Simpsons* to become a smash hit, so Dave wondered what might happen if he combined humor with rap music.

Compared to Coss Marte, Dave had every advantage. Great education, loving parents, no childhood trauma. But trying to become a professional rapper with Dave's background is like Coss trying to become a Rhodes Scholar after getting a full-ride scholarship to Oxford. White privilege was a liability in the rap game, and for the first time in his life, Dave was the underdog.

"I always dreamed of being an entertainer," said Burd in a 2015 interview in *The Guardian*. "It felt like the right dream to have, because becoming a legitimate rapper felt as unrealistic as playing in the NBA. But rapping works like a sport...the more you do it, the better you get at it."

Lacking nearly every attribute traditionally needed to become a rapper, Dave had to innovate his way into the crowded field. It took a couple years of experimentation, tinkering with the various elements of his would-be rap persona. In the same way the fictious Austin Powers was an ill-equipped and satirical version of James Bond, Dave used his weaknesses as the hook. Carefully examining every aspect of the rap game, he decided to turn each element on its head in order to be decidedly different.

Machismo is the bedrock of rappers, boasting of their sexual prowess and always referring to their extraordinary physical endowment. That is why Dave chose "Lil Dicky" as the perfect name; it is the foil to his braggadocios competitors. Instead of exaggerating the size of his equipment, he launched his hilarious rap persona as being extremely small in the category that matters most to other rappers.

While Dave had a decent job and came from a nice family, he didn't have excess resources. No trust fund or fabulously rich uncle to fund his pet project. To the chagrin of his overly protective parents, Dave used his bar mitzvah savings to produce his very first video. It was his entire life's savings, and the risk of failure was looming high.

The song was called "Ex-Boyfriend," which broke every unwritten rule of rap. Dave tells the story of his beautiful new girlfriend, someone he's really excited about and is about to sleep with for the first time that night. As the evening unfolds, they run into her ex-boyfriend, which increases Dave's feelings of inferiority. To Dave, the ex appears to be the most handsome man he's ever seen. His flowing hair, chiseled body, and perfect face remind Dave of a Greek god.

They share a drink and Dave's feeling of inadequacy continues to grow. The ex is gorgeous, charismatic, and wealthy while Dave is homely, nervous, and broke. A bit later, they end up next to each other at the urinal and Dave sneaks a look at the ex-boyfriend's "private area." To his horror, Dave is beyond intimidated by what he sees.

The rest of the song hysterically describes the contrast between the ex's surplus and Dave's shortcomings as his angst continues to grow. The song is the antithesis of most boastful rap stories, portraying himself as completely inadequate, and that is exactly why it took off. Within a day, more than one million people had watched and shared the video. Lil Dicky had officially hit the scene.

An overnight success. But as we've seen from Simply Gum's Caron Proschan, overnight successes are usually far from overnight. In fact, Dave Burd worked on "Ex-Boyfriend" for nearly two years. Over two hundred versions and thousands of hours were invested to refine his creativity into a song that seems like it was spoken off the cuff. Thousands of *Big Little Breakthroughs* later, the work felt natural and was finally ready for release.

"I'm very much a no-stone-unturned kind of guy," Dave explains. "Even if there's a moment where the take is perfect, I'll still look at every other take, just to make sure there's not one that's maybe slightly better. I really do exhaust every option, so that way I have the internal peace of mind that this moment in this piece of art cannot be better. It's very nitpicky and hyper-neurotic and exhausting. But for me, it yields the ultimate peace of mind. Once I do that and I have that feeling, then I'm okay with the results."

With each new musical release, Dave continued to push the creative boundaries. Instead of emulating previous rap success, he set out to pioneer a new style all his own. His video entitled "Professional Rapper" features Lil Dicky being interviewed by the legendary Snoop Dogg for a job as a rapper. The hilarious exchange between the two illustrates the brilliant creative strategy.

Snoop Dogg suggests that Lil Dicky stop acting like a nebbish, insecure wimp and start playing the part of the prototypical macho rapper. Lil Dicky respectfully disagrees, suggesting that his highly unusual approach will appeal to a whole new target audience, one that traditional rappers have missed.

"Professional Rapper" has now been viewed nearly two hundred million times on YouTube.

Most rappers are boastful about their unending wealth, often "making it rain" by tossing hundred dollar bills into the air at a crowded nightclub. In contrast, Dave created a song called "$ave Dat Money" that centers on his cheapness. The lyrics describe how he seeks out generic medications, uses his cousin Greg's Netflix log-in, and double-checks restaurant bills to ensure he hasn't been overcharged. He essentially pokes fun at the rapper lifestyle while focusing on his own frugality. His sheets are low thread count, his gym membership is a free trial, his clothes are all hand-me-downs.

"I didn't just make the song for irony's sake," explained Burd. "I genuinely do have pride in the way in which I save money. The song in a nutshell is about how all rap songs are about spending money, so this is an ironic twist on that. I thought it'd be cool to flip it on its head."

Unlike other rappers who invest millions in fancy video productions, this one was made for free. The video begins with Dave going around begging people for permission to shoot his epic rap video at their fancy house in Beverly Hills for nothing in return. He cajoles a car dealer to let him borrow a Lamborghini in exchange for advertising credit at the end of the video. At one point, he crashes the high-budget set of another rap video being filmed and then uses their equipment, models, and props for his own video. The refrain "$ave Dat Money" continues to remind us how very different—and creative—this rapper is.

As other rappers were busy making songs about their private jets blowing carbon emissions through the skies, Dave made a song about preserving the environment. Cameo appearances by Justin Bieber, Ariana Grande, Halsey, Zac Brown, Kevin Hart, Sia, Adam Levine, Wiz Khalifa, Miley Cyrus, Katy Perry, Ed Sheeran, and Leonardo DiCaprio make the song irresistible. It encourages listeners to protect Mother Earth, suggesting they visit a website Dave created called WeLoveTheEarth.org to learn more and donate. It's estimated that the song has raised more than $7.5 million for environmental causes.

As if becoming a rap legend wasn't enough, Dave is now the star of a television show about his own life. *Dave*, the show, has the same hysterical rawness of *Curb Your Enthusiasm*. It also tackles social issues such as mental health and addiction while remaining wildly funny. As of this writing, the show's first season was the most successful show ever launched on the FXX Network and has been renewed for a second season.

The Old Way vs. The New Way

The fundamental basis for Dave's success is his relentless pursuit for doing things differently. A good way to frame his thinking is a simple fill-in-the-blank model:

Everyone else does _____ (old way) _____, so a creative twist could be _____ (new way) _____.

All the other rappers boast about being wealthy, so Dave boasted about being cheap. All the other rappers showcased their physical gifts, so Dave featured his flaws. Typical rappers put themselves at the center of the universe, so Dave made a song about protecting the Earth. The simple formula, repeated at every turn, is what launched Dave into the upper echelons of his industry, despite his long list of disadvantages in the field. The willingness to push the creative boundaries and smash established norms generated his success.

This simple formula certainly has played a pivotal role in my own career over the last three decades. Here's my professional background encapsulated in this unassuming model.

- Everyone else learned to play rock guitar, so I studied jazz.
- Everyone else got a degree and professional experience, so I started a company at age twenty having never taken a business class.
- At the beginning of the internet craze, everyone else focused on internet advertising, so I started an internet promotion company.
- Everyone else does venture capital in Silicon Valley, New York, or Boston, so I started my venture fund in my hometown of Detroit.
- Everyone else focuses on big innovations, so I focus on little ones.

Looking back, it was the moments when I embraced this oppositional stance that led to my successes, whereas the times when I followed the herd led to my biggest setbacks. And believe me, I've had my share of stinging defeats. When I followed the pack in 2006 and tried to launch a self-service tech solution for small businesses, I failed miserably. When I launched a new company back in 2015 that was basically like Coachella for businesspeople, it was a total bust. In fact, it was the moments when I tried to play it safe by copying others that led to my most painful losses, while the career-defining wins were achieved through our simple yet defiant formula.

And each of us can adopt the same approach. Try taking the fill-in-the-blank formula for a spin in your own business. For example, if you manufacture office furniture, what dramatically different approach could you take on your product design? Pricing model? Sales approach? Marketing efforts? Manufacturing process? Hiring practices? Leadership structure? You don't need to be completely opposite in every area of your business to win, but exploring oppositional approaches in all aspects may help you surface one or two actionable ideas.

If all the other candidates for that big job promotion you want pursue the opportunity in the same way, how could your approach stand out? The same formula can apply in your personal life. When our kids make the case for something they want, citing "all the *other* kids get to…" as the basis of their argument, we parents shut it down quickly. But as adults, why do we let ourselves fall into the same follow-the-leader trap that we forbid our kids from pursuing?

The Underdog

From an early age, Mat Ishbia was underestimated. Most people felt he was decidedly average, making his dream of playing basketball for an elite team like the Michigan State Spartans seem far-fetched. Top schools like MSU recruit from around the globe, enjoying their pick of the absolute best athletic talent. Mat, on the other hand, wasn't recruited, received no scholarship, and had to beg to try out as a walk-on.

While he lacked the physical characteristics of most elite athletes, legendary coach Tom Izzo saw something special in Mat. Despite being six inches shorter than the average player on the team, Mat demonstrated a rare level of intensity and determination. Against all logic, Izzo gave the kid a shot, a decision that would eventually have a far bigger impact on the world than the team's collegiate standings.

Under Izzo's leadership, Mat ended up playing in three consecutive Final Four tournaments before ultimately helping the team win a National Championship. Coach Izzo mentored this unlikely hero into both a fierce competitor and a creative leader. Their connection ran so deep that Mat hung around for a year after college to work as an assistant for Izzo.

Through his continued successes working with Coach Izzo, Mat was offered his dream job as a full-time coach of a Division I team. He would have been the youngest D1 coach in NCAA history, a remarkable feat based on Mat's background. It was the chance of a lifetime, but he had also developed a love for business during his undergraduate studies. Coach Izzo encouraged him by saying, "Maybe instead of basketball, you can take some of the things you learned here and turn them into something bigger than being a head coach." At this pivotal moment, Mat chose the more difficult and less glamorous path, forgoing the coaching offer and joining a small mortgage company.

At the time of Mat's start date back in 2003, United Shore Mortgage looked just like thousands of others in the home loan business. Joining as employee number twelve, Mat learned the business from the ground up, from cold-calling potential clients to processing loans. Sitting at his cold metal desk, he wondered if he made the wrong decision to pursue business over sports.

I sat down with Mat during the COVID-19 pandemic, so our face-to-face conversation was a video call instead of an in-person session. As he popped on my screen, I was startled by his professionalism. In the midst of a pandemic, Mat sat in his well-organized office, perfectly groomed and wearing a neatly pressed suit and tie. I, on the other hand, sat unshaven in a ratty sweatshirt, and I'm not completely sure I was even wearing pants.

While attire may be a trivial thing, it speaks volumes about Mat as a leader. "Dominate by being different," Mat told me, sharing his core philosophy immediately as we began our discussion. Just like David Burd, when Mat examined the behavior of his competitors, his first instinct was to do the opposite. If they dress casually, he and his team would wear suits. If they pursue the obvious strategy, Mat looks to take a radically different approach.

Back when Mat joined the company, United Shore sold mortgages to homebuyers just like the slew of other look-alike competitors. In fact, the company wasn't even in the top five hundred mortgage companies in the US. Craving a better opportunity, Mat convinced the owner to shift the entire business to wholesale lending. In other words, United Shore decided to sell their loans to small, independent mortgage brokers instead of selling directly to consumers. The independent brokers, in turn, rebrand the offerings and sell directly to homebuyers.

"I went the opposite of everyone else," Mat tells me as a smile tries to peek out from his determined profile. "We went against the grain. Everyone said we couldn't do it, that we'd fail."

As Mat continued to share his strategy with me, it struck me how similar it was to both Coss and Dave, despite the differences in geography, industry, and customer base. They each embraced creative approaches to differentiate in crowded competitive markets. They each applied imagination to both the big strategic decisions and also the small daily choices that moved their businesses forward one step at a time.

Seeing firsthand how frustrating delays can be in the mortgage underwriting process, Mat obliterated the industry's typical seven-day time frame, replacing it with a brisk twenty-four-hour turnaround. This, among other *Big Little Breakthroughs*, made United Shore the go-to choice for independent mortgage brokers. As success continued, Mat was able to buy the business and officially take the helm.

"Being creative is thinking that you don't have to do what everyone else does. Just thinking freely is a big thing. So, that was kind of what we did, and we focused on it, and thought differently," Mat explains.

Mat's intense focus on inventive thinking shows itself in a number of inspiring leadership practices, such the company-wide program called Brilliant Ideas. While most companies offer a standard-issue suggestion box, Mat adds public recognition to reward the creative process. Mat explains, "I don't know what the next big thing is, but my team members know. They're actually doing the job. So, we created the Brilliant Ideas program to encourage every team member to share every new idea they can think of, big or small."

For every idea submitted, the employee receives a Brilliant Idea Lightbulb trophy to display on his or her desk. These visual indicators serve as a badge of honor to colleagues while pushing team members to share more ideas and earn more public recognition. "People actually keep track of how many little light bulbs they get on their desk. It doesn't cost much, and as we implement their ideas, it's empowering people to take ownership and say, hey, brilliant ideas can be from anywhere. It doesn't matter if it is a small idea or a big one...we encourage people to challenge the way we work and bring their creativity to the job daily."

Mat recently expanded the program to include clients, vendors, and partners. He actively solicits suggestions from everyone in his orbit, rewarding them with a heartfelt lightbulb trophy. In the same way he cherished every award he won as an athlete, he now engenders the same excitement and feelings of accomplishment he had in sports as a part of the idea-generation process.

In an effort to recruit top talent to their growing business, Mat launched the Business Innovation Group (BIG) eight years ago. Instead of only hiring to fill specific roles, the company hires people they think are a good cultural fit but who haven't yet found the perfect position. The BIG program is a twelve-month apprenticeship rotation, where new team members get to work in fourteen different parts of the business in order to decide which represents the best permanent fit.

This decidedly different approach to talent development has paid off. "One of the guys that started in the first or the second BIG class is now my SVP of Operations. Twelve hundred people now report to him, and he's thirty years old," Mat explains. "Traditionally, you hire someone based on their skills. In our case, we're hiring them based on their character and then helping them figure out where they fit best. It's back to our philosophy of being different by design."

From product offering and facilities to technology and talent, United Shore's immense success is achieved through hundreds of *Big Little Breakthroughs*. Mat shared a fun example of this with me, explaining how they navigate the five thousand job applicants the company receives each month. "We sit them right near the security people, who ask them, 'Hey, how are you?' We carefully observe how the job candidate responds. Do they blow off the security person or smile and engage? The security person then shares their notes about the job candidate with the recruiting team, so we know right away if this person is going to fit within our family."

Mat views himself as a kind, supportive leader. But he bristles when people blindly follow previous successes. "I can't stand it when people say, 'Oh, that's because we've always done it that way.' That's the biggest loser saying of all time. We should just do something because we've always done it that way? Yeah. I'm just not accepting that. We've got to get better. We've got to improve."

Mat's creative approach has driven explosive growth. With $180 billion in annual mortgage origination and $5 billion in company revenue, United Shore now has 6,300 employees and has been ranked as the largest wholesale mortgage company for six years in a row. In fact, they are second in overall mortgage volume only to fellow Detroit-based mortgage company Quicken Loans, and as you might guess, second place doesn't sit well with Mat.

He has an insatiable appetite to be a champion. "I want us to be the number one overall lender in the country," Mat tells me. "We're already the largest wholesale lender in the country. Now, it's like, okay, we've done that. Let's go take down Quicken Loans next."

Without a hint of boastfulness or bravado in his voice, as if he were simply stating a scientifically proven fact, he continues, "We'll beat them, whether it's this year, or next year, or the year after, we'll beat them overall. The next thing is to take over the number one spot, and once again, I'm very competitive and we will do it. I'm not being arrogant. We're going to do it for sure." For the record, I wouldn't bet against him.

Mat's confidence lies at the intersection of two powerful forces: creativity and grit. As we've seen in the cases of Coss and Dave, work ethic drives far more progress than God-given talent. Mat explains, "My thing is, I'm not the smartest guy and you'll learn that about me quickly. My competitors, they're all smarter than me and they have more money than me, but no one can outwork me." The intense work ethic that was cultivated by Coach Izzo is apparent in Mat's daily routine: every single day, as he's done for the last seventeen years, Mat arrives at the office in his suit and tie at 4:00 a.m., heading home at 6:45 p.m. sharp.

"And that's how we built it from the ground up. One day at a time. Nobody pays any attention to us for years, and years, and years, and next thing you know, we've built to where we are today."

My kind of win...one Big Little Breakthrough at a time.

Through the stories of Coss Marte, Dave Burd, and Mat Ishbia, we see that creativity is the great equalizer and is accessible to every one of us looking to pursue change, growth, and success. While we don't all have ambitions of running billion-dollar companies or becoming rap superstars, their stories help us understand how powerful our own creative skills can be toward achieving whatever success looks like for each of us.

For some, it's getting a job promotion and a raise. For others, it's becoming a more effective parent and raising independent kids. Maybe your goal is to launch a podcast and connect with others around your passion for miniature model sailboats. Or maybe you want to use your creativity to get more done in less time so you can finally make your favorite 5:15 p.m. yoga class.

In chapter 3, we'll explore why creativity has become the currency of success in the modern business era and what we can do to harness it. We'll take a scientistic view of the importance of inventive thinking while examining the traps and obstacles that can trip us up. And we'll see firsthand how two scrappy entrepreneurs from England created a multibillion-dollar company while disrupting one of the world's most revered professional sports.

CHAPTER 3

The Frogger Principle

Charles married Diana, the Iran hostage crisis ended, and the Post-it Note was born. But the thing about 1981 that I'll remember most: *Frogger*.

One month before my eleventh birthday, the iconic arcade game came to life and I was hooked. Often blowing off homework, friends, food, and semiregular bathing, I became obsessed with *Frogger*. Despite graphics that today could be designed by my four-year-old daughter, Tallia, the game was addictive to millions just like me.

With my Atari joystick in hand, I was in control of the heroic amphibian who was determined to cross the river. But there was a problem. My inept little frog couldn't swim. He was only able to secure safe passage by hopping from one solid surface to the next. He went from the back of a lily pad to a floating log to a cagey alligator swimming by.

The challenge, as some of you may remember along with Tab cola and Pop Rocks, is that these hard surfaces weren't stationary. In fact, they flowed down the river at an increasingly faster and faster pace, creating a dangerous environment for my jumpy little friend. Our protagonist had to quickly leap from one point of safety to the next or he'd meet his maker in the raging river of death. Standing still—even for a moment—was tantamount to suicide.

The frog in *Frogger* couldn't rest on his successes for more than a millisecond; he had to keep hopping ahead in order to survive his hostile environment. The quest for forward progress in the midst of imminent danger is what made the game so compelling. Navigating chaos in order to reach a new destination. *Frogger* contributed to my embarrassingly low report card marks in sixth grade, but I learned far more from *Frogger* than doing long division in Mrs. Morrison's math class.

If you really think about it, we are all playing a giant three-dimensional game of *Frogger*.

Our successes aren't permanent but rather a temporary state in the context of unprecedented change and increasingly difficult circumstances. That fleeting moment of success is the equivalent of our Kermit-esque buddy landing on the back of a turtle. It simply can't be savored indefinitely. Instead, we must leap from one success…to the next…to the next, unless we're prepared to be swept into the rapids.

Standing still doesn't only kill frogs. The comfort and satisfaction of a successful leap lures too many smart people into thinking they don't need to *keep on hoppin'*. (Sounds like a catchy name for a country song, no?)

None of us need to drown in complacency. By making *Big Little Breakthroughs* part of your daily routine, you won't just gain a life jacket; your reward will be the vroom of a 655 hp speedboat with a titanium ski bar and eleven cup holders.

A Muddy Driving Range Meets a Microchip

Leaders in the golf industry were enjoying a blissful existence. Since the first eighteen-hole course was built back in 1764, the business of golf was—quite literally—a walk in the park. Knicker-clad customers often loved a day on the links more than their firstborn child. Business deals were consummated on the golf course, elaborate golf buddy man-cations became the norm, and the sport even had its own TV channel. The game itself rarely changed, but for the advent of some new club that could drive the ball from Milwaukee to Switzerland.

Just as complacent leaders were sipping their Arnold Palmers, two brothers in the UK began to cook up a disruptive approach. Rather than marveling at the sport's current success, they instead focused on a transformation that has since gone on to shake the industry incumbents right down to their knee-high plaid socks.

Steve Jolliffe and his brother Dave came to a realization in 1997: "Golf is not much fun if you aren't very good at it." Instead of leaving it alone and ordering up another round of extra-dry martinis with blue cheese olives, the brothers turned their attention toward the long list of golf's pain points. People of different skill levels had a lousy time playing together. The game took too long. It consumed huge amounts of land. It was slow. It was expensive. It required years of practice. Compared to more modern sports, it was boring to watch.

The Jolliffes weren't the only ones getting frustrated. In the US alone, the number of players slumped 22 percent from 30 million back in 2005 down to 23.4 million today. Since 2006, more golf courses close each year than open. The game felt old school and out of touch, especially to younger players.

Craving a fresh approach, Steve and Dave started to experiment with creative twists to the stuffy sport. What if we created an experience that was fun for all skill levels? How could we speed up the game? Bring down the costs? Attract new players instead of repelling them? The brothers spotted an opportunity while complacent leaders smoked their stubby cigars and chewed on overcooked steaks.

They realized the game of *Frogger* was in full play and the fat cat incumbents were vulnerable.

Trackable microchips were just becoming a widespread thing, which gave the budding entrepreneurs an idea. Could we insert a chip into a golf ball in order to track distance and accuracy? Now this was a big idea—using imbedded technology to track the speed, height, and trajectory of an individual ball. Voilà. Eureka. Mission accomplished...pour the champagne and cue Queen's anthem "We Are the Champions."

But this initial idea—as powerful as it was—didn't alone change the sport. If used only to help existing golfers improve their swings, it wouldn't exactly put a dent in the universe. Instead, the brothers sought to use microchips as the basis of a new type of golf game altogether.

The pair purchased a driving range in London's working-class suburb of Watford and got to work reimagining golf. Instead of smacking balls into the great unknown, huge colorful targets were installed to give golfers a fresh challenge. "We wanted to create a compelling and addictive game, so when a child hits one into the front target, they're way more excited than an experienced golfer hitting one into a back target," Steve said in a 2018 interview. In order to make balls roll more smoothly and keep costs low, they replaced grass with artificial turf. Their once-haggard driving range became an innovation laboratory, a test kitchen for a completely new golf experience.

The early days were difficult. The new sport was hard to explain. Seasoned golfers scoffed at the concept, while newbies didn't understand it. Neither potential investors nor possible sponsors would even return a phone call.

They endured more slammed doors than a ketchup-stained encyclopedia salesman, but the brothers persisted through rough times. A small tweak here. A new idea over there. Should we serve food? What about adding music? One *Big Little Breakthrough* after the next, momentum started to build.

In their first year, revenue was up eightfold compared to the location's previous life as a muddy driving range. Anecdotal feedback was positive, and they saw something rarely seen at most practice locations—people were actually having fun. From kids who had never before picked up a club to semipro weekend warriors, laughter and smiles replaced the furrowed-brow grumpiness of the past.

In the cool London fog, a monster was born. The phrase "Target-Oriented-Practice" was soon condensed into an acronym: TOP for Topgolf. But even with a hip new name and a little early success, the old guard still had no idea what was coming.

The brothers continued to endure rejection. Richard Grogan, a prominent industry investor, turned down the Jolliffes twice. "It's a lot of fun, it's interesting technology, and there were a lot of people there, but I'm sorry to say it's just not going to make it," said Grogan to his partners after paying Topgolf a visit. Yet Steve and Dave wore Richard Grogan down, and he eventually decided to buy the rights to bring Topgolf to the United States.

The highly anticipated US launch in 2005 turned out to be a fizzle instead of a bang. The long line of customers Grogan dreamed about did not appear at the DC-area location. High hopes in Chicago and Dallas were also met with a frigid reception. Grogan was on the verge of a catastrophic failure, the worst in his otherwise successful career.

The team knew the game was fun, but they just couldn't get customers to pay attention. Reverting to a low-tech approach, employees started walking around town wearing sandwich board signs advertising the delight to be had at Topgolf. Incredibly, the seemingly unimaginative tactic worked. People finally started to show up and fell in love with the game. Lines formed; word spread. It was this one small idea, not a giant innovation, that got the momentum started.

A series of additional *Big Little Breakthroughs* over the next few years drove breathtaking growth. The facilities were expanded to support large-scale kitchens, each with an executive chef to drive nongaming revenue and delight customers. Huge TVs were placed in each suite, along with comfortable couches and an endless string of creature comforts. Players connected their physical games to a mobile app, complete with social media integration to further expand player enjoyment. Topgolf went on to acquire the online multiplayer game *World Golf Tour*, deeply integrating Topgolf into customers' lives. The core technology advanced to analyze every swing, helping players improve their games.

Today, Topgolf appears unstoppable. Soon to go public, the company is now worth more than $4 billion. With sixty-nine venues throughout the US, Canada, Mexico, Europe, and Australia, the company plans to open one hundred new locations in the next five years in a growing segment with no competition to speak of. It's the biggest change to golf since the motorized cart.

Not only did they create a beast of a company (I sure wish I was an early investor), they're elevating the very sport that first rejected the concept outright. Fifty-four percent of Topgolf customers are ages eighteen to thirty-four, representing the highly coveted demographic that traditional golf was losing fast. Twenty-three percent of all new golfers today say their first experience holding a club was at a Topgolf facility, and a whopping 75 percent say Topgolf influenced their decision to play.

On the surface, the company's remarkable success appears to be the manifestation of a lone, cargo tanker–sized innovation. Yet it was dozens of *Big Little Breakthroughs* that formed the growth juggernaut we now admire. It wasn't just the microchip. Or the food. Or the low-tech signs. Or the music. It wasn't only the TVs or the couches. The speed of play, the lower costs, the integration of all skill levels, the appeal to young players each contributed to success. Instead, it was the fusion of each little innovation—not any single idea itself—that enabled the company's massive success.

All Signs Point to "C"

But what if you're not starting a new company or swinging to disrupt an entire industry? Perhaps you run a small business or work as a manager at a large company. Maybe you're focused on raising your kids, keeping the dog clean, taking out the trash, and just hoping you have a free hour to binge your favorite cooking show. You could be a new college grad still trying to figure out your path or maybe you're further along in your career, looking to make that long overdue change.

Like most of us, you were probably ordered to steer clear of creative ideas, with the same stern warning you received about the risks of smoking Camel Lights or sniffing Elmer's Glue. As if cultivating our creative abilities was the equivalent of releasing some untamed, animalistic impulse that would earn a spot in juvenile detention, we were repeatedly instructed to follow the rules instead of following our hearts. Yet this misguided advice is right up there with arranged marriages and treating infectious disease with leeches—well-intentioned counsel that proved far from ideal.

In the past, creativity was optional for most. Get a good job, follow the rules, keep your head down, don't make waves, listen to your boss, retire in thirty-five years with a fourteen-carat gold-plated Seiko. Unfortunately, the outdated strategies we've been taught are a recipe for mediocrity at best and vast underachievement at worst. We can no more afford to follow yesterday's advice than we can rely on tarot cards to offer accurate driving directions (turn right at the Two of Swords and then hang a sharp left at the Six of Wands).

Different times call for different approaches and different skill sets. The olive-green shag carpeting that worked beautifully for Greg Brady would hardly do the trick for Kourtney Kardashian. The proven strategy developed on an adding machine, discussed on a rotary phone, and printed on carbon paper is not going to help us reach the promise land in today's era of digital transformation, change, and upheaval.

According to a 2019 research survey on the "skills gap" by the Society for Human Resource Management (SHRM), the number one top missing skill set in the global workforce is "creativity, innovation, and problem solving with critical thinking." The number two most missing skill set: "ability to deal with complexity and ambiguity" (which is fancy code-speak for creativity).

What topped the list of LinkedIn's research on the most needed skills in 2020? You guessed it: creativity.

Aiming for the C-suite? An IBM study of 1,500 CEOs across sixty countries cited creativity as the most important leadership quality.

Just hoping to get a job? A 2015 study published by the Association of American Colleges & Universities revealed that "a candidate's demonstrated capacity to think critically, and solve complex problems is *more important than his or her undergraduate major.*" And that insight is coming from the folks in the actual business of undergraduate majors. That's the equivalent of Ronald McDonald suggesting you become a vegan.

Forrester Research, in a 2019 report on artificial intelligence and automation, said that a human worker's only way to hold on to a job in the future against a digital competitor is to be creative, indicating that it's the "creative skills that give—and will continue to give—humans an edge over robots." Take that, R2-D2.

Herein lies the disconnect. We've been taught to suppress our creative instincts in the same way prepubescent teens are instructed to suppress their desire to make out with their brace-toothed counterparts. But that advice is wildly out of date by all indications. In fact, if we want to land a job, have a productive career, reach our full potential, and even optimize our personal lives, embracing our creative voice is no longer optional.

And the numbers prove out this disconnect. An *Ad Age* study of five thousand adult professionals reported that "eight in ten people feel that unlocking creativity is critical to economic growth, yet a striking minority—only 25 percent—believe they are living up to their own creative potential."

McKinsey, the notoriously analytical consulting giant, decided to explore the impact of creativity and innovation on business performance. The data scientists poured over the numbers, wearing out their pocket protectors and squinting so much that their black plastic glasses needed fresh white tape to remain intact. What they discovered made their gigantic linear brains explode.

Companies with higher scores on creativity were twice as likely to deliver above-average total return to shareholders and delivered above average growth 2.3 times more often than their less-creative counterparts. The report conclusively states that "creative leaders outperform their peers on key financial metrics" and that "the most creative firms had better financial performance; creativity matters for the bottom line."

I think the McKinsey folks will soon be trading in their protractors for paint brushes.

In PwC's 2019 22nd Annual Global CEO Survey, the top of the skills gap list was "the ability to effectively innovate," as the majority of leaders identified their current capacity as insufficient.

The 2020 C-Suite Challenge report, published by the Conference Board, listed "building an innovative culture" among top three most pressing internal concerns of 740 CEOs surveyed globally.

Yet most companies are still not fully cultivating creativity. A 2015 McKinsey study revealed, "Ninety-four percent of the managers surveyed said they were dissatisfied with their company's innovation performance."

I don't know about you, but my head is spinning. The key takeaways for those like me who are numerically challenged:

1. People, teams, and companies that are more creative have better financial outcomes across the board.
2. Most people, teams, and companies don't invest enough in expanding those capabilities and don't feel they have an adequate system in place to build creative capacity.

A $73 Billion Reward

All these reports and stats are impressive, to be sure. But the granddaddy of number-crunching joy is the *Forbes*/MIT "innovation premium."

The analytical wizards at *Forbes* teamed up with the super geniuses at MIT to examine how innovation impacts a company's stock price. They wanted to model out if a stock value was boosted based on how innovative a company is perceived to be. Jeff Dyer, one of the original architects of the model, explains, "The innovation premium is the proportion of a company's market value that cannot be accounted for from the net present value of cash flows of its current products in its current markets. Put another way, it's the premium the stock market gives a company because investors expect it to launch new offerings and enter new markets that will generate even bigger income streams."

To reach an accurate number, the model factors in an insane amount of data. They leverage a proprietary algorithm from Credit Suisse that includes historical cash flow analysis of forty-five thousand companies and more than five hundred thousand data points. The team reviews a minimum of six years' financial data, correcting for company size, industry, and geography. They factor the forward-looking two-year consensus estimate of return on investment (ROI), projected cash flow, and reinvestment rate. They adjust for market volatility, industry trends, supply chain factors, and I'm pretty sure zodiac sign just to be safe. Essentially, they consider every logical factor that should determine a stock's price and then compare it to the actual price to see how big of a value premium investors ascribe to the company's perceived innovation prowess. And wow do investors pay up for creativity.

Let's look at Salesforce, which is currently number three on *Forbes's* annual list of the most innovative companies. As of this writing, the company is valued at $161 billion. But here's the thing: based on all rational data, the company should be worth only $88 billion. (Side note: you don't get to use the phrase "worth only $88 billion" very often.) This means that investors are paying an 82.27 percent innovation premium as investors bid up the stock based on their perception that Salesforce will continue to innovative. Put simply, Salesforce is worth $73 billion more than the core business metrics dictate.

The *Forbes* list ranks companies in order of their innovation premium. ServiceNow tops this year's list with an 89.22 percent innovation premium. This means that the company's $87 billion value is comprised of $38 billion based on their *actual* performance and a whopping $34 billion based on *how innovative the company is perceived to be.*

Tesla, as you might imagine, also made the list, coming in fourth with an innovation premium of 78.27 percent. Here, shareholders enjoy a $65 billion bonus in value attributed only to the company's innovation chops. Compare Tesla to General Motors and folks like me from Detroit get a little seasick. Valued at just $33 billion, the nation's largest car company is only worth 22 percent of Tesla, which only has 18 percent of GM's revenue.

Wait...what? Tesla and GM *both make cars.* They're in the identical manufacturing business. GM had $137.2 billion in revenue in 2019 with $6.6 billion in profits. In the same year, Tesla had just $24.6 billion in sales while losing nearly a billion dollars. Based on all rational measures, GM should be worth more. They have nearly five times the revenue and a much longer history of success, and they actually make money rather than chalk up losses. Yet Tesla enjoys a massive premium because even someone who has never even been in a car would agree that Tesla is just more innovative than GM. Said differently, General Motors is paying an *innovation tax* as their share price is battered by the company's inability to convince investors that the gang can still be innovative.

The innovation premium/innovation tax concept applies to all businesses, not just publicly traded behemoths. While employees of smaller private companies don't monitor their daily stock price, they vote with their feet. Companies that demonstrate innovative approaches attract, engage, and retain talent far more effectively than their stodgier counterparts. Private companies that fully embrace creativity and purposefully build an innovative culture enjoy faster growth, happier customers, and bigger exits when they eventually cash out. Whether you run a barbershop, a mill working plant, or a boutique cybersecurity consultancy, your company is simply worth more as you become more innovative.

The same is true for individuals. The person who regularly demonstrates inventive thinking and creative problem solving is the one who gets promoted faster and reaches higher levels of career success. And if your goal is impact over profits (raising successful kids, making a difference in your community, improving the environment), the innovation premium concept still holds. Regardless of your field, craft, or pursuit, an investment in growing your individual innovation premium delivers a whopping return.

Think of any other investment you might make—a stock, real estate, part ownership in your brother-in-law's new Italian restaurant. In any investment, you invest resources (money, time, effort) in exchange for an expected reward (financial gain, a house that's the envy of your neighbors, a free bowl of baked ziti since you now own 12 percent of Fantastica Pasta over on Birch Street). The other factor of any investment is risk. Investing in a blue-chip stock is lower risk than in an upstart Sicilian joint. So, we're looking at three factors: investment, anticipated reward, and risk.

Let's compare an external investment, such as buying 173 shares of ExxonMobil stock, to investing in your own creativity. The cost of your creativity investment is minimal, especially since you've already purchased this book (thank you, by the way). Sure, there's a time investment to boost your skills, but your creativity investment won't interfere with making this month's rent.

Once you develop your skill set, it's yours to keep. Unlike a stock that must be sold to enjoy the profits, your creativity investment just keeps paying dividends while you still own the underlying asset. As the economy becomes more automated, complex, and competitive, your expanded creative skills will deliver a consistently larger and larger payback. All the while, you savor the internal rewards since the expression of creativity is intrinsically satisfying. Plus, it is renewable, unlike the gas company that invests billions in an offshore well that will eventually run dry.

And your ExxonMobil shares? Subject to innumerous forces outside your control, the investment proves volatile. In case you're wondering, the stock is currently trading at a five-year low due to the collapsing oil market and low consumption trend caused by COVID-19. Your investment is subject to geopolitical turmoil, regulatory burdens, terrorist attacks, climate change, competitive pressures, and weather patterns. Not to mention another catastrophe like the *Exxon Valdez* tanker disaster. In comparison, your creativity investment is durable against these threatening external forces. Back to investment basics, isn't it a no-brainer which bet will cost you the least with the lowest risk and highest possible reward?

Quite a different strategy than what we've been taught to believe. What used to feel safe has become risky, and the other way around. In fact, a flip-flop has been brewing at a massive scale. Growing up, we were taught that hard skills were the golden ticket, only to discover most skills in that category have become automated or commoditized (I guess they aren't so "hard" after all). We were taught, on the other hand, to ditch the soft skills relating to our imagination in the pursuit of "real work." The truth is, these skills are the ones in highest demand and most correlated to financial gain, high performance, and maximum impact. Your MacBook Air can quickly calculate the fault tolerance of a bridge but isn't any good at composing a Broadway musical.

The 70/30 Rule

We've all heard of the old 80/20 rule: 80 percent of your profits come from 20 percent of your best customers; 20 percent of your employees generate 80 percent of the productivity; 80 percent of your headaches come from 20 percent of your problems. Vilfredo Pareto was certainly perceptive back in 1896 when he realized that 80 percent of the land in Italy was held by just 20 percent of the population. Pareto earned the naming rights to this well-known and generally accurate concept.

But let's examine a modern variant of the Pareto principle that applies to existing knowledge, progress, and creativity. As a general rule, I'm convinced that our current training, experience, and well-laid plans will only deliver 70 percent of the results we seek, whereas the remaining 30 percent gap can only be achieved through creativity.

Imagine you run a food distribution business that's been around for forty-six years. It employs 735 people, has a strong history of profits, and a great reputation. With this enviable set of circumstances, it's only logical to believe you should keep doing what's been working. Hey, if it ain't broke, don't fix it. Why rock the apple cart?

The problem is that the world is changing around you, faster than any other time in history. You haven't cracked some imaginary code, but instead you're currently on dry footing in a life-sized game of *Frogger*. Like the frog, you have to leap forward into uncharted waters if you plan to make it home for dinner.

The big annual strategy rollout is met with great enthusiasm as your senior team gobbles down the cocktail shrimp in a fluorescent-lit, beach-themed Orlando ballroom. Leaders from each functional area explain the details, and you can just taste that juicy year-end bonus. We've done it before; we know what we're doing. This is going to be a layup.

But shortly after you leave the comforting embrace of pastel wallpaper, things start to go south. A mushroom shortage means your costs are now out of whack, putting intense pressure on your sales force. That new eco-friendly competitor who got a massive investment from Silicon Valley just developed a new tech-enabled distribution system that makes yours look like it was built during the Nixon administration. Your senior vice president of operations—the rock that you could always count on—had a midlife crisis and ditched her corporate gig to become a yoga instructor. And just when you think it can't get any messier, your restaurant customers are cutting orders in half due to a strange virus that requires them to embrace social distancing, a concept you hadn't even heard of back in the warm sun of Orlando.

As John Lennon famously said, "Life is what happens when you're busy making other plans." For you and your food distribution business, the plans that were ratified just a few months ago are now woefully inadequate. The experiences of the past may be instructive, but the challenges you now face have never been tackled before. The game plan was strong, thankfully, and will allow you to deliver 70 percent of your targets. But who wants to just squeak by with a C-minus grade?

Now you're staring down the creativity gap—the 30 percent that wasn't scripted. To conquer it, you'll have to make decisions in the face of ambiguity. You'll need to improvise, adapting to rapidly changing circumstances in real time. You'll need creative problem solving to battle through the setbacks and inventive thinking to hunt down new growth opportunities.

Your frog needs to learn to hop in new directions, and fast.

Being a creative leader, you figure it out...one *Big Little Breakthrough* at a time. You line up a cloud-based tech platform to battle your savvy new competitor. You scour the earth, finding an even better source of mushrooms, cutting a multiyear deal that lowers cost and creates a competitive advantage. You bring in an industry outsider to fill the open SVP slot, providing a fresh perspective and new set of experiences. And the dwindling demand from socially distanced restaurants opens up the idea to distribute food to hospitals, first responders, and institutional buyers. Some ideas are bold, but many are not individually spectacular. It is the volume of ideas—not the magnitude of any single one—that enables you, our heroic leader, to outperform the industry norms, chalking up the biggest growth year in the company's history.

Of course, the 70/30 rule could have been ignored. Imagine instead you froze, unable to adapt to changing circumstances. Since creativity was never spoken of or developed, you and the company hold steadfast to the original plan. Due to previous wins and strong momentum, your team delivers 70 percent of the original forecast and manage to remain solvent. For now.

The problem is, the 70/30 rule compounds annually. If the company only delivered 70 percent of the target, you are now coming from a very different place when you enter the subsequent year. With the unsteadiness of a wounded dog, the business limps into the new year lacking confidence. Poor performance has the board breathing down your neck, creating a tense environment with no room for creative risk taking. Better batten down the hatches and stick to our knitting, the theory goes. You and the team decide to play it safe, only to discover that was the riskiest move of all. Year two ends with another 30 percent miss, which is met with layoffs, leadership changes, and the annual January strategy off-site held at the Comfort Inn just outside Chicago's O'Hare Airport. So much for those delicious blackberry margaritas in Orlando.

But what if this compounding interest went in your favor instead? Imagine how coming off a banner year, even in tough times, would bolster your creative confidence. With the 30 percent gap closed and conquered, year two is the continuation of an innovation renaissance. From the CEO down to the associate trucking supervisor, new ideas and fresh thinking become the norm. New customer segments are won as market share in existing accounts increases steadily. The cash surplus enables bold investments in future tech and infrastructure, deepening competitive advantage while having plenty left over for jumbo company-wide bonuses.

The results of each 70/30 cycle compound, either in your favor or against it.

And like most concepts in this book, the same principle applies individually. Conquering the 30 percent gap each year compounds in your favor, paying an ever-increasing dividend in the form of role promotions, earnings growth, and greater job satisfaction. Each glorious win over the 30 percent creativity gap pushes you toward your full potential, building your skills and confidence, making next year's fight that much easier. On the other hand, you don't want to get into the negative spiral that a few back-to-back lost years will create. This doom cycle can devolve quickly into quiet desperation, making a comeback increasingly difficult.

The Formulaic Flop

Formulas work great for romantic comedies, boy bands, and the perfect mojito. The whole reason a formula exists is to deliver a predictable result. When the outcome is positive—like that incredible mojito I get at Casa Fuente on nearly every trip to Vegas—formulas are terrific. Which makes we wonder why so many formulaic failures exist when the pattern is so obvious as to clearly be avoided.

How many times have you seen this sequence play out?

Act 1: "The Young Innovator" A new business—let's call it Company A—is wildly innovative. Customers love it. The firm is the darling of Wall Street, attracts the best talent, and is wildly profitable. This new market leader crushes the sleepy industry incumbents, who are sent out to pasture.

Act 2: "The Challenge" A few years later, a new competitor— we'll call it Company Z—enters the scene, uncovering a vulnerability that our hero missed. This challenger finds a new way to deliver value to customers. The company takes a creative approach and starts to win, while the original company—now the market leader—tries to hold its ground. The new challenger, Company Z, is nimbler and more innovative, forging ahead unencumbered by the past.

Act 3: "The Undetected Decline" Based on previous momentum, Company A continues to grow, but much more slowly. Leaders utter platitudes such as, "We'll be fine. We've been through this before." Their arrogance distorts the truth of the situation as shareholder value erodes. All the while, the new challenger, Company Z, continues to chip away at the market leader, poaching key employees and romancing away key customers.

Act 4: "The Final Breath" By the time the once scrappy but now entitled leaders of Company A finally accept the gravity of the situation, it's too late. A series of blunders, missed opportunities, and play-it-safe bets lead to the company's ultimate demise. Executives scramble to find their golden parachutes, while shareholders and customers pay the ultimate price. The challenger—Company Z—has become the champion.

Let's put it to the test. Plug in any of these companies, and the formulaic flop fits perfectly:

Company A	Company Z
Polaroid	Instagram
Rand McNally	Waze
Blockbuster	Netflix
Saturn	Tesla
Eastern Airlines	JetBlue
Atari	Xbox
JCPenney	Zara

Baskin-Robbins	Pinkberry
Blackberry	iPhone
MySpace	Facebook
Borders Books	Amazon
Toys R Us	Target
The Flintstones	*The Simpsons*
Golf	Topgolf

While these are the most obvious and notable flops, finding this formula in nearly every industry, geography, and company size is easier than Googling the weather. The clunky, old-school personal injury law firm is disrupted by the modern, fast, tech-enabled practice. The out-of-touch specialty software incumbent falls prey to the more innovative upstart. The pattern happens to careers too. And universities. And churches, communities, even nations. So why in the world do we continue to repeat the pattern when it is so obvious that a fifth-grade paper on the topic would earn a B-minus for lack of imagination? Why do we keep making the same mistake, especially when it is more cliché than a Hallmark card?

We simply cannot lose sight of *Frogger*, our amphibian inspiration. His message is clear: develop creative skills in order to keep hopping ahead, or risk losing it all. Standing still is outrageously dangerous, while high-frequency, controlled creative steps deliver a clear and much safer path forward.

There's never been a more important time to build your creativity muscles, and there's never been a more exciting time to flex them.

In the next chapter, we'll explore how our creative heroes use daily habits to foster their extraordinary work. In the same way athletes use training techniques to develop their abilities, we'll see how prolific innovators build their skills. Our gym may seem more like an artist's studio, but the notion of doing the reps to achieve mastery remains intact.

Together, we'll peek behind the curtain to examine the training rituals of Lady Gaga, Banksy, and Steven Spielberg. Let's study how legendary artists, musicians, authors, inventors, and business leaders cultivate their imagination through simple daily habits.

I'll also share my five-minute-a-day routine that you're welcome to borrow to boost your own creative abilities. No gym equipment needed.

CHAPTER 4

Build the Muscle

The British poet Edith Sitwell began each morning by lying in an open coffin before writing her first words of the day.

Dr. Yoshiro Nakamatsu, whose invention of the floppy disk is just one of his 3,300 patents, places himself underwater and only generates ideas while close to drowning.

The celebrated novelist Franz Kafka was unable to write until first standing completely naked in an open window, performing a ten-minute exercise routine for the world to see.

Patricia Highsmith, author of several beloved psychological thrillers, typically wrote two thousand words each day, but only in the presence of three hundred live snails.

Francis Bacon, the English scientist and philosopher credited with developing the scientific method, lived by a daily routine that included six or more bottles of wine, multiple gluttonous meals, pills by the fistful, and regular gambling.

Less important than their ritualistic oddities, these creative legends used the power of habits to stoke their imagination.

Consistent routines are practiced by prolific musicians, film-makers, and inventors to harness creative abilities and deliver stunning work.

For us, creative habits don't need to be bizarre. In his book *Atomic Habits*, bestselling author and habits expert James Clear describes habits as "good decisions on autopilot." He points to research from Duke University that cites habits as accounting for more than 40 percent of our behaviors on a given day. Said plainly, if we want to build our creativity abilities, we should start by examining our habits.

When I studied jazz guitar, it was the consistency of practice that accounted for nearly all my progress. An inspired lesson from a brilliant teacher paled in comparison to the countless hours I spent alone with the hypnotic click of my secondhand metronome.

We've been led to believe that it takes ten thousand hours of practice to learn a new skill, as evidenced by the "10,000-hour rule" made famous by author Malcolm Gladwell. While it may take that long to achieve mastery in some fields, I'm a bigger fan of the twenty-hour rule, developed by author Joshua Kaufman.

In his hilarious 2013 TED Talk, Kaufman challenges the validity of the 10,000-hour rule while offering up an alternative. He suggests that just twenty hours of deliberate practice will allow you to learn the basics of almost any new skill. While you may not become a master sommelier, you could certainly learn the basics of wine appreciation. Twenty hours won't get you playing the cello like virtuoso Yo-Yo Ma, but you'd easily rock out "Twinkle, Twinkle" while gaining a preliminary understanding of the curva-ceous instrument.

The twenty-hour concept is liberating when we realize that investing just a few hours toward our creative growth can deliver many of the juicy benefits we seek. To unleash *Big Little Break-throughs*, you won't need a PhD in creative studies since these small imaginative nuggets are accessible to us all.

Let's further break down our twenty hours into manageable chunks. Twenty minutes a day for two months—or ten minutes a day for four months—is an investment that each of us can make that will move us decidedly closer to our *5 percent Creativity Upgrade*. For the low time investment of skipping a few episodes of your favorite reality show, you can be well on your way to a powerful creative boost.

We'll examine the habits and mindsets of creators who were able to achieve INNOVATION (all-caps), but the same approaches can apply to normal folks like you and me as we discover an abundance of everyday innovations (lowercase).

An Apeeling Peel

Born to Chinese immigrants who fled to Canada for a better life, Jenny Du grew up in what she'd later describe as a "super blue-collar family." Though her parents lacked formal education of their own, the Dus pushed their four daughters to pursue rigorous academic studies. With her dad often working seven days a week as a welder and her mom taking every job she could to help pay the bills, the girls had to learn independence at an early age.

Jenny's sisters followed traditional paths, with two becoming optometrists and one becoming a dentist. Jenny, on the hand, still wasn't sure what she wanted to do after earning her PhD in chemistry.

Along with fellow postdoctoral students James Rogers and Lou Perez at UC Santa Barbara, Jenny was drawn to attack one of the world's biggest problems: food waste. A staggering 40 percent of the world's food is squandered, largely due to spoilage, with a whopping 10 percent of all greenhouse gases linked to food waste. Even worse than the economic and environmental impacts, wasted food means that people go hungry.

According to the World Health Organization, 821 million people—one of every nine people on the planet—go to bed hungry each night. As our population continues to grow, the problem will only intensify. By 2050, our global population is expected to reach 10 billion, which will require 56 percent more food than we currently produce.

The stark disconnect between massive food waste and the desperate need to feed hungry people led Jenny, James, and Lou to start asking questions. How do we protect food today? Is refrigeration really the best we can do? How do plants protect themselves? Why do plants start to decay once they are off the vine? What causes food spoilage? Jenny and the team persisted, with each question splintering into three more.

The questions began to morph from "why" and "how" to "what if?" What if we could create a way to protect produce after it was harvested? Since every fruit and vegetable has a peel to protect it, what if we could make the natural peel more effective?

Questions led to experiments, which in turn led to a big idea: What if we could develop an all-natural plant-based coating that could dramatically slow the spoilage process? The idea to improve nature's peels drove the three young scientists to action. After two years of late-night coffee- and pizza-infused tinkering in the lab, Apeel Sciences was founded in 2012 with a small grant from the Bill & Melinda Gates Foundation.

Initial ideas were a good start, but it was a series of *Big Little Breakthrough* after the initial spark that allowed the team to forge their vision into a reality. It took six more years before their first product—a spray-on peel for avocados—was approved by the FDA for commercial use.

"The joke with the avocado is: not now, not now, not now. Now? Too late," cofounder James Rogers laughs. "But when you get an Apeel avocado, the joke no longer makes sense because the fruit stays ripe for so long." Avocados treated with Apeel's plant-based coating last up to three times longer than their nontreated counterparts. Rogers continues, "You can't see it, smell it, taste it, or feel it. And it's just plants. We use food to preserve food."

The small, nerdy company on the outskirts of Santa Barbara continued to gain momentum and garner attention. After the Gates Foundation provided additional funding to support further research and development, the three cofounders landed on the radar of the media, scientific community, and eager venture capital investors. Silicon Valley's Andreessen Horowitz, which famously backed Facebook, Airbnb, and Twitter, led a $70-million investment in the company, joined by celebrity investors Katy Perry and Oprah Winfrey.

"I hate to see food wasted, when there are so many people in the world who are going without," said Winfrey in a public statement tied to her investment. "Apeel can extend the life of fresh produce, which is critical to our food supply and our planet."

Time magazine named Apeel Sciences one of TIME's 50 Genius Companies in 2018, while the World Economic Forum included the company on its annual Technology Pioneers list at a ceremony in Davos, Switzerland. In 2019, *Fast Company* inducted Apeel to the number seven spot on its Most Innovative Companies list, ahead of Apple, Peloton, and Universal Music Group.

On May 26, 2020, during the scariest times of the COVID-19 pandemic, Apeel Sciences reached the milestone that every startup founder dreams of. A $250 million investment, led by

Singapore's sovereign wealth fund, placed the company's valuation at more than $1 billion. Jenny, James, and Lou's creative idea had officially become a "unicorn," Silicon Valley slang for a startup company that reaches a billion-dollar valuation.

With plenty of capital and notoriety, Apeel is now well on the way to making a meaningful impact. "Food waste is an invisible tax imposed on everyone that participates in the food system," said the founders in a company statement. "Eliminating global food waste can free up to $2.6 trillion annually, allowing us to make the food ecosystem better for growers, distributors, retailers, consumers and our planet. Together, we're putting time back on the industry's side to help deal with the food waste crisis."

At a tour of the company's glimmering 100,000-square-foot headquarters, team member Daniel Costanza (no relation to George) explains that one of their customers no longer needs to use plastic wrap on cucumbers due to the Apeel protective spray. Just this change alone—with one cucumber producer—will save as much plastic as it would take to wrap the Empire State Building eleven times around. "Imagine adding that to each food category throughout the globe," Costanza says. "That's a huge paradigm shift away from single-use plastics. It's pretty crazy."

How did a renegade group of postdoc researchers at UC Santa Barbara create such a wildly successful company? Their fruitfulness (sorry, I couldn't resist) came by way of growing and harvesting their own creative capacity through a series of daily habits. Just like the fruits and vegetables the company protects, creativity itself grows through *inputs*, *conditions*, and *repetitions*, the same building blocks we'll use to expand our own abilities.

For produce, positive inputs such as sunlight, water, fertilizer, and soil support growth while negative ones such as insects and disease stimulate decay. To grow healthy produce, farmers work to optimize external conditions such as climate and proximity to other crops while keeping the surroundings safe from harmful influences like rodents with the munchies. And from seed to harvest, produce needs adequate time to grow. The perfect strawberry only ripens through the repetition of sunlight and water over a several-week period.

The same three components fostered Apeel's growth and success. The initial idea emerged through relentless curiosity, with the questions themselves becoming the inputs along with extensive research into the problems of food waste and world hunger. Inputs also included the years Jenny spent at home with her three sisters, developing a strong sense of independence and problem-solving skills. Prior to forming Apeel, she and her cofounders spent countless hours in the chemistry lab, gaining a deep understanding of the scientific process. And as the company grew, inputs came in the form of capital, additional team members, public recognition, and research findings from around the globe.

From the proximity to a major research university to their swanky new headquarters, conditions played a key role in the company's good fortune. Internally, Jenny helped shape the company culture as a condition to foster inventive thinking and creative problem solving. "It was an outstanding opportunity to do meaningful work, work in an interesting technical field, and build the company's culture and values from scratch—what more could anyone ask for?" Jenny said in a 2020 *Forbes* interview.

She set out to build the culture around transparency and trust, encouraging team members to share any and all ideas. "We have an all-hands meeting every Monday," Jenny said in a 2019 presentation at UCSB. "You get to hear from all different parts of the organization...it's like open season. We are transparent and honest and a little bit vulnerable."

The repetitions component is often excluded from our romantic notion of artistic brilliance, yet doing the reps is what develops individual and organizational creative muscle mass. Jenny and the team toiled with the Apeel formulas for years, day in and day out. To develop a thin peel of organic, edible plant material that can be sprayed onto produce and significantly eliminate water loss and oxidation is much easier said than done. Without sustained persistence, Apeel could have easily ended up among the millions of other good initial ideas that never get off the ground.

Whether you're setting out to eradicate world hunger or you just want to learn to play "American Pie" on the banjo, there's a systematic way to build creative might. Studying history's greatest innovators—from composers and playwrights to inventors and business icons—most geniuses are rather practical in how they build their creativity muscles. They have a systematic approach, cultivated through daily habits, that serves as the foundation of their creative discovery.

Deconstructing our practice habits into inputs, conditions, and repetitions—the same three components that drove Jenny Du's success with Apeel Sciences—we can formulate our own training regimen to expand creative capacity. These are the same three habitual factors that enable us to juggle chain saws, learn to dance the tango, or speak Portuguese. And they'll do the trick quite nicely for each of us to become more creative.

Inputs

When the mysterious graffiti artist Banksy was eighteen, a near miss with the police transformed his artistic process. He was spraying his art on a parked train in his hometown of Bristol, England, with a group of fellow artists when the authorities caught them by surprise. "The rest of my mates made it to the car," Banksy recalled in a 2003 interview, "so I spent over an hour hidden under a dumper truck with engine oil leaking all over me. As I lay there listening to the cops on the tracks, I realized I had to cut my painting time in half or give it up altogether. I was staring straight up at the stenciled plate on the bottom of the fuel tank when I realized I could just copy that style and make each letter three feet high. As soon as I cut my first stencil, I could feel the power there. I also like the political edge. All graffiti is low-level dissent, but stencils have an extra history. They've been used to start revolutions and to stop wars."

Currently one of the most celebrated artists in the world, Banksy's distinctive style began with the input of this hour-long stare down. Stenciling became his technique of choice, making his work instantly recognizable. The graffiti artist, activist, painter, and filmmaker was named one of the world's most influential people by Time magazine in 2010, and his works now fetch millions from insatiable art collectors.

When you examine Banksy's incredible body of work, the inputs are as clear as the artist's own signature. One of the most notable elements of Banksy lore is that he is anonymous. In an era where people manufacture drama just to garner publicity, nobody knows Banksy's real name or what he looks like. He refuses exposure of any kind, hiding in the shadows instead of lusting after the limelight. Mysterious and compelling to be sure, but it turns out Banksy's anonymity came by way of inputs from others.

The painting *Nursing Madonna* from the late fifteenth century sold at auction for $2.5 million in February 2019. It was created by an anonymous artist known only as "Master of the Embroidered Foliage," one of dozens from that period who kept their identity hidden behind a pseudonym. When Elena Ferrante was nominated for a Nobel Prize in Literature, the organizers were concerned what would happen if she won because she has been writing under a fictitious name since 1992 and no one knew how to find her to present her the award.

Being a prankster is another one of Banksy's idiosyncratic characteristics. He once snuck into the Louvre and mounted a replica image of the *Mona Lisa* plastered with a smiley-face sticker. He was somehow able to remain undetected when he hung a small portrait of a woman wearing a gas mask on a wall at the Metropolitan Museum of Art in New York. One time, he installed a blow-up doll of a Guantanamo prisoner, complete with an orange prison jumpsuit, on a ride at Disneyland, where it remained for ninety minutes until park officials had it removed.

Banksy's most famous prank made headlines around the world while arguably elevating his notoriety beyond any other living artist. As soon as the Sotheby auctioneer's gavel signified the sale of Banksy's painting *Girl with Balloon* at a 2018 auction, stunned onlookers were horrified as the painting began to self-destruct. Undetected by Sotheby staff, Banksy had secretly installed a mini paper shredder inside the frame of his painting, which had been in the auction house's possession for years. The device was triggered through a remote control that Banksy was somehow able to activate the precise moment his painting was sold. The "final sale" work dropped through the bottom of its frame until it stopped halfway through to reveal a half-shredded painting hanging under its original mounting.

Imagine the shock of the buyer who'd just spent $1.4 million. Banksy's motivation for the prank is unclear. Was it an "example of artists deploying guerrilla tactics to expose their disdain for the critics, dealers, gallery owners, and museum curators on whom they depend on for their livelihood," as art historian Kelsey

Campbell-Dollaghan suggested? Or was it a brilliant marketing mind looking to elevate his brand and raise the value of his art? In this case, the buyer apparently has the last laugh since *Fortune* magazine estimates the value of the painting has more than doubled since the prank occurred.

But Banksy isn't the original prankster pioneer. The artist Harvey Stromberg, posing as a photojournalist in the 1970s, installed more than three hundred stickers of ordinary objects such as light switches, bricks, and power outlets throughout New York's Museum of Modern Art. It took the staff over two years to identify and remove all the stickers, which were applied with exacting detail to conceal their existence.

Believe it or not, Banksy wasn't even the first prankster with a self-destructing work of art. Back in 1960, artist Jean Tinguely's sculpture *Homage to New York* debuted in a garden ceremony at the city's Museum of Modern Art. The mechanical contraption was set in motion in front of distinguished collectors, including John D. Rockefeller III, as the mischief unfolded. The haughty crowd was bewildered when the work burst into flames before their eyes. Here's how the museum curators described the scene at the time:

> A meteorological trial balloon inflated and burst, colored smoke was discharged, paintings were made and destroyed, and bottles crashed to the ground. A player piano, metal drums, a radio broadcast, a recording of the artist explaining his work, and a competing shrill voice correcting him provided the cacophonic soundtrack to the machine's self-destruction— until it was stopped short by the fire department.

From his stenciling to his pseudonym to his pranks, Banksy used inspiration from other creators as the inputs to develop his own unique blend of artistry. The same is true for his subversive subject matter. The idea to paint a living 8,000-pound elephant bright red and then overlay a gold fleur-de-lis pattern on its massive body was hatched in a response to the input of global poverty. While placing a live elephant in the middle of an art gallery drew the ire of animal rights activists, Banksy's message couldn't be ignored. "The elephant in the room is that 1.3 billion people live below the poverty line," Banksy said in a written statement.

A painting of little girls cuddling up to missiles is a statement on geopolitical turmoil. Two male police officers engaged in a passionate kiss was based on Banksy's observation of homophobia among British authorities. From his provocative imagery to his clever puns, his art is a reflection of the various inputs he gathers. Whether it's a pastoral landscape ensconced in crime-scene tape or a portrait of Winston Churchill with a Mohawk, each work is the visual manifestation of converging inputs.

Inputs are critical in any training regimen. If you want to get in shape, your inputs include food, water, and nutritional supplements. Inputs may also include a personal trainer, your workout buddy to hold you accountable, and a subscription to *Weight Watchers* magazine.

Using inputs to elevate my own creativity, I love consuming art in many forms, from music to literature to fine art. I also try to ingest inputs that have nothing to do with my work or existing passions. You'd be surprised the impact you can gain from reading *Popular Woodworking* or watching instructional videos on how to prune a bonsai tree. Random inputs can actually have a dramatic impact on creativity.

George Harrison, the legendary Beatles guitarist, was studying Eastern philosophy and learned about a core principle called relativism. "It seemed to me to be based on the Eastern concept that everything is relative to everything else as opposed to the Western view that things are merely coincidental," Harrison said in his 2002 autobiography, *I, Me, Mine*. He decided to test the concept by writing a song based on the first words he'd find when opening a random book. Flipping open a dusty hardcover, he happened to see the words "gently weeps" printed in the center of the page. The resulting song, "While My Guitar Gently Weeps," is now included as one of *Rolling Stone*'s "500 Greatest Songs of All Time" and widely considered to be Harrison's best work.

As a peculiar input, the German poet and playwright Friedrich Schiller filled his desk drawers with rotting apples, requiring the decaying stench before writing a single word. From traditional to unorthodox, consider what inputs will best suit you as you craft your ideal creative habits.

Conditions

Steven Spielberg was only twenty years old when he secured a seven-year contract to make films for Universal Pictures. Spielberg was young and impressionable, and his now iconic status was far from inevitable. His boss at the time, Universal's president Sid Sheinberg, made a promise to young Steven that he credits as the key to his ability to unleash creativity. "I will support you as strongly in failure as I will in success," Sheinberg told the younger man. Had Spielberg landed in a different environment, we can't be sure his creative accomplishments would have been as monumental. Sheinberg gave Spielberg the ideal conditions for him to take creative risks, which built his confidence and elevated his art.

Following inputs, conditions are as important as the work itself. In the same way a greenhouse creates the ideal conditions to grow certain plants, creative conditions are a crucial factor in our ability to grow artistically. Your conditions include factors such as physical environment, rituals and rewards, equipment, outside pressures and demands, deadlines, and the people around you.

The legendary rock band Aerosmith uses conditions to drive the band's creativity. Every week, they have a meeting called "Dare to Suck." Lead singer Steven Tyler explains, "Each one of us brings an idea that we think is probably terrible, and that we are embarrassed that we even have the idea. But we present it. And nine times out of ten, the idea is actually terrible. But one time out of ten you get 'Dude Looks Like a Lady' or 'Love in an Elevator.'" The ritual of the Dare to Suck meeting allows bandmembers to fearlessly share their crazy ideas, helping them become better artists while uncovering new material for the band.

In a closely related ritual, Ballot Bin inventor Trewin Restorick has a standing team meeting called "F*ck Up Fridays." During their weekly brown bag lunch, each team member shares what they f*cked up that week. The mistakes are applauded, not criticized. The whole team embraces and examines each stumble, looking for nuggets of insight that may be helpful in the future. If someone didn't F something up, Trewin asks them why not and presses them to take more creative risks the following week. The Friday ritual helps cultivate the team's creative courage while expanding their tolerance for failure.

Conditions played a critical factor for Lin-Manuel Miranda as he wrote "How Far I'll Go," one of the songs for Disney's animated film *Moana*. He set out to write an "I want" song, sung by the film's lead character who was in her teens. To find inspiration, he returned to his own childhood home. "I was writing a teenage character and I needed to connect with that angsty part of myself that feels like the future is forever away and everything is life or death. So, I went and locked myself in my childhood bedroom," Lin-Manuel said in a 2017 interview with the *Washington Post*.

Long before his fame and success, Lin-Manuel established the ideal conditions to hone his craft. Along with a few musical buddies, he formed an improvisational group to help build creative muscle mass. Since 2004, Freestyle Love Supreme meets regularly to practice and perform improvised hip-hop music based on input from the crowd. Someone in the audience may toss out the verb "cajole" while another guest proposes the noun "refrigerator." In real time, the troupe composes and performs a rap song—complete with beat boxing—using the audience's suggestions. Lin-Manuel's improv gang created the perfect training conditions that ultimately enabled his historic success.

I picked up a terrific conditions-based ritual from my good friend and fellow author Neil Pasricha. In his 2019 book, *You Are Awesome*, Neil describes one of his favorite approaches, which he calls "untouchable days." He explains that most of us have five workdays each week that appear very similar to one another. Each day is a scattering of calls and meetings, with small pockets of time in between. The problem is, it's very hard to get into the creative groove when your next phone call is eleven minutes away. To free up time for deep, creative work, Neil restructured his calendar. He now squishes all meetings and calls into four jam-packed days, leaving one day each week as untouchable.

During his untouchable day, Neil removes every distraction so he can focus all his energies on creative efforts. He turns the Wi-Fi off on his computer to avoid email and social media distractions. He puts his phone on airplane mode to prevent interference from texts or calls. With a completely clear calendar and no intrusions, he's able to do his best creative work. He points out that he's not actually working any more hours, but rather he's simply making a more efficient use of the same time. Other than his wife's ability to find him in the event of an emergency, Neil completely shuts out the outside world to go deep inside his creative mind.

I borrowed Neil's untouchable day ritual and have now been practicing it religiously for more than a year. This shift has been the single biggest boost to my creative output in the last ten years, giving me the time to focus on work that requires more than fifteen-minute increments. By changing conditions, my creative output accelerated dramatically. If you can't slot out an entire day, you can always try a modified schedule. Even if your version is an untouchable morning once a month, the improved conditions will yield improved *Big Little Breakthroughs*.

Leonardo da Vinci routinely took up to five naps a day to boost his creative abilities. And it turns out there's some science to support the slumberly genius. Dr. Sara C. Mednick, an associate professor of psychology at the University of California, Irvine, and author of the book *Take a Nap! Change Your Life*, conducted a survey in which she gave a creativity test to a group of participants. After the scores were tallied, the group was divided, with half of the subjects taking a nap while the others rested without sleep. Later in the day, the same creativity tests were administered again to measure the nap's impact on creative output. Dr. Mednick's research revealed that the sleepers improved their scores by 40 percent while the groggy non-sleepers enjoyed no gain.

We may think napping is for the lazy, but sleep is a condition that can pay big dividends. The artist Salvador Dalí famously took several naps a day to refresh his creative mind. To ensure he didn't sleep too long, he built a habit he referred to as "slumber with keys." Dalí would sit back in a comfortable chair while holding a large ring of keys in his hand, which he'd purposely hold directly over a metal plate. When he drifted off, he would eventually lose his grip, dropping the keys loudly to jolt him awake. "Not a second more is needed for your physical and psychic being to be revivified by just the necessary amount of repose," Dalí wrote in his 1948 book, *50 Secrets of Magic Craftsmanship*.

Bestselling author Dan Pink developed a productive sleep ritual, which he lovingly calls a "Nappuccino." Dan gulps down a large cup of coffee in the midafternoon and then promptly puts on his eye mask and lies down for some shut-eye. Setting an alarm for twenty minutes later, he drifts off without the worry of oversleeping. The buzzer rings precisely when the caffeine starts to affect his body, allowing him to awaken with a giant boost of energy. With new evidence pointing to an ideal nap length of eighteen to twenty-two minutes, Dan's technique is an efficient way for him to recharge his creativity and enjoy highly productive afternoons.

Optimal conditions for creativity are a matter of personal taste. Some creators love working in public places, gleaning inspiration from the hustle and bustle, while others insist on quiet solitude. Certain artists' studios remain messy, in a chaotic state of disarray, while others keep their surroundings immaculate and orderly.

Virginia Woolf, one of the most prominent authors of the twentieth century, only wrote when standing up, while Igor Stravinsky stood on his head for fifteen minutes each morning before composing music. The playwright Tom Stoppard literally chained himself to his desk for at least seven hours each day to ensure his writing continued at a steady pace, a condition that few of us would choose to emulate. The key takeaway: design your own conditions in a way that's right for you, which will play a crucial role in your creative advancement.

Do the Reps

Just before she won the Academy Award for Best Original Song, I watched Lady Gaga dazzle the live audience with a pitch-perfect performance of her hit "Shallow." From her stage skills to her vocal ability, the talented performer made it all look so easy.

When we see people performing at the top of their fields—from Broadway to business—they often make it look simple. But people who achieve Lady Gaga levels of success arrive at the top by way of rigorous training. They refuse the elevator, preferring to take the stairs.

The romantic notion of a wildly talented genius who effortlessly reaches the epitome of achievement has about as much practical validity as the Easter Bunny. Rather, it's the unglamorous, repetitive practice regimen that unlocks creative brilliance.

Stefani Joanne Angelina Germanotta, now known as Lady Gaga, was born on March 28, 1986, into an Italian American family in New York. Her ascent to stardom was less about raw talent and more closely aligned with her relentless work ethic. She began playing piano at age four and became driven to become a star before her tiny legs could reach the piano pedals. In a 2009 interview, she told a London reporter, "I've always been famous—you just didn't know it yet!" She already viewed success as part of her being, which drove her to extreme levels of training and practice.

While her elaborate outfits and theatrical performances may appear to be the child of whimsy, Lady Gaga is meticulous and deliberate about every aspect of her music and brand. Growing up, she spent hours honing her craft. Pushing aside the customary pleasures of childhood, she studied piano, singing, and dance with the intensity of a Zen monk. When she wasn't practicing performance skills, she studied the legends of fashion design, theatrical staging, choreography, and visual artists. Her training inputs were a strange mix—from David Bowie to Bach, from Andy Warhol to Cher. She drew inspiration from an eclectic mix of artists, later weaving their ideas together into her own unique style.

"To be completely candid, the creative process is approximately fifteen minutes of vomiting my creative ideas," Lady Gaga said in a 2011 *Gagavision* interview. "It all happens in approximately fifteen minutes of this giant regurgitation of my thoughts and feelings, and then there are days, months, and years spent fine-tuning." To put this in perspective, if creating a hit Gaga song takes five hundred hours in total, the ideation process is only .05 percent while the vast majority of her creative time is spent shaping and refining her work. And if you include the thousands of hours she invested in deliberate practice before the song was initially spewed onto the page, the contrast would be even more glaring.

It's the ritual of refinement that's often the difference between mediocre and legendary work.

It's been said that the one thing all great authors have in common is lousy first drafts. The difference between a bad book, a decent book, and a breakaway bestseller is often directly linked to the amount of time invested in the refinement stage. When a writer quickly dumps her ideas onto a page and ships them to print, the end result isn't usually her best work. In contrast, her masterpiece comes by doing the reps in the unglamorous and painstaking process of refinement.

We all know that doing the reps is required to build physical muscle mass in the gym. Regrettably, none of us are born with "six-pack abs." Yet most of us garble the translation when it comes to creativity, thinking that it is a fixed talent rather than a malleable skill. And skills of any kind only become deeply ingrained by way of repetition.

At age sixteen, Stefani began working with famed vocal coach Don Lawrence, who had also worked with Billy Joel, Christina Aguilera, and Mick Jagger. Behind the glitz of her dramatic performances, Lady Gaga still does the reps and continues to work with Lawrence. For a single high-profile performance in 2017, she trained with her coach every single day for six months leading up to the show.

Today, her training regimen continues with enviable discipline and consistency. To keep up with the physical demands of the job, she exercises five days a week doing yoga, Pilates, and strength training. She carves out time to write music and rehearse daily. Lady Gaga is the product of intense and consistent practice, an amalgamation of her countless hours doing the reps. Each *Big Little Breakthrough* she achieved fused together into the megastar we now love. In the words of Aristotle, "We are what we repeatedly do. Excellence, then, is not an act but a habit."

It's often been said that it takes twenty-one days to form a habit. Flipping that around, I believe it takes twenty-one habits to make each day productive. When we ensure our habits are deliberate and directed toward our intentions, the habits stack together to deliver great outcomes.

Daily rituals are the polar opposite of a magnificent performance. They aren't your moment of glory, but rather they're the unglamorous tasks you do in order to win the prize in the first place. Bestselling author Seth Godin might have put it best when he said, "Lots and lots of people are creative when they feel like it, but you are only going to become a professional if you do it when you're not in the mood."

My Creative Rituals

While I consider myself an artist (and I hope you do too), there are days that I don't feel creative at all. I have the same emotional ups and downs that all artists have: on some good days I feel like I'm rock legend Mick Jagger, while on the bad ones I feel more like the lip-synching '80s fraud band Milli Vanilli. There are times I'm ashamed of my work, times when I feel like an imposter, and times when I think no one will care what I have to say.

Doubt is a persistent bedfellow, but habits can help us rejuvenate. I find my rituals helpful on the good days but absolutely essential to get me through the tough ones. Although each person should develop his or her own individually optimized training program, I share mine with you in the hopes that it can provide a decent point of reference.

As mentioned earlier, untouchable days have become a crucial habit for me when cranking out meaningful creative work. Much of this book, for example, was written during distraction-free untouchable days.

In addition to larger efforts such as writing a book, composing a song, or crafting a new business plan, I practice a short daily ritual to keep my imagination fresh. Think of it as a five-minute daily exercise routine to maintain creative fitness. My little ritual has been tweaked over the years through trial and error, and with lots of ideas (inputs) from others. I practice this simple and effective system a minimum of five times per week to keep my creativity sharp. Here's the high-level system, followed by an explanation of each step:

Josh's Five-Minute Creativity Workout

1. **Centering Breath** (thirty seconds)
2. **The Daily 3** (sixty seconds)
3. **Guzzle Inputs** (sixty seconds)
4. **Creative Calisthenics** (sixty seconds)
5. **Highlight Reel** (thirty seconds)
6. **Battle Cry** (thirty seconds)
7. **Centering Breath** (thirty seconds)

Now that we've seen the overview, let's unpack each of the components:

Centering Breath. Just as the name indicates, this a quick breathing exercise to get grounded and focused. I borrowed the concept from one of the top pro-athlete performance coaches, Jason Selk. In his book, *10-Minute Toughness*, he shares this approach, which is simple to implement and extremely effective. Take a deep breath for six seconds, hold it in for two, and then release for seven seconds. Jason has helped pro MLB pitchers throw no-hitters during high-pressure games by using this technique, and I find it to be a powerful way to start and end my five-minute routine.

The Daily 3. I borrowed this one from Neil Pasricha (previously mentioned inventor of untouchable days). His ritual is to start each day by answering three questions: What am I *grateful for*, what will I *focus on today*, and what will I *let go of*? I answer these quickly, in a stream-of-consciousness manner where I respond with the first thing that comes to mind. My only rule is that I can't repeat an answer for thirty days, so it makes me focus on smaller, more tangible things. For example, instead of being grateful for my health (which I am, by the way), I may indicate gratitude for the extra-crispy old-world pepperoni I plan to enjoy later that evening on a Detroit-style square pizza. Or instead of letting go of something enormous like all human envy, my quick release may be letting go of the frustration I felt while waiting in the security line at the airport during yesterday's trip home.

Guzzle Inputs. We've covered the importance of inputs as a factor in boosting creative capacity. In this ritual, I simply swallow down sixty seconds of creative inputs to stimulate my thinking. Mine is often a burst of John Coltrane's raw saxophone or the smooth guitar of Wes Montgomery. Other times, I'll read a random article on a subject I know nothing about. I suggest you vary your inputs from your own artistic muse (mine is jazz music; yours may be viewing impressionist paintings or watching *South Park* reruns) and ingest material from outside your normal worldview. If you're looking for a new one, search online for Freestyle Love Supreme, Lin-Manuel Miranda's improv group.

Creative Calisthenics. Growing up, I loved a book series called *Two-Minute Mysteries*, in which I'd read a very short passage (often just a few paragraphs) and then have to solve a mystery that it posed. Today, I do a sixty-second sprint of inventive thinking (playing offense innovation) or creative problem solving (playing defense innovation). Basically, I give myself a one-minute mystery such as, "What are eleven nontraditional uses for a pen?" or "How would I advertise toothpaste to a tribal village where nobody's ever seen a toothbrush?" Think of these as jumping jacks for your creativity muscle, keeping you fit and in practice.

Highlight Reel. Also adapted from Jason Selk, I've created a thirty-second highlight reel that I play on the LED screen in my mind. Imagine watching a highlight reel from your favorite sport, but instead of featuring yesterday's tennis match, it features you performing at your best. I do a fifteen-second burst of an existing accomplishment, followed by a fifteen-second burst of something I've yet to achieve. The combination of these two—watching something I've already done and then something I want to do—burns powerful images into my mind and helps me create the best path toward future results. This exercise ties directly to innoplasticity (covered in chapter 1), opening new brain pathways and unlocking potential.

Battle Cry. Throughout ancient warfare tradition, soldiers would chant out a series of inspiring words just before marching into combat. In my case, I created a short manifesto that I read out loud. It is based on two ideals that are core to the person I aspire to become: a warrior (grit, tenacity, resilience, persistence, courage) and an artist (creativity, imagination, inventiveness). Reciting these words further grounds me into my ideal creative state of mind:

THE WARRIOR ARTIST
Today is my day
Today, I'll show up fully
Today, I'll make the right choices instead of the easy ones

Today, I will learn and grow
Today, I hold myself to the highest standards
Today, I'll take my challenges head-on and refuse to
    back down or procrastinate
Today, I remain committed to helping others become
    their very best

Today, I will unleash bold, creative, and unconventional
    ideas
Today, I will support those I care about the most
Today, I'll discover something new

Today, I'll push myself to a new level of focus and
    achievement
Today, I will demonstrate patience and empathy,
    grit and resilience

Today will make me stronger and tougher
Today, I'll deliver tangible results
Today, I will make the world a better place
Today, I will take action

Today…I am the Warrior Artist

After a final centering breath, I'm off to tackle my creative challenges. This five-minute daily ritual helps me fight off negativity, centering my mind on what's possible. Obviously, you should experiment with your own training ritual. The point is, a simple five-minute daily routine can set you up for creative success.

Yes, this may feel strange at first; getting going is always the hardest part. Bestselling author Robin Sharma likes to say, "All change is hard at first, messy in the middle, and beautiful at the end." The good news is that elevating your creative skill set is absolutely within your grasp if you're willing to do the reps.

In the same way Apeel Sciences' technology helps protect fruit and veggies from decay, your training regimen will protect you from imagination atrophy. Like the delicious avocado, we need to defend the creative capacity that's already inside us with a strong protective peel.

To achieve our *5 percent Creativity Upgrade*, it makes sense to train like those who have already been there. From Apeel Sciences' Jenny Du to Lin-Manuel Miranda, from Banksy to Lady Gaga, from Steven Spielberg to Aerosmith's Steven Tyler, let's build habits around creativity in order to maximize our abilities. Let's craft a deliberate training program, factoring in productive inputs, conditions, and repetitions in order to unlock a flood of *Big Little Breakthroughs*.

For additional training resources and techniques, including worksheets and team exercises, visit BigLittleBreakthroughs.com /toolkit.

Now that we understand the science of creativity and the need for everyday innovation, it's time to shift from *why* to *how*.

For the rest of this book, we'll explore how to cultivate creative skills and deploy them in our lives and careers. We'll discover the *Eight Obsessions of Everyday Innovators* to understand the mindsets that will help us fully realize our *5 percent Creativity Upgrade*. We'll also peek into the *Innovation Tool Kit* to gain some practical and highly effective tactics to unlock fresh ideas.

Together, we'll sit down with a wide range of characters from all over the world. You'll meet entrepreneurs disrupting the establishment in pharmaceuticals, motorcycles, infant care, and apparel. We'll chat with nonprofit leaders taking on massive challenges including global education, women's empowerment, and prison reform. We'll learn insider secrets from LEGO, P&G,

Microsoft, and other multinational giants. And we'll emerge with a systematic approach to boost your creativity to new heights.

So, grab your paint brush, saxophone, lab gear, or sculptor's clay. There's a vault inside you that's filled with unimaginable treasures. Let's go crack the combination lock.

PART TWO

THE EIGHT OBSESSIONS
OF EVERYDAY INNOVATORS

How do innovators—of all shapes and sizes—think and act? How can we all enjoy a meaningful *Creativity Upgrade*, elevating our performance in both business and life? What should we do to build creative capacity and discover an abundance of *Big Little Breakthroughs*?

Now that we've set the foundation in Part One, we'll answer these questions by uncovering the *Eight Obsessions of Everyday Innovators*. These core mindsets drive daily behavior, elevate creative output, and propel ordinary people like you and me to greatness:

1. **Fall in love with the problem.** Rather than prematurely landing on a specific solution, this means taking the time to carefully examine and understand the challenge at hand. It means being more committed to solving the problem than to a particular manner of solving it and remaining flexible and open-minded in order to find the optimal approach.

2. **Start before you're ready.** Everyday innovators take the initiative to get started now instead of waiting for permission, detailed instructions, or ideal conditions. They are willing to course-correct along the way, adapt to changing circumstances in real time, and operate with agility.

3. **Open a test kitchen.** Innovation is both strengthened and de-risked through experimentation. By building a framework and conditions for testing and creative exploration, ideas are cultivated and optimized.

4. **Break it to fix it.** Ditching the "if it ain't broke, don't fix it" advice of the past, everyday innovators proactively deconstruct, examine, and rebuild to deliver superior products, systems, processes, and works of art.

5. **Reach for weird.** Preferring the unexpected approaches to the obvious ones, everyday innovators challenge conventional wisdom by searching for unorthodox ideas. They have a penchant for discovering oddball, sometimes even bizarre ideas in order to discover better outcomes.

6. **Use every drop of toothpaste.** Consider this a scrappy approach of doing more with less. Counterintuitively, being resource-constrained can fuel creative breakthroughs. Resourcefulness and ingenuity become powerful weapons in the fight for superior innovation.

7. **Don't forget the dinner mint.** Adding small, creative flourishes can yield significantly improved results. An extra dose of surprise and delight enables new invention, competitive victory, and individual achievement.

8. **Fall seven times, stand eight.** Realizing that setbacks are inevitable, everyday innovators use creative resilience to overcome adversity. Mistakes are a natural and important part of the innovation process and can be flipped into advantages when studied and embraced.

We'll travel the globe, hearing the stories of underdogs and visionaries, misfits and creators. By deconstructing the beliefs and tactics of extraordinary innovators, we'll demystify creative brilliance.

Ready to dive in? Let's go stir things up.

Chapter 5

Fall in Love with the Problem

As his frustration boiled over, Chad Price reached the breaking point. His legs were numb from sitting in the worn plastic seat for nearly two hours, yet there were still sixteen people ahead of him on the list. The pale fluorescent lighting was making his eyes water amidst the angry flare-ups of other customers impatiently waiting their turns. Two rows over, the four-year-old was having yet another temper tantrum, while the large man to his left sloppily gobbled down a ham-and-cheese sandwich. From the blistering, stale air to the lingering smell of overheating photocopy machines, the soul-sucking experience was all he could take.

We've all had the painful experience of waiting at the dreaded Department of Motor Vehicles. Consistently ranked as the number one worst customer experience in endless "hall of shame" reports, even ahead of budget airlines and cable companies, most of us would rather get a root canal than have to suffer through a visit to the DMV.

As Chad squirmed in his government-issued chair, he just knew there had to be a better way. Why must this experience be so unbearable? At that moment, Chad *fell in love with the problem*.

Several months after his agonizing visit, Chad learned that his home state of North Carolina decided to privatize DMV operations. The state would pay a small transaction fee to new operators who were willing to brave the challenges of running their own DMV. Despite the discouraging warnings of his friends, Chad decided to take on the bureaucratic mess and see if he could do it better.

From a purely economic standpoint, the problem seemed unsolvable. A DMV location supports a certain geographic area, presumably serving a fixed number of customers. The prevailing wisdom is to keep costs as low as humanly possible, since people have to visit whether they like it or not. After all, there's no competition for a governmental agency, and since the fees are set by the state, there is no way to raise prices in order to deliver a better experience.

Fully understanding the cost stalemate, Chad decided to push the creative boundaries. He set the constraints aside, imagining an ideal DMV experience without limits. What if the experience rivaled a visit to a high-end hotel, or even a theme park? As he thought about it, he said to himself that he'd drive for miles—right past other DMVs—if he could visit his dream location. "What if other people would do the same?" Chad thought. "Wait a minute… what if the market size isn't fixed after all?"

Because he was so deeply rooted in the problem of a lousy DMV experience, Chad decided to flip things upside down when he opened his own location in Holly Springs, North Carolina. What made it remarkable wasn't just one special touch but a series of *Big Little Breakthrough* ideas that elevated the customer experience to otherworldly.

When you first walk in, you wonder if you're even in the right place since Chad's DMV feels nothing like the Cold War interrogation chamber you expected. The smell of fresh-baked cupcakes and French-press coffee fills your nose, while your eye catches the colorful fresh-cut flowers and vibrant area rugs. You notice a children's play area with toys and games as a small group of kids pleasantly giggle in the corner. Instead of hiding behind bullet-proof glass, a well-trained team member welcomes you with a warm smile. After checking in on an easy-to-use iPad, you relax in a comfy leather chair to peruse a wide selection of current and uncrumpled magazines. Not sure if it's a prank or if you've just entered an episode of *The Twilight Zone*, you look for the hidden cameras that must be documenting your surreal experience.

"People drive over an hour to get to us," Chad explained to me as we began our conversation. Speaking with Chad, remarkably amped up to share his story, is like having a conversation with the Energizer Bunny after he's chased three Red Bulls with a double espresso. "We asked ourselves, could we pull people from different counties? Could we make the experience so good that folks would drive past two or three other DMVs just to get to us?"

Looking beyond the prevailing wisdom, Chad created a DMV like no other. Customers started posting selfies online, and people would stop in for a delicious smoothie even if they didn't need to renew their tags. Though Chad couldn't raise prices, he firmly believed that a better experience could grow customer volume. Instead of making it 3 percent better, he made it 1,000 percent better, and the results were dramatic.

Today, Chad Price's Holly Springs DMV does almost double the transaction volume of any other location in the state, making it far more profitable than his bureaucratic counterparts. Even in a highly regulated environment with more rules than a medium-security prison, Chad's creativity led to a far better outcome.

We often think that brilliant creators begin with a magical lightbulb moment of invention. But just like Chad Price, the best innovators start by closely connecting to the problem they plan to topple long before they uncover novel ideas to solve it.

"Fall in love with the problem, not the solution" is a quote that's been attributed to several different business legends, from Waze cofounder Uri Levine to Intuit's founder and former CEO Scott Cook. It's the notion that the problem should be the focus of invention far more than any specific solution. The best creative minds refuse to commit to a certain answer, preferring to remain flexible while obsessing on the problem they're trying to solve. Simply put, the more time you spend examining the problem, the more innovative your solution will become.

We've been taught to be solution-focused and to look past problems; to demonstrate unwavering optimism. Yet it's only when we remove our rose-colored Ray-Bans and deeply examine the problem itself that we're able to discover fresh ways to attack it.

A tormenting DMV experience wasn't the only problem that Chad uncovered. Solely responsible for his thirty-seven-year-old sister who suffers from a debilitating medical condition, Chad started to spot many problems in the health-care field as he provided care for his sister. "I was taking my sister to the doctor, and because she now lives with me, I have to take her to all of her medical appointments," Chad told me. "We would go to an appointment, and we'd wait. We would go into a room, we would wait. We would then go into another room and wait to get lab work. One day, we had an issue with lab work where we waited an extremely long time. I just felt like the service was horrible. And then a mistake was made so I got a call a couple days later that something went wrong and we had to go back to the office to redo the blood work. It reminded me of the DMV."

Always the consummate problem lover, Chad decided to investigate further. It turned out that the $20 billion US lab testing industry was dominated by two corporate behemoths—LabCorp and Quest Diagnostics—who've held a tight grip on the field for decades. Chad wondered if there was a way he could take on these giants with the same creative verve he used to reinvent the DMV.

Entering the medical lab testing market seemed like a fool's bet. Chad had no health-care experience, no lab training, and no capital. As if he were taking a peashooter to a machine gun fight, he'd be going up against two goliaths with unlimited resources to defend their turf. Realizing the mismatch, Chad first locked his sights on the problem he was trying to solve instead of sprinting into battle.

Chad and his buddy Joshua Arant, who would later become his cofounder, hopped in a van and went on a road trip. The pair spent three months driving around the country to experience the myriad of problems in medical testing firsthand. They'd show up at testing clinics and speak to frustrated patients in waiting rooms. Enticing lab techs with burgers and fries, they heard stories of rampant inefficiency and poor morale. After getting kicked out of many doctors' offices, they convinced a few physicians to share their lab testing frustrations—from timing delays to inaccurate results to cost overruns.

It was only after months of immersion, studying the industry's problems from every possible angle, that the pair decided they were ready to start their own lab testing company. "There were already two whales in the industry," Chad told me with a smirk. "If they're the whales, we'll be the shark." To solidify their sharklike attitude, Chad named the company Mako Medical. It was time to become the predator.

Chad's careful examination of the problematic status quo led to a series of *Big Little Breakthrough* ideas. Chad explains, "We made a list of everything—I mean every single thing—the competition did. And we challenged ourselves to do the opposite."

Industry norms are seven-day turnaround times, so Mako figured out how to do it in twenty-four hours. Transportation and logistics are traditionally outsourced, so Mako invested in a fleet of cars, each with a shark fin prominently attached to its roof. The sleeping giants delivered lab results in one standard format, so Mako customized their reports for every single client.

"Their salespeople wear suits and ties, so we decided that everybody on our team should wear scrubs. Every single day, every position, doesn't matter if you're the CEO or the janitor, you wear medical scrubs," Chad told me. "They're publicly traded, we're private. They use their profit to give back to shareholders, so we set our goal to give back to local charities, military veterans, and faith-based nonprofits."

"At Mako, we picked a handful of charities, making commitments to help fund these organizations. So, when things got tough, it was funding those causes that we were committed to," Chad explained. "It never was about making money so we could go buy a big home or a fancy car. It was the fact that we wanted to build something for the blind or the handicapped."

As you might imagine, taking on multibillion-dollar corporations isn't easy. At first, the company struggled just to stay afloat. "There were so many late nights," Chad recalled. "We would go several twenty-hour days in a row. Some days, we didn't even sleep. We worked every single day like it was our last day in business. For the first year, it was extremely tough. The second year, extremely tough. We were working seven days a week, taking zero salary. It was only by the third year that we really gained market momentum. And that's when things started to take off."

And take off they did. By 2017, just three years after the company was founded, Mako Medical earned $92 million in revenue. In 2018 it grew to $125 million, and with thirty-four-year-old Chad Price still at the helm, the company will top $200 million in 2020.

Getting curiously close to a burning problem—first at the DMV and then at the medical lab—led Chad Price to launch two wildly successful businesses. But as you might imagine, the problem-hunting Chad Price was just getting started.

"Being in health care, there's not a day that goes by without me hearing from someone who can't afford their medications." Chad frowned as he explained his latest frustration to me. "Why would you have to go to Canada to get affordable drugs? It doesn't make any sense."

"What pushed me over the edge was a story that a cardiologist told me about a hospice patient. When you go into hospice, the hospice company gets just two hundred dollars a day to take care of you as you begin to die. A lot of these patients are on medication, but because the costs of the drugs are so high, the hospice company is unable to continue to administer them. So, a lot of these patients who are dying are no longer on the medicines they desperately need. Then they begin to have other complications: They feel like they're drowning. Their lungs begin to fill up with fluid. And so even though they know they're dying and they're in hospice, the quality of their death is greatly impacted because of the cost of the meds."

Chad continues, "When I found out that the cost to produce those meds are pennies, I said to myself, 'I'm going to break this. I'm going to go head-to-head against the biggest pharmaceutical companies in America.' I discovered that there are thousands of medications in America you could buy for one penny when you take out every piece of unnecessary markup. So, the pills that those people need in hospice, I could give those pills to them for less than a dollar a week."

Chad took on the DMV, and then the lab testing field, because he was deeply frustrated with a horrible experience. Now, because he grew so close to the core problem, he's taking on the pharmacy industry. In early 2020, Chad Price launched his new company: Mako Rx. "I didn't set out to be in the pharmacy business or lab business. Quite frankly, I could think of ten other things I would rather do that would be way more exciting. But these are real problems and if you can fix them, you impact millions and millions of people."

With the same curiosity he had when starting Mako Medical, Chad studied the problem. He immersed himself in the industry, decoding its opaque processes from drug manufacturing through distribution. Making a list of every single prescription medication in America, he tracked the cost and subsequent markup through each stage of the value chain. His anger rose when he learned that drugs that sell for $200 per pill sometimes cost only ten cents to manufacture. Through carefully studying the problem, he learned that there are no fewer than ten points of cost markup before a medication reaches the consumer. "What if only two people marked it up?" he thought. If he could solve this, the heartbreaking stories of patients forced to decide between taking their insulin and feeding their children would become a distant memory.

It took a few years of rigorous study and streetfighter grit, but Mako Rx is now up and running with a radical new model: for a fixed $25 per month subscription, patients can get an unlimited supply of over three hundred common medications with *no additional cost* whatsoever. If they need meds outside this list, they pay only a small fraction of the normal retail cost.

How is Chad different than your Aunt Sally who spends all day complaining about an endless stream of problems yet never gets up from her floral couch to do anything about them? Innovators like Chad become problem solvers instead of chronic complainers by coupling two mindsets to the problems they seek to topple: *belief* and *empathy*.

As Chad became aggravated by the situations he encountered, he only pivoted his frustration into action because he believed he could improve things. I'm sure he was irritated about the rainy downpour that ruined his Sunday afternoon beach volleyball game, but Chad didn't launch a weather company. Everyday innovators are always on the lookout for problems, but they are drawn to the ones they believe they can solve.

In my previous book, *Hacking Innovation: The New Growth Model from the Sinister World of Hackers*, I uncovered a core belief shared by a notorious but highly creative gang of cybercriminals. No matter how impenetrable a security system may seem, hackers insist that every barrier can be penetrated. This is the belief that gives them the moxie to attempt their most difficult escapades.

Regardless of complexity, risk, or probability of success, Chad developed a love affair with problems he believed he could tackle. And by shining a bright light on those problems, he was able to uncover their vulnerabilities. As the title of Marie Forleo's bestselling book professes, *Everything Is Figureoutable*.

Added to his belief that the problems he was addressing were solvable, Chad's empathy helped him discover enduring breakthroughs. The ability to sense other people's feelings and emotions is a highly valuable asset when it comes to innovation, as evidenced by a new study published in the *Journal of Consumer Research*.

Marketing professors Kelly Herd (University of Connecticut) and Ravi Mehta (University of Illinois) set out to measure how empathy affects creativity. In a study of more than two hundred adults, participants were asked to create ideas for a new potato chip for pregnant women. Half of the group was instructed to generate ideas using logic and cognitive skills, while the other half was instructed to let empathy guide the way. The empathic cohorts were asked to close their eyes for thirty seconds to imagine what the women were going through during pregnancy. How would she *feel* when eating the snack?

After a panel of experts was enlisted to judge the ideas, the empathetic group dramatically outperformed their logical counterparts. The simple thirty-second empathy exercise yielded flavor ideas such as "pickles and ice cream," something a mom-to-be might be craving. Other winning ideas included "sushi with wasabi" and "margarita for moms," since women are asked to abstain from raw fish and alcohol during their pregnancy and may be yearning for those flavors.

"A lot of people are told to be very objective. 'You're a professional. Think about this in an objective way. Don't get caught up in emotions,'" said Professor Herd. "But what we find is that the empathetic process actually leads to more creativity.

"We've shown that empathy can change the way you think," Herd continues. "We've looked at it in a somewhat narrow context of product design, but it appears that subtle things, such as imagining how someone else would feel, can have a huge impact on creativity in general." She concludes, "Eliciting empathy has inherent value in maximizing creativity."

Chad brought a potent mixture of empathy and belief to the fight. These attributes, combined with his focus on identifying, deconstructing, and examining the problems around him, led to the successful launch of three businesses (and counting).

As kids, many of us played the game Hot and Cold. One person would hide something—a neon yellow yo-yo for example—while the others had to find the item by asking a series of questions. The person holding the secret could only respond with "you're getting hotter" or "you're getting colder" until one of the hunters deduced the yo-yo's location.

"Is it in the kitchen"?
You're getting colder.
"Is it in the garage?"
You're getting hotter.
"Is it in the storage chest?"
You're burning up!

As you pursue *Big Little Breakthroughs*, the closer you get to a problem, the closer you are to a creative discovery. When you identify pain points that are acutely bothersome, innovation is right around the corner.

"Is it a small problem that's not a big deal?"
You're getting colder.
"Is it something that really bugs me?"
You're getting warmer.
"Is it pervasive, widespread, and deeply problematic?"
You're burning up!

At the root of every successful innovation—from minute to gargantuan—lies a problem waiting to be solved. We learned from Chad Price that we must study and probe each problem in order to discover the most effective solution. What upstream activity caused the problem in the first place? What new problems might emerge if the original problem were solved? Who will be impacted most if the problem were eradicated tomorrow?

To Best a Problem, Bathe in It

Ryan O'Neill, who leads Expedia's customer service group, was shocked to learn that 58 percent of its customers called the help center after booking a reservation. Keep in mind, Expedia is supposed to be a self-service digital platform. The team was so focused on reducing call times that they hadn't stopped to explore ways to eliminate the calls altogether. Driven to improve things, Ryan assembled a team of people from different parts of the company and created a war room to immerse themselves in the problem.

Trying to uncover the main reasons people called in the first place, the team assembled data and interviewed both customers and call center staff. Through an extensive investigation, it turned out the number one reason people called the company was to get a copy of their traveler's itinerary. In 2012 alone, over twenty million calls were made with this request. Since Expedia's cost to handle each call was around $5, the team was facing a $100 million annual problem.

At first glance, the itinerary issue was dismissed since Expedia already auto-emailed customers their travel details. But if itineraries were emailed, why were customers still calling? Immersing themselves in the problem, the team learned that sometimes customers typed an incorrect email address during the booking process. Other times, travel itineraries ended up in people's junk mail folder or were deleted accidentally.

The solutions only came to life after the team spent an extended time investigating the problem. Once the issue was fully understood, two *Big Little Breakthroughs* solved the challenge quite nicely. First, the company added a highly visible button on the site to help customers easily retrieve their own details. Next, a simple prompt on the call center recording, "Press two to resend your itinerary," ended up making a massive difference. Once the simple fixes were implemented, call center volume dropped from 58 percent straight down to 15 percent, saving the company millions while boosting customer satisfaction.

When I'm investigating a problem, I like to think of myself as a detective hunting down a major case. How would *SVU's* Captain Olivia Benson investigate the crime? How would *CSI's* Gil Grissom piece together the evidence?

To learn the best way to investigate a problem, I spoke with FBI counterterrorism specialist and Senior Special Agent Jack Bauer. Naturally, Jack Bauer isn't his real name. The folks at the Bureau aren't too keen about actual agent names showing up in books, so I changed his name to protect his anonymity. That said, the expert I interviewed is a ten-year FBI veteran, a real-world version of the fictitious Jack Bauer played by the Emmy-winning actor Kiefer Sutherland on the hit TV series 24.

I learned that the first part of a good investigation is to resist the diabolical temptation to prematurely solve the case. "A common rookie mistake is jumping to a conclusion too quickly," Special Agent Bauer told me with steely conviction. "Just because a person is an obvious suspect doesn't mean they did it. It comes down to knowing the difference between what you *think* happened and what you *know* happened."

The FBI's deliberate investigative process produces an astounding success rate. In 2019, 90 percent of defendants in federal crimes pleaded guilty before trial, realizing the evidence against them left no other option. Of those who actually went to trial, fewer than 1 percent won their defense in the form of an acquittal.

To achieve such a remarkable win rate, the FBI takes time to study the crime and gather the facts before rushing an arrest. Each investigation begins with an assessment phase, where the team takes an inventory of what they know and what they don't know. Investigators start by examining the situation, asking basic questions such as "What has occurred?" and "What information do we have right in front of us?"

After the initial assessment, the next investigative phase involves gathering evidence. In a crime scene, a good forensic investigator examines the situation from every angle. There may be physical artifacts such as bullet casings, blood, or a broken window. The CSI team notes what's present, documenting the findings with photos, diagrams, and videos. The fingerprints on the nightstand, hair follicles in the shower, and bloody footprints on the back porch are all cataloged into evidence.

Great detective work also involves noticing what's missing or out of place. If the front door hadn't been busted, perhaps the killer was familiar to the victim. An empty garage could tip off investigators to a possible getaway car. If the crime was a robbery gone wrong, why is the victim's gold and diamond Rolex still in plain sight on the bedroom dresser?

"A big part of this phase is identifying what information is missing and then establishing a plan to find it," Special Agent Bauer explains. Here, the team may examine phone records and bank statements or engage in physical surveillance of a suspect.

By studying the crime while relentlessly asking questions, investigators uncover additional clues as they form the body of evidence.

After physical evidence is gathered, the investigators canvass the area for witnesses. Did the victim have a boyfriend? Who supplied her with the drugs that were found in her system? Did she owe unpaid gambling debts to her bookie? As witnesses are interviewed and persons of interest interrogated, new fact patterns emerge that help fill in the blanks of the physical evidence.

Only after all the physical evidence and eyewitness testimony is assembled can the investigation shift toward putting all the pieces together and forming a conclusion. Think how many TV murder mysteries were solved after the obvious suspect's alibi checked out and a new wrinkle in the case led to an unexpected guilty party. Truth isn't found by initial instinct but rather through the disciplined process of reaching conclusions only after all the facts are studied.

One of Arthur Conan Doyle's most popular Sherlock Holmes stories is that of "The Adventure of Silver Blaze." As Holmes was investigating the theft of a prized racehorse, others close to the case quickly concluded that it must have been a stranger that had stolen the animal. During an interview with a stable hand, however, a fact was uncovered that allowed the brilliant detective to crack the case in a surprising way. As the interview commenced, the large dog that lived in the barn was quietly resting in the corner. Holmes pressed his subject to describe everything about the evening of the theft, but the man insisted the dog had never barked.

According to Holmes, "I had grasped the significance of the silence of the dog, for one true inference invariably suggests others.... Obviously the midnight visitor was someone whom the dog knew well." In the end, Holmes was able to deduce that it wasn't a stranger at all but the horse's trainer who perpetrated the crime. Holmes identified and arrested the guilty man by carefully examining the problem and its clues before reaching his conclusion.

After gathering all the evidence of a case, seasoned investigators test their conclusions before appearing in front of a judge in the same way a detergent company test-markets their new triple-whitening cleaner before rolling it out to every Walmart in North America. "We consult with prosecutors, lawyers, and experts to learn what holes we still need to fill in order to make an airtight case," explains Special Agent Bauer. "Our conviction rate is so high due to the rigor of our investigations. If we just went on hunch or instinct, the success rate would be closer to a coin toss."

Despite the intense focus on facts, a successful investigation requires creativity. Special Agent Bauer elaborates, "Problem solving is my gig. Curiosity and creativity are among the top necessary traits needed to excel in law enforcement. Collecting data is only a small part of the job. The art form is interpreting the information, finding creative ways to gather evidence, and putting it all together."

Successful investigators obsess over every detail of a crime, and they won't ease up until the perpetrator is behind bars. In other words, they *fall in love with the problem*. Let's put this approach to the test as we explore how innovative leaders took on two of the world's toughest challenges: reducing recidivism among ex-cons and boosting the graduation rates of inner-city kids.

Redirect the Hustle

With 2.3 million inmates housed in the United States prison system, mass incarceration is a mammoth problem. Taxpayers spend over $80 billion each year in what seems to be a never-ending cycle, with new prisoners maxing out prison capacity and released felons quickly reoffending, only to enter the system yet again. Although 95 percent of prisoners will reenter society after serving their time, the recidivism rate (those that end up back in jail) offers a bleak outlook. According to a 2018 Department of Justice study, 83 percent of those leaving prison were arrested at least once in the nine months following their release. Nearly 70 percent of all discharged prisoners end up back in jail, a clear indication that the system isn't working.

Catherine Hoke, a prominent private equity investor, was an unlikely candidate to tackle the issue of inmate reform. Never having set foot in a prison, she spent years in Silicon Valley listening to eager entrepreneurs pitch their business ideas for investment. She saw firsthand what it took to run and grow a successful company but hadn't even considered what it took to survive behind bars.

Wanting to give back to her community, she began volunteering in local prisons in her spare time. Before long, she grasped the enormity of the problems at hand, spending an increasing amount of her time behind the prison gates helping inmates improve their post-release chances. Her immersion into this unknown world helped her better understand the complex web of interconnected problems. Like a good detective, she gathered evidence and investigated the situation. She interviewed the warden, corrections officers, street cops, and inmates trying to garner a comprehensive view of the issues before attempting any fix.

To her surprise, sitting across the table from a convicted felon was strikingly similar to speaking with a startup executive. Both shared many traits—grit, tenacity, vision, and leadership skills. What if the inmates could redirect their hustle into a legitimate effort? What if the skills needed to lead a criminal enterprise could be repurposed? Perhaps the prisoner in front of her, wearing an orange jumpsuit and sitting in a cold metal chair, could become the next great entrepreneurial leader.

The more Catherine learned, the more she became committed to driving desperately needed change. Studying the problem further, she was troubled to learn that almost half of incarcerated people had themselves been the victim of a physical trauma. Many came from a cycle of poverty and misconduct, with parents and sometimes even grandparents involved in criminal activities. We often hear of second chances, but most of the prison population had never been given a legitimate first chance. Despite the desire for the majority of ex-cons to lead a legitimate life after prison, opportunities are scarce. Only 15 percent find employment within a year after serving their time, which turns out to be one of the biggest factors driving high recidivism rates. As a last resort, ex-cons often return to a life of crime.

Catherine truly believed she could drive positive change for ex-cons just as Chad believed he could make a difference in health care. After months of careful examination and planning, she founded the Prison Entrepreneurship Program (PEP) in 2004. Catherine moved to Houston to partner with the Texas Department of Criminal Justice to implement her training and rehabilitation program. She and her team began teaching inmates how to redirect their drive, thinking of themselves as entrepreneurs instead of criminals.

As she learned more about the nuances of crime, poverty, gangs, and prison life, she continued to improve her approach. Over the next five years, five hundred inmates graduated from her program, with 60 percent of them starting a business upon their release. Incredibly, the recidivism among her graduates dropped to just 10 percent, a record-breaking figure in the world of crime and punishment. Texas governor Rick Perry and President George W. Bush both honored Catherine with awards for her service and impact.

But just like the inmates she helped who had made a bad decision and then had to pay the price, Catherine ran into her own trouble. After a painful divorce that left her financially and emotionally devastated, Catherine was accused of having inappropriate relationships with four of the ex-cons she served. Although each was a consenting adult relationship that occurred after the inmate's release, Catherine was forced to resign from PEP and was barred from entering any prison in the state of Texas.

Publicly humiliated and at the lowest point of her life, she empathized with the millions of inmates who had similarly been labeled by their worst decision. She made a terrible mistake during a vulnerable period in her life, an error that she deeply regretted. But despite her own personal difficulties, she decided to continue her work helping inmates transform their lives. The problem was just too important to quit. Risking everything, she moved to New York and established a new and improved version of her program, this time called Defy Ventures.

Defy Ventures launched in 2014 with the same focus of helping inmates become legitimate entrepreneurs after their release. Having spent a decade studying the complex series of problems that convicted felons face when reentering society, and also better empathizing with their struggles from the shame of her own mistakes, she was able to refine her approach. The closer she got to the problem, the better she understood how to solve it.

When an inmate begins the program today, he or she is immediately given the title of "entrepreneur in training." Shifting the label from criminal to future entrepreneur has an immediate effect on participants' identities. During their prison terms, participants engage in coursework, mentorship, and direct instruction from Defy Ventures staff. The entrepreneurs in training learn life skills, helping them reframe their past and envision a better path forward. The business instruction centers on launching their own business, from identifying a market need to raising capital. In the same way Catherine was focusing on a big problem to solve, participants learn to focus on the problems of their potential customers before developing a business idea. The program culminates in a *Shark Tank*–style pitch, where graduates compete for startup funds to get their ideas off the ground upon their release.

One of Defy Ventures' most successful graduates is Coss Marte, the founder of CONBODY, whom we spoke with in chapter 2. Coss told me that Defy gave him both the practical training and the belief in himself that he needed to pursue his dream, crediting the program with his ability to launch and succeed.

As a result of their relentless focus on the problem, Defy Ventures graduates have a recidivism rate of only 7.2 percent, roughly *one-tenth* the national average. The program has expanded to seven states, working in eighteen prisons with 4,800 volunteers, with plans to expand to twenty-five states over the next five years.

Defy's mission of redirecting the hustle isn't only for those who want to start their own business. The program also teaches skills around getting and keeping a job. In contrast to the troubling national average of 15 percent post-incarceration employment rates, 84 percent of Defy graduates find work within ninety days of their release.

Tackling recidivism by training inmates to become entrepreneurial is a creative and highly effective approach. Could a similarly nontraditional approach work upstream of the prison system to combat educational deficiencies in at-risk communities?

A Fighting Chance

Khali Sweeney grew up in one of the most violent and crime-infested areas of Detroit. Abandoned by his parents at birth, he bounced from one foster home to the next throughout his especially unpleasant childhood. Just like many of the people that Catherine Hoke helped at Defy Ventures, Khali's upbringing was marked by poverty, failing schools, and crime. With few options and a bleak future, he dropped out of school after the sixth grade to join a Detroit street gang. By the time Khali turned sixteen, he had already suffered a gunshot wound and a stabbing.

At age twenty, a friend's casual remark that "nearly everyone we know is either dead or in jail" changed Khali's life. It was exactly the wake-up call he needed. At that moment, he decided to take responsibility for his future and craft a legitimate life for himself and his young son. With no formal education or marketable skills, he took every manual labor job he could find to turn his life around. A full ten years of hard work and sacrifice later, Khali was a responsible, tax-paying citizen.

Khali could have easily ended up in prison or in the morgue, like so many others around him. Now transformed, he wanted to help other troubled kids turn things around, but how could a guy with no resources, education, or support help inner-city youth?

Detroit's 48207 zip code was named one of the top three most dangerous neighborhoods in America in a 2013 FBI ranking. The study said the chances of becoming a victim of violent crime in this community over the course of a year were one in seven, while the high school graduation rate hovered at an abysmal 37 percent.

Reflecting back on his own circumstances, Khali credited the time he spent learning boxing in a local youth program for giving him the inner strength and discipline he needed to change his life. Because he was so close to the problem and his own solution—having lived them both personally—he was able to unlock a powerful new idea. In 2007, Khali Sweeney opened the Downtown Boxing Gym in the same rough neighborhood where he'd grown up.

Appearances aren't always as they seem. What appears to be a boxing business is actually a nonprofit organization dedicated to helping at-risk kids get on the right track. Boxing is simply the lure to get kids in the door, but they're not allowed to train in the ring until they spend one to two hours working with an academic coach in the back room. Kids who previously had no support now spend up to six days a week working on literacy, math, and personal development. Until the program began, some kids had never heard the words "I believe in you" or "you can choose the life you want to lead."

As word spread about the program, Khali faced new challenges. The dilapidated building couldn't accommodate the hundreds of kids now on the waiting list. Tackling this problem, Khali reached out to corporate and philanthropic donors, eventually receiving grants that allowed him to expand his operations. Getting to the gym was another big problem, because most of his students lacked access to reliable transportation. Walking a mile or two in the summer isn't a huge deal, but a snowy January in Detroit created too big an obstacle. To address the issue, Khali convinced Detroit's car companies to donate vehicles. The program now operates a fleet of vans that travels into the neighborhoods every afternoon, providing safe and free transportation to students.

"Every kid deserves a fighting chance," Khali told me when we first met back in 2012. Because he experienced the debilitating problems of poverty and failing schools himself and had the belief that he could make a difference, he took a creative approach that paid off. While the high school graduation rates within a three-mile radius of his gym are still some of the worst in the country, the kids who attend Khali's program have a *100 percent graduation rate!* For *ten years in a row*, the students who participated enjoyed a 100 percent graduation rate!

In 2017, CNN honored Khali Sweeney as one of their top ten CNN Heroes, drawing further attention to the incredible progress he's making in Detroit. Today, Khali still works and lives in the neighborhood, choosing to stay immersed in the problem he's fighting so hard to conquer.

Now that we've seen how romancing a problem can lead to breakthroughs—both big and little—we're ready to examine the next obsession of everyday innovators. Together, let's find out how the principle *start before you're ready* led to a major disruption in the baby-care industry, a women's empowerment awakening in Ethiopia, and a David versus Goliath victory in the brutally competitive arena of e-commerce.

Chapter 6

Start Before You're Ready

The noise from the rocket engines was deafening as the eager crowd watched in amazement. Billows of smoke began to plume from the launchpad while the ground vibrated like a vintage alarm clock refusing to be silenced. "3, 2, 1...Blast off. *To infinity and beyond!*"

Technically, this was NASA's 2008 STS-124 space shuttle mission. But for millions of Disney fans around the world, it was the moment when Buzz Lightyear would actually travel into space. The foot-long action figure joined the shuttle crew as they blasted toward the international space station for a fifteen-month mission of discovery.

Even after launching Buzz Lightyear into space, Duncan Wardle hadn't yet figured out how to bring the toy home. Duncan, who was Disney's head of innovation at the time, had convinced NASA to allow his son's action figure to ride as a stowaway on the space shuttle, but there was no reentry plan in place. Duncan explained to me what happened next.

"I had no idea how to bring him home, so I phoned up the director of communications at NASA. I said, 'When are you bringing Buzz back?' and there was total silence on the other end of the phone. After a long pause, he told me that was never part of the contract and they planned to just discard him in space along with other nonessential items before returning to Earth. I couldn't let this happen, so I threatened to leak word to the international press that NASA incinerated Buzz Lightyear in the Earth's atmosphere."

Naturally, the improvised plan worked. Apollo 11 moonwalker Buzz Aldrin was among the celebrities who marched in the ticker-tape parade that welcomed home Buzz Lightyear at Orlando's Disney World. A few months later, the action figure was enshrined at the Smithsonian's National Air and Space Museum in Washington, DC, in a star-studded celebration.

Duncan Wardle reminds me of Walt Disney himself. His child-like wonder made me want to start sketching cartoons...until he showed me the set of intimidatingly great illustrations that he'd drawn earlier that day. For the record, I can barely draw a stick figure. Duncan's well-trimmed beard and charming British accent can't subdue his enthusiasm. Leading innovation for one of the most innovative companies in the world, he embodies the second obsession of everyday innovators: *start before you're ready*.

"Throughout my thirty years at Disney, I went for the things that I had no idea if I could pull off," Duncan explained. "I built a swimming pool down Main Street USA for Michael Phelps to swim down, but I hadn't spoken to Michael about it first. I designed a Super Bowl halftime show before I'd been in touch with anyone at the NFL."

Innovators like Duncan don't wait for permission or direction. Instead of postponing until conditions are ideal, they leap into action and figure out the unknowns along the way. They believe that it's better to take the initiative and get moving before you have a detailed plan, relying on their ability to course-correct while in motion. The most effective innovators—from big to small—*start before they're ready*.

Mat Ishbia, United Shore's suit-and-tie-wearing CEO from chapter 2, explains his philosophy: "Most people think, 'I'm going to get it right. I'm going to measure twelve times and cut once.' Let's say that takes them six months, but you jumped at it immediately. In that six months, you could have forty different cycles. If you start immediately, your first couple attempts are not so good. But you keep adjusting, and by the time you get six months later, you are way ahead of that person who's taking their first swing. Way ahead. I tell my people to start now and figure it out as you go."

$3 Million or One Penny?

Given the choice, would you rather receive $3 million right now or one penny that doubles every day for thirty days? When researchers have asked this question in countless studies, participants overwhelming snag the $3 million. But if your instincts are telling you to take the quick cash, let's examine what you'd be missing.

Doubling each day, the meager penny gets a slow start. After a week, its only worth 64 cents. Checking the balance three weeks in, you'd probably be kicking yourself for making this choice since the balance only sits at $10,485.76. But compounding interest starts to really work to your advantage the longer you're in the game. By day twenty-eight, you're over $1.3 million. And on day thirty, your eyes open wide to see your stunning balance of $5,368,709.12.

Compounding interest, just like innovation, is all about getting going quickly. For fun, let's run the same experiment while thinking of our bet as the value of an idea, not just a numerical monetary value. Imagine you waited just ten days to start with an idea that was one hundred times better. Ten days seems brief, and a 100X improvement feels like a massive advantage. But your vastly improved idea is no match for the capacious value of time. After thirty days, your far superior—but slightly delayed—idea is only worth $1,048,576.

Let's say you waited a bit longer but started with an absolutely killer idea. Instead of a hundred times better with a ten-day delay, let's run the numbers starting fifteen days later with an idea that is ten thousand times better. Even with a starting point that is ten thousand times better, you're still worse off by waiting. By day thirty, you're only up to $3,276,800, more than $2 million behind. Here, starting two weeks later with an entry point that was *ten thousand times* better delivered an end result that was 39 percent worse than getting started immediately. Think of this phenomenon as *compounding innovation interest*. You're far better off starting quickly and adjusting as you go instead of waiting until things are just right. Keep in mind, the starting point—one penny—couldn't be smaller and more accessible. A microscopic *Big Little Breakthrough* set in motion quickly can multiply to epic proportion.

Yes, I realize the flaws of this illustration. For example, a terrific idea may accelerate in value at a faster clip than a mediocre one, eventually surpassing the speedier launch. The key takeaway isn't the precision (or lack thereof) of one experiment but rather the notion that the ultimate value of an idea is directly linked to how quickly you get after it.

Leap Before Looking

When a catastrophic earthquake struck Nepal in 2015, Mallory Brown had to change everything. The 7.8 magnitude quake was devastating, killing nearly nine thousand people and crippling the country's already shaky economy. Her plan to help electrify a remote village now seemed insignificant compared to the new troubles that ravaged the area. Instead of going back to the drawing board, retooling her game plan and wasting precious time, Mallory boarded her previously booked flight to Kathmandu and raced into the postapocalyptic chaos.

Years prior, Mallory had no plans to pursue humanitarian work as her profession. She was a business major in college and never imagined she'd be rushing into Nepal's earthquake devastation less than a decade after her fun-loving university days. But an unexpected injury in a foreign land would change her career trajectory and help thousands of people around the world as a result.

"I took a backpacking trip just for fun when I graduated from college," Mallory told me as we began our conversation. "I was in Indonesia when I flipped over the handlebars of my bicycle, falling face-first into the ground. It could have been much worse, but I busted open my chin and needed stitches. The accident shook me out of vacation mode and into real life. The doctors told me to go to a clinic every other day because of the risk of infection, and I saw the health-care quality that people received. I started to see what it looked like for people living in poverty."

While her friends snorkeled and frolicked in the sun, Mallory wandered through local villages. She ate strange food and immersed herself in foreign culture. She loved the way she felt as she learned and explored, but she also realized how difficult life could be for people without the advantages she had grown up with in an upper-middle-class family in the United States.

As her poorly stitched chin began to swell in the sweltering hot sun of a rural Indonesian village, Mallory had an epiphany. "This is what I want to do with my life," she told herself as she tried to contain the smile from overtaking her street-dirtied face. Amidst the pungent smell of spices from a local market and the noise from half-broken bicycles colliding with potholes, Mallory decided to shift her life's work to the nonprofit sector, pursuing humanitarian progress over materialistic profits. Crucially, she *fell in love with the problem*. And with great zeal for the challenge ahead of her, Mallory Brown *started before she was ready*.

"I started traveling to very impoverished places, and I was immediately surrounded by need," Mallory explained. "You see houses that you can't even imagine living in. The first time I actually saw someone carrying water on their head was very different from the *National Geographic* moment I'd imagined…you're seeing this person struggling to carry a super-heavy, super-dirty container on top of their head, and it looks brutal. I quickly saw that there were endless needs to tackle. We need schooling, we need health care, we need water, we need transportation, we need housing."

Lacking a meticulously crafted five-year plan, Mallory decided to leap in. She wondered how she could make the biggest possible impact for the largest number of people. Drawing on her background in amateur filmmaking, she decided to create and share videos as a component of her strategy. Getting large numbers of people to donate to causes around the world was a tall order, but when Mallory puts the audience inside the scene, everything changes. "When you watch a film, you can actually see it and feel it. With the music and the emotion that a film can convey, you feel like you're there and then feel compelled to help." This creative approach quickly became her signature fundraising methodology. As this idea layered on top of each additional *Big Little Breakthrough*, compounding innovation interest started to pay dividends.

An example of her creative strategy occurred in a rodent-infested tunnel beneath the Las Vegas Strip. "Hundreds of people are living in these tunnels; it's like a real-life version of Teenage Mutant Ninja Turtles," Mallory tells me. "There's no electricity, there's no running water. It's a very unpleasant living situation. I met a man living in the tunnels who had been homeless for twenty years, and I decided I would try to help him. I raised funds to buy him some basic supplies, and I was able to get him some dentures because he only had four teeth left in his mouth."

"I asked him what he'd want if he could have anything in the world, and he told me he just wanted to hold his children before he died. I had goose bumps. I was blown away. I was expecting him to say, 'I want a house,' or 'I want to feel what it's like to be rich for one day,' or some other superficial thing." The man had no idea where his children lived or how to contact them, so Mallory published a film of his story online. "His daughter contacted me within a couple days and said, 'I think the man in your video is my father, who I haven't seen in twenty years.' It was unbelievable, it was a miracle."

"I connected this man to his daughter, and they reunited after decades," Mallory shared with well-deserved pride. "I bought him a bus ticket to go visit her in Texas, and she was able to help him land a job. Now he lives down the street from her and he sees his grandchildren multiple times a week. He is a new man. If you saw before and after photos you wouldn't recognize him."

On her thirtieth birthday, Mallory traveled to Ethiopia to spend a week helping women obtain small business loans in order to break the cycle of poverty. She helped secure $42,000 for a small group of women while discovering a new sense of purpose and focus for herself. "I just felt so connected to these women," Mallory explains, "and I realized that women's empowerment would become my mission. It took me a while to get to that point, but helping women lift up their families and communities resonated with me so deeply and now it's my main focus." Mallory's quest didn't begin with women's empowerment as part of an intricate initial plan. By starting before she was ready and figuring it out as she progressed, her focal point was discovered midflight.

Back to the devastating earthquake in Nepal, Mallory flew to the point of greatest need long before she was ready. "I showed up with no plan; zero idea as to what I was going to do on the ground," Mallory remembers. "All I had was a friend of a friend of a friend who sent a Facebook message to some Nepalese woman asking if she could pick me up from the airport. I spent three weeks in Nepal, living in this random woman's home. On the ground, we figured out how to bring sanitation supplies to survivors in communities that had lost their homes. It turned out to be one of the most beautiful campaigns, and it came from the most chaotic three weeks of my life. Keep in mind, I'm not sent to these places by the UN or the Red Cross. I'm just Mallory Brown who buys a plane ticket on Delta, flies to a troubled location, meets a stranger who doesn't speak my language, and shows up with an open heart."

Mallory's newest effort is her most audacious yet. "It is a global marathon for women's empowerment called *Walk a Mile*," she tells me. "It's based on the concept of empathy, walking a mile in someone else's shoes. *Walk a Mile* is a twenty-six-part documentary series and in every mile, I step into the shoes of an impoverished woman. Every mile is filmed in a different country and highlights a different struggle that women face, raising money for a local women's charity. So, it's twenty-six episodes, twenty-six miles, twenty-six women, twenty-six charities."

Spending a week in each location, Mallory films every moment to later craft into one of her breathtaking documentaries. In Tanzania, she walks with a woman named Elizabeth to learn about her life and her challenges. Mallory decides to help make hand-molded stoves out of clay so Elizabeth and her community have a safe way to cook without inhaling toxic smoke. In Guatemala, Mallory focused on feeding malnourished families and in Serbia, it's about teaching women to read. Currently in year two of the *Walk a Mile* project, Mallory continues to *start before she's ready* as she takes on each new challenge.

Why We Wait

If starting before you're ready is so important, why do most of us wait? There are several tightly wound hindrances, tied together in a knot that would require breaking your left thumbnail to loosen. But just like that stubborn extra loop in your shoelace, it starts to unwind quickly if you can pry it just a little bit free.

One of the biggest obstacles to getting started is that the effort can seem...well...like too much effort. When a new project feels daunting for me, I'm a master at coming up with every reason not to start. "I'm not feeling it...I had an extra drink last night" stops me on Thursday, while "I'm not feeling it...I didn't even have a drink last night" is my excuse on Friday. The truth is, sometimes the only way to bust the stalemate of inaction is to just get moving.

In my case, I developed an easy hack that I inelegantly named "the fifteen-minute trick." (How creative, right?) When I just don't feel like getting started on a new project or picking up where I left off on an old one, I force myself to give it an honest fifteen minutes. If I still don't feel like I'm in the groove when the timer rings, I put down the work guilt-free and come back at a later time. But way more often than not, I'm cranking along and in the zone by the time I hear the buzzer. If you're feeling stuck or stale or grumpy or afraid, forcing yourself to begin for a short, finite period can give you the momentum you need to continue.

The instruction we've had throughout our lives—both formal and informal—can also impede initiative. The whole "measure twice, cut once" thing may apply if you're pouring concrete on a construction site, but the optimal approach as it relates to imagination is actually the opposite. We'll cover experimentation in the next chapter, but the modern-day truism should be "cut twice, measure twice, keep cutting." We are better off getting started quickly, testing several versions of an idea concurrently, and then refining our approach based on the results of our experiments. Great innovators of all shapes and sizes get going quickly, testing and refining along the way.

Fear, of course, is the granddaddy of all procrastination. I've justified and rationalized countless delays over the years, while the real constraint was that shoulder devil whispering scary things in my ear. None of us want to fail, stumble, look foolish, or get it wrong, but if we let those concerns hold us back, we're empowering fear to win. To subdue the Fear Monster, we don't need to develop the courage of a comic book superhero. Instead, it's about finding creative ways to de-risk the start.

Putting myself through college as a working musician, I took every gig I could land. I'd sometimes get weird requests that I really wasn't sure I could handle, such as the time I was asked to perform in a Cajun zydeco accordion band. Or the time when I got the call to be a fill-in guitarist for an '80s heavy-metal "big hair" band. I spent a couple of years traveling around the rural south in a rusted-out nine-passenger van with an all African American (other than me) soul and funk band. I was not only the youngest member of the group by thirty years, but I was also required to deliver any and all spoken word (rap) lyrics during performances. In each of these experiences, I was uncomfortable and frightened at first. I had major doubts and was sure I'd screw it up, becoming a punch line for the audience. But despite my impending sense of doom, I pushed myself to at least give it a shot. Making the decision to try was by far the hardest part. Once I got over that, it was just a matter of trying my best, making mistakes, and adapting quickly.

We tend to think that getting started is all about generating the absolute perfect plan, but it's really more about getting every possible idea out of your head so you can later sort the good from the bad. Chuck Jones, the famous Warner Bros. animator whose creations include Wile E. Coyote, the Road Runner, and Tom and Jerry, said it best, "Every artist has thousands of bad drawings in them, and the only way to get rid of them is to draw them out."

A Fast Start

It was 3:00 a.m. in Tel Aviv, and baby Daniel made it abundantly clear he was hungry. The infant's piercing cry jolted both his parents from a deep sleep, but this feeding was dad's turn. Ayal Lanternari was bleary-eyed as he stumbled to the kitchen to warm his son's bottle, counting the minutes until he could return to bed for a little more shut-eye. Unfortunately, it wouldn't be anytime soon since heating breast milk or formula in a microwave depletes nutritional value. Instead, Ayal began the universally dreaded bottle-heating dance just as millions of sleep-deprived moms and dads have done for generations.

Get a pot, fill it with water, heat it to a boil on the stovetop. Pour the boiling water into a glass container, insert the bottle, wait for fifteen minutes as your kid screams his face off while you question your life choices. It's agonizing, and every one of us who's been a parent has suffered through it.

An idea popped into Ayal's head after he'd clumsily completed the heating ritual and his three-month-old was gulping down the night's third feeding. In a sleepy daze, he imagined a radically different baby bottle that heated quickly. Remembering from grade-school science class that an increase in surface area would decrease heating time, he cycled through every shape he could imagine. As Daniel's belly grew full, Ayal landed on a bold idea.

Ayal envisioned a bottle shaped like a human breast that was hollowed out in the middle. The milk would be held in a thin, even layer over the entire surface area, allowing it to heat quickly. Further, the concave shape would make it easy for kids to hold and easy for grown-ups to stack. Daniel quickly fell back to sleep after the feeding, but Ayal's mind raced through the night.

By early morning, Ayal could wait no longer to share the idea with his pal, Asaf Kehat. Best friends since the age of five, Ayal and Asaf grew up in the same Israeli town of Haifa. The pair were raised in a rough neighborhood, often having to fight to survive. In this war-torn region, the friends tuned out the sounds of explosions by filling their minds with the vision of an exciting future together.

They both became biomedical engineers, working for different companies but still never giving up on their childhood dream of collaborating. When the two discussed Ayal's bottle idea that morning, they realized it could finally be their big shot. They feverishly examined the world of baby feeding and were delighted to find that no similar product existed. At that moment, with only a few hours of research and no specific plan, the two decided to *start before they were ready.*

In February 2013, nanobébé was born with the mission to create a better bottle. Crucially, *starting* before you're ready and *launching* before you're ready are two very different things. For nearly a year before the company was founded, the two partners worked tirelessly on the design and conducted extensive research. After the company was formed, the new entrepreneurs spent the next five full years testing their bottle with hundreds of parents, infants, lactation consultants, and pediatricians. They tweaked the design, researched competitors, and developed a precision manufacturing process.

"There's a huge difference between an idea and a product that is ready to satisfy millions of customers," Ayal told me as I sat down with him and his cofounder, Asaf. "We had to make it dead simple in how you present it, explain it, and produce it. We worked for years to strike a balance between being original and being simple." While tempted to hit the market earlier, they wanted to make sure every aspect of their product was just right before placing their bottles in babies' mouths.

Ayal and Asaf raced to begin work on their idea but took their time before sharing it with the world. By the product's 2018 debut, the packaging was perfect. The bottle and all its accessories such as plastic milk liners and breast pump adapters required no instructions since the product line was refined and simple. Before hitting store shelves, global distribution deals were forged, product designs were perfected, and manufacturing capacity was secured. With their deliberate and creative approach, the partners started quickly and launched slow.

In a mature industry with deeply entrenched market leaders, nanobébé instantly stood out from the crowded competitive herd. Despite costing 35 percent more than a traditional bottle, nanobébé sold out twice in their first month of business. The story of two dads reinventing baby feeding was irresistible, making the company a media darling and helping them land feature stories with *Business Insider*, CNN, and endless mom blogs. And when nanobébé was featured on the cover of *Time* as one of the magazine's Best Inventions of 2018, the two pals fully realized their childhood dream of building something special together.

Had Ayal and Asaf waited to start, infants around the world would still be chugging down their dinners from the same old-school cylindrical bottles of the past. And parents would still suffer through countless hours of heating, warming, and waiting while their infants' tiny mouths produced gigantic shrieks and screams.

The Shoe King

When you think of the most influential leaders in the $366 billion global footwear industry, you probably imagine luxe designers such as Christian Louboutin, Jimmy Choo, or Louis Vuitton. Or maybe you conjure up images of athletes like Michael Jordan or celebrities like Kayne West. But I'm pretty sure that Greg Schwartz didn't make your top 100 list.

Reminiscent of Baloo, the tall and lovable bear featured in Disney's *Jungle Book* movie, you're more likely to imagine Greg as a tax lawyer than a shoe icon. Greg doesn't sport $2,500 Yeezy sneakers; he's the guy wearing loose-fitting khakis and decade-old brown loafers. But just five years after cofounding StockX, he's one of the most important leaders in the field.

Just like Apeel Sciences, StockX has achieved "unicorn" status as a company valued at over $1 billion. With more than one thousand employees, StockX has over $1 billion in annual revenue and serves customers in two hundred countries around the world. This young Detroit-based tech company competes head-to-head with industry giants such as Foot Locker, eBay, and Amazon... and wins.

"StockX is an e-commerce platform, a global marketplace that connects buyers and sellers," Greg explains as we sat down to catch up on his remarkable success. Greg and his wife, Nikki, are dear friends of ours, so I've had a front-row seat to his incredible ascent. Since I first invested in his prior company back in 2011, we've shared meals and wine, successes and frustrations. "At our core, we call ourselves a stock market of things. We launched with sneakers, which is still our largest category, but today we also offer apparel, collectables, watches, and handbags."

Since he was a kid, Greg loved building things. He built an electric car in high school, which was far more appealing to him than his coursework. Back in the early days of the internet, he daydreamed about starting a tech company. He got his first taste when he designed a very early mobile app called Mobile Checkbook. Long before iPhones hit the scene, Greg built software that ended up on thousands of clunky Nextel flip phones around the world. This was a passion project on the side of his corporate gig, feeling more like play than work. It wasn't a massive commercial success, but it gave him an early sense of what was possible.

After spending a few years in New York's corporate scene, Greg couldn't wait to get back to building things. He returned to his hometown of Detroit, eager to launch a tech company. I met Greg in the spring of 2011 when he approached me to invest in his new idea. For context, I had just founded Detroit Venture Partners a year earlier with the goal of helping passionate entrepreneurs launch and scale their businesses while making a positive impact on the city of Detroit. From the time I started the fund in 2010 until I left at the end of 2014, we evaluated more than three thousand entrepreneurial pitches. While many presentations piqued my interest, Greg's was one of the most memorable.

Greg's initial idea at the time wasn't all that great, but Greg himself was as impressive as they come. Articulate, bright, and humble, he had a drive to win that transcended his calm demeanor. Captivated with him but not his idea, I shared honest feedback and invited him to join me for an extended whiteboard session where we could explore ways to improve his proposal. After graciously accepting the offer, we spent several hours together reworking the idea, and I could tell that Greg was special. He was open-minded, coachable, smart, and driven, making him an ideal entrepreneur to back. Once his idea was refined and improved, my partners and I made the investment, and his company, UpTo, was off to the races.

UpTo sought to become the social network that looks forward in time. If Facebook was memorializing what you've already done and Twitter was centered on what you were currently doing, UpTo would allow you to interact with friends about what you were going to do in the future. Wouldn't it be cool to know what your friends are "up to" next weekend? And for companies, how incredible would it be to target ads to people based on their intent? If a person shared their plans to go house hunting next weekend, what a perfect time to deliver ads for mortgages, furniture, and moving services.

UpTo launched with great fanfare, quickly becoming a center-piece of the Detroit tech scene. Unfortunately, user growth was slow and the business ended up as a highly publicized fizzle. "It was really hard," Greg shares. "It was hard because there were employees at this company, there were investors that bet on us. There was a lot of pressure to deliver and we missed the mark. At the same time, you can't feel bad about that forever. I had to learn from the experience and move on. I said to myself that the one thing that I could do for family, for colleagues, for the people that bet on me, and frankly for the city of Detroit, was to get back after it and deliver a huge outcome. I just wanted one more crack at it."

One Friday evening as UpTo was winding down and Greg was contemplating his uncertain future, my former partner at Detroit Venture Partners pulled Greg aside. Dan Gilbert, the billionaire owner of the NBA's Cleveland Cavaliers and founder of Rocket Mortgage (previously Quicken Loans), shared a rough idea for a new company and asked Greg to run it. Before either man made it home for dinner that night, StockX was born.

Saying that the idea for a shoe-trading e-commerce site was half-baked would be an insult to things that are actually half-baked. A better analogy would be that the oven wasn't turned on, the ingredients hadn't yet been purchased, and an inexperienced baker had a craving for a molasses cookie. It was up to Greg to figure it all out. He had *to start before he was ready.*

Over the years, Greg and I have often discussed how initial ideas are often overrated. We both agreed that while initial ideas can be directionally important, they are not the panacea that most people think. The majority of value, in fact, is created as the idea evolves. One idea leads to another idea that morphs into something altogether different. Conceptual ideas only come to life through hundreds of *Big Little Breakthroughs*, which can only be discovered once you're in hot pursuit.

"You have to go through that process, iterate, and bring it to market even if it's half broken," Greg explains. "The only way an idea becomes valuable is by tweaking it, putting it in front of people, and getting critical feedback. You take one step and then figure out the next. Unfortunately, too many people have great ideas but then just sit on them instead of getting started."

As Greg got started on StockX, he had far more questions than answers. Key to their ability to win against eBay was the concept of authenticating each pair of sneakers. Since you're buying shoes directly from an individual instead of a company, how do you know if that $1,900 pair of Jordan 10 Retro SoleFly is legit or a fake? As a direct buyer-seller marketplace, StockX had to eliminate the risk of fraud in order to keep the transactions flowing.

"We had to figure out how we'd sit in the middle of each transaction, which was going to double our shipping costs for every sale. Unlike eBay, we also incur warehousing and inspection costs. Most people we talked to early on told us we were crazy. That it would be nuts to touch every product. That we were doomed out of the gate."

Greg continues, "So, we started with a lot of critics, and yet we had this belief that we could fight through it. And if we could scale the model, costs would come down. But it started with a lot of unanswered questions and unsolved problems. Instead of trying to tackle them all at once, we just kept putting one foot in front of the other." Each small win built on the next, as StockX's compounding innovation interest continued to fortify their foundation.

Once Greg got the website launched, he had the classic chicken-and-egg problem of any marketplace: delighting "customer zero." Buyers only show up when there's a wide selection of stuff to buy, but sellers only come when there are plenty of buyers. Greg had to figure out how to make a market, ensuring that no one felt like they were visiting an empty store. To bust the deadlock, Greg would manually place bids on any shoe that was offered for sale by a user on the platform. Even if he had to buy the shoes himself and resell them later, he did what was needed to create a fluid marketplace. These days with thousands of transactions a day, the marketplace is alive with activity. But to reach that point, Greg had to get it started before things were fully ready.

The seemingly glamorous joyride of building a startup is far messier than most people think. "Early on, we didn't have any sense of the challenges around running a supply chain," Greg reminisces. "I remember how we botched Black Friday back in 2017. We had tens of thousands of items coming through in a short period of time, but we only had a handful of authenticators. Boxes were just piling up, and we simply didn't have the capacity to deliver on our customer promise. We came out of it realizing that it was a step backwards, but it created an opportunity for us to learn and fix it going forward."

Recently the company expanded to support customers preferring Chinese over English. Due to the complex nature of the language and its specialized characters, the task seemed daunting. Naturally, Greg and his team started before they were ready. "We could have waited two years to have every bell and whistle, but we decided it was more important to launch quickly and delight our customers in China," Greg explains. The team got started fast and figured it out along the way, launching a simplified Chinese language version while meeting their intimidating deadline.

If you could put StockX under a microscope, you'd see that the company is a compilation of setbacks and solutions, pivots and adjustments. A thousand interconnected *Big Little Breakthroughs*. From day one, Greg and his team *started before they were ready*, preferring to iterate in the real world instead of waiting until everything was perfect on the drawing board. As they continue to expand into new product categories and geographies, the StockX crew will chase down each opportunity with the speed of the athletes they equip with the latest sneakers. You don't create a billion-dollar company in less than five years, while battling the biggest competitors in the world, by taking your time.

Whether you're growing a global tech company in Detroit, fighting for women's empowerment in Sudan, reinventing the baby bottle in Israel, or sending your son's Buzz Lightyear into outer space, *starting before you're ready* is an obsession that leads to mouthwatering outcomes. And once we get started, it is a series of *Big Little Breakthroughs* that will guide us through the uncharted waters of opportunity.

Now that our engines are revving, let's race toward the next obsession of everyday innovators. How did a single hot dog cart in Madison Square Park transform into the beloved $2 billion Shake Shack restaurant chain? Against all odds, how did the underdog Team New Zealand achieve a decisive victory in the America's Cup yachting race? How did a tiny experiment drive a $100 million profit boost for Microsoft's Bing? Let's find out together as we explore our next key principle: *open a test kitchen.*

Chapter 7

Open a Test Kitchen

Do you prefer the crispy mozzarella, tempura watercress, and black garlic mayonnaise cheeseburger or the pumpkin mustard, bacon, cranberries, and sage hot dog? For something sweet, would you rather try the black sesame milkshake, the pancake and bacon frozen custard, or stick with a cold brew float? What sounds like a scene from the Culinary Institute of Paris is actually playing out at the Shake Shack over on Varick Street in Greenwich Village, Manhattan.

These strange dishes are not on the burger chain's permanent menu. Instead, they emerge from the Shake Shack Innovation Kitchen located in the basement directly underneath the bustling restaurant. Opened in 2018, the underground kitchen is a culinary playground, equipped with a cornucopia of high-tech gear, unusual ingredients, and the ethos of creative experimentation.

The Innovation Kitchen is the brainchild of Shake Shack's culinary director, Mark Rosati. He explains, "One of the biggest things any company has to think about as it grows is how to stay nimble and able to push boundaries. We ask ourselves, if we started Shake Shack today, what would we do differently?"

In fact, the company looks nothing like it did when it got its start. In 2001, high-end restaurateur Danny Meyer launched a hot dog stand in Madison Square Park, adjacent to one of his swanky upscale restaurants. It was fun for him to offer his signature culinary playfulness at a lower cost and faster speed compared to his far pricier dining options at the Gramercy Tavern, Union Square Cafe, or Maialino Mare. As the hot dog stand grew in popularity, Danny added burgers and crinkle-cut fries to the menu, eventually changing the name to Shake Shack in 2004. A long way from its humble roots, the burger chain has expanded to more than 250 locations around the world, enjoys more than $600 million of annual revenue, and boasts a market value of more than $3 billion. The company's per-store sales are more than double that of an average McDonald's location, and its growth rate is giving Ronald McDonald some serious heartburn.

Despite their runaway success, the Shake Shack team works hard to maintain the creativity of a startup. At corporate headquarters, a prominent sign hangs on the wall reinforcing their entrepreneurial roots: "The bigger you get, the smaller you have to act." To drive the principles of creative exploration, Shake Shack's wild success comes directly from our third obsession of everyday innovators: open a test kitchen.

From regional restaurants to global conglomerates, food industry leaders rely on test kitchens to drive innovation. The industry's equivalent of a scientific laboratory, they're designed to provide a safe, well-equipped environment for inventive thinking. Recognizing it would be impossible to dream up a complex new dish during the Saturday evening dinner rush, test kitchens provide the time and resources required to invent a delicious future. From unrestricted ideation sessions to rigorous testing and measurement protocols, test kitchens drive growth while reducing risk.

With a live restaurant only a flight of stairs away, the five-person crew at Shake Shack's test kitchen has access to immediate feedback from real customers. This allows the team to cook up wild ideas, test them quickly, and then have customers play a crucial role in the invention process. "There are risks when you bring customers into the testing process," Rosati explains, "but in the end, their feedback will always make the food better."

Inside the Innovation Kitchen, the chefs are cooking up a wide array of *Big Little Breakthroughs*. In addition to running experiments on new menu items, the team also spends time innovating on process improvements, training upgrades, and customer experience enhancements. How will customers respond to a digital self-serve ordering kiosk? What would happen if we used 4 percent more seasoning during the burger prep stage? How could we shave just five seconds off the cooking process? Ideate, experiment, refine. Rinse and repeat.

Shake Shack's remarkable success is directly tied to their experimentation mindset. Whether they're exploring something really odd, like the time they created a hot dog poached in sparkling wine and topped it with caviar, crème fraîche, and crumbled potato chips, or they're investigating a more efficient way to clean the countertops at the end of a shift, the company's test kitchen approach has helped them become one of the most beloved restaurant chains in the world.

Luckily, you don't need to be in the food business to open a test kitchen. Lawyers conduct mock trials to test out their arguments in a safe environment before making their case to a live jury. Surgeons now hone their skills using augmented reality goggles as they practice experimental procedures on robotic patients. Car companies prefer to bang up test dummies rather than real customers, while life insurance sales professionals conduct simulated presentations so they can optimize their approach before stepping in front of paying customers. Your test kitchen may be a designated physical space like Shake Shack's Innovation Kitchen, or it could be a metaphorical one that lives only in the hearts and minds of your team. The common thread is a safe, well-equipped environment where you can invent, test, and refine.

The 10,000 Experiment Rule

In chapter 4, we referenced the 10,000-hour rule, popularized by Malcolm Gladwell. As a reminder, Gladwell suggests that mastery in a particular endeavor is achieved through ten thousand hours of deliberate practice. But bestselling author and *Harvard Business Review* contributor Michael Simmons thinks that *experiments* are the far more valuable metric of success. "Creative persons, even the so-called geniuses, cannot ever foresee which of their intellectual or aesthetic creations will win acclaim," Michael explains. Accordingly, he coined the "10,000-experiment rule," which states that creative success is directly correlated to the number of experiments conducted. For us, it isn't about achieving the literal ten thousand numerical target but rather embracing the mindset of ongoing experimentation. The higher the volume of experiments we run, the more likely we'll be to unlock the *Big Little Breakthroughs* we seek.

Mark Zuckerberg, CEO and founder of Facebook, agrees. "One of the things I'm most proud of and that is really key to our success is our testing framework," he says. "At any given point in time, there isn't just one version of Facebook running. There are probably ten thousand." In fact, high-velocity experimentation has become a catalyst of success for the majority of tech giants, with Amazon, Google, and Microsoft each conducing tens of thousands of experiments each year.

"Our success at Amazon is a function of how many experiments we do per year, per month, per week, per day," said Jeff Bezos, Amazon's CEO and currently the richest person on the planet. "If you can increase the number of experiments you try from a hundred to a thousand, you dramatically increase the number of innovations you produce."

Amazon's AWS (Amazon Web Services) cloud computing division started as a small experiment in 2006. Since the company had invested heavily in its own infrastructure, leaders wondered if they could lease out some excess capacity to other companies. At the time, this was just one of dozens of experiments the company was testing as it pursued its quest for growth. Despite the fact that the vast majority of the experiments Amazon conducted failed, AWS is a bold reminder of how powerful a winning idea can be. In 2019, the AWS division generated $35 billion in revenue with $7.2 billion of profit. AWS wasn't Amazon's only massive win that started as a tiny experiment. In fact, Prime, Echo, Kindle, and third-party sellers were each born from experiments.

To get into the experimentation groove, Simmons suggests keeping a daily *to-test* list alongside your typical to-do list. To build your experimentation mindset and skills, he recommends conducting three experiments every day, even if they are tiny little tests. For example, you might run an experiment to help choose the highest performing color for the "Buy Now" button on your corporate website.

Individually, you could test the productivity effect of only checking email twice daily. I just ran a test to measure the impact of eating a fistful of mini M&M's on my four-year-old twins' bedtime routine. As any sane person should have foreseen, the experiment failed miserably. Avi and Tallia rode their sugar high for an extra seventy-five minutes before finally crashing, making me wish I'd tried a sedative on them instead. Maybe that'll be my next experiment.

Kidding aside, in our efforts to cultivate high volumes of small ideas (*Big Little Breakthroughs*), conducting a high volume of experiments (*Big Little Experiments*) is the ideal approach.

In 2010 alone, Google conducted 13,311 experiments just on its search algorithm. Instead of backing the ideas from those in the company with the most organizational seniority, Google prefers to let experimental results drive decision-making. Notably, only 516 changes were implemented from the more than 13,000 experiments Google ran, resulting in a 96.1 percent "failure" rate.

When most of us hear of a failure rate over 95 percent, we squirm in our chairs as if we'd been caught cheating on the SAT exam. We mistakenly believe that successful companies and smart people always get it right the first time, so any failure rate above 0 percent suggests total-loser status. The truth is, a 100 percent success rate is not a success at all. If every single attempted idea is a winner, you're playing it so safe that you won't ever enjoy the creative breakthroughs you seek. A higher failure rate, on the other hand, suggests a better system of experimentation, along with an abundance of creative ideas worth testing. I'd sure love to be as big of a "failure" as Google—how about you?

Microsoft reports that approximately one-third of its experiments prove effective, one-third have a neutral outcome, and one-third have a negative result. According to Stefan Thomke, Harvard professor and author of *Experimentation Works*, companies that have a failure rate of less than 20 percent are not taking enough creative risks to keep up with increasingly competitive market pressures.

An Open Letter—A Sperm's Advice on Improving Your Odds

Hi, my name is Samuel J. Sperm Jr. I know you're hoping to have successful innovation up there, so I figured I'd drop some wisdom. If human conception is the ultimate act of invention, I'm clearly a qualified expert since my entire life's focus is on that one thing. I don't play golf, watch reruns, or eat potato chips. I spend every moment of every day with a single-minded objective.

You humans crack me up sometimes. When you want to innovate, you take the Mega Millions Lotto approach. You think that one single pick, played once, is going to deliver untold riches. Sorry to spoil the fun, but you've got a 1 in 302,575,350 chance of hitting the jackpot. That's the same likelihood of getting struck by lightning 433 times. Good luck with that.

Now if there were just one of me, my odds would be even worse. When I leap into action, I'm contending with as many as six hundred million direct competitors. And even if one of us hits a bull's-eye on the perfect day of the month, there's still only 30 percent chance things work out. So, my individual odds are closer to one in two billion.

But me and my buddies, we're all about high-velocity experimentation. If we took your Mega Millions Lotto approach, the human race would soon be extinct. We prefer the more effective method of deploying high-frequency, high-quantity trials. In the end, this reduces risk, allows us to try many different experiments at once, saves time, and ultimately ensures that we'll be successful in the end.

Take it from me and my six hundred million fellow *Big Little Breakthroughs* in training. It takes lots of tiny experiments to deliver predictable success.

Yours truly,

Samuel J. Sperm Jr.

Let's Run the Experiment

Flying high above the endless sea of workstations in Mass Mutual's 100,000-square-foot call center, hundreds of helium balloons appear to be reaching toward the sky as if they're longing to be set free. These restless balloons aren't celebrating a national holiday; they're celebrating widespread experimentation.

"Everywhere there's a balloon taped to a desk, it's evidence that someone's running an experiment," said Amy Ferrero, VP of claims for the 180-year-old, $30 billion insurance and investment giant. "The balloon is there not only to say, 'I'm running the experiment,' but the balloon is also an invitation for others to stop by and talk about the experiment."

One person's balloon-flying desk is manned by a nineteen-year veteran of the company whom we'll call Susan. "Well, I'm the last stop before we cut the beneficiary check. Before I release funds, I have to perform three steps—A, B, and C—which I was trained to do in that order. If I find an error in step C, I have to go back and redo step B, which is the longest step in the process. Since each step is independent, my experiment is to do A and then C before doing B." She'd done it the old way for nearly two decades, wasting time while her frustration boiled over. Now, simple experiments like this one have changed everything for her.

"I hated my job. I hated coming to work. I was counting the days to retirement. I kept taking longer and longer drives to work.

I'd show up late. I'd leave early and I'd just dread coming in," Susan explained. "But now, we can run experiments! Every idea I ever imagined before had to go up five levels and ended up dying on the vine. After a while, you just stop bringing ideas to work. Over time, I concluded it was just a job. It was a paycheck. I could express my creativity somewhere else. But now...I love my job."

To drive a culture of open experimentation through the hundreds of people on Amy Ferraro's team, she didn't create a complex experimentation database. She didn't create a massive spreadsheet or craft a rigorous corporate experiment policy. Instead, she bought a tank of helium and a few hundred Mylar balloons. She shared her philosophy about experimentation and implored the team to run as many experiments as they wanted. The balloon strategy created an infectious feeling of energy, creativity, and fun that had previously been dormant. With some low-cost supplies, Amy Ferraro created a test kitchen.

Amy's inspiration came from Rich Sheridan, CEO and cofounder of Menlo Innovations, a software design and development firm in Ann Arbor, Michigan. The company tackles an eclectic variety of projects, such as building the heads-up display for the 2018 Lincoln MKZ, writing the code for the Accuri flow cytometer medical device, and designing a handheld diesel motor diagnostic tool for people who repair eighteen-wheeler rigs. In addition to running his company, Rich is also the bestselling author of *Joy, Inc.: How to Build a Workplace People Love* and coauthor of *Chief Joy Officer: How Great Leaders Elevate Human Energy and Eliminate Fear*.

Sitting down with Rich is intimidating at first. He's whip-smart and about seven feet tall. Being five foot five on a good day, I couldn't stop thinking about one of those "evolution of man" graphics with me on one side, eleven people between us, and Rich on the other end. Luckily, the warm smile that's permanently affixed to his bespectacled face makes him abundantly welcoming. He speaks with the excitement of a nine-year-old who can't wait to share a newly learned secret. If Indiana Jones and Nikola Tesla somehow had a love child, I think it would be Rich Sheridan.

Rich's message of returning joy to the workplace is what inspired Mass Mutual's Amy Ferraro to build her helium balloon approach to experimentation. Rich is a chronic, compulsive experimenter and has built one of the most effective test kitchens in the world. He summons the concept of "let's try it before we defeat it" with religious zeal. With his trademark grin, Rich explains, "The phrase 'let's run the experiment' is almost as common at Menlo as, 'Good morning. How are you?'"

"One of our grandest, most famous experiments was when Tracey had little Maggie. After three months of maternity leave, she came to me and said, 'I'm ready to come back to work, but there's only one problem. The day care we were planning to use is full, grandparents live too far away to help, and my husband and I don't know what to do.' I told her to bring Maggie into work. If I'd only had a camera in that moment; the look of bewilderment on her face. She said, 'All day? Every day? Rich, you know at some point she's going to make a big baby fuss and it will disturb everything.' I told her, 'Let's run the experiment.'

"That was eight years ago. Oliver is in today; he's Menlo baby number thirteen. It has been a wonderful experiment...talk about energizing a team. And then we found out that customers behave better when you bring babies to the meetings! This is an example of how we live at Menlo. Let's see what happens. Let's run the experiment."

Rich's entire operation is a living, breathing test kitchen, but it isn't a separate physical space like Shake Shack's Innovation Kitchen. Instead, Menlo Innovations embraces a wide-sweeping mindset of continuous experimentation. Rich deliberately built his corporate culture to avoid the gravitational pull of knee-jerk reactions in favor of his mantra—let's run the experiment.

Sometimes the test kitchen mindset yields gigantic INNO-VATIONS (all caps), but they can also deliver a steady stream of micro-innovations. Rich describes a recent *Big Little Breakthrough*: "Team members were reading articles about how 'sitting is the new smoking' and that we should be standing at our desks. Instead of buying everyone a $2,000 stand-up desk that we weren't even sure they'd like, we decided to run the experiment. One day, I looked across the room and one of our software engineers had a chair up on a table with a board on it, along with her computer and keyboard. That was the first standing desk experiment. Took about three seconds and zero dollars to try."

Rich continues, "All of a sudden, I started seeing chairs everywhere. Next, somebody went home and built a box to try out instead of the chair. Eventually we ended up with these little $400 adjustable VariDesks that you could add to any table you want. This speaks to our attitude of let's not formalize it. Let's just try it. Let's not form a committee to investigate and analyze four hundred different versions of standing desks. Instead, let's just see if we like standing all day, see if it actually works, and see if we can get our work done."

Menlo Innovation's physical environment is actually a continuous-flow experiment. Every desk and piece of equipment is on wheels, allowing team members to reconfigure the space anytime they feel the urge. The full team works in a single gigantic open space with concrete flooring and no walls, making it the office version of a blank canvas. Three people might break off into a pod one day to work on a project, while the next day they might experiment with an eight-person octagon of desks, all facing in to foster communication. Rich tells me that the space changes every day, and that no individual person is in charge of facilities. Instead, they all are.

As you might guess, Menlo Innovation's hiring practice is also experimental. Rich and I agree that the typical job interview process is broken. "I describe it as two people lying to each other for an hour," Rich laughs. Deciding to recruit for cultural fit over résumé match, Rich tells me he's looking for people with good kindergarten skills. "You know…plays well with others, doesn't hit, bite, scratch, swear, run through the room with scissors in their hand. We need good team players." To find the best candidates, Menlo ditched the conventional interview in favor of an audition.

Candidates are paired in groups of two and instructed that their assignment is to help the person with whom they've been matched get invited back for a second interview. The interviewing pairs are assigned various projects in twenty-minute intervals while being observed by Menlo team members (referred to as "Menlonians"). The observation is focused more on how well the candidates collaborate and support one another than their individual work product. Instead of hiring based on a résumé or references, Menlo Innovations hires based on how well candidates perform in a live experimental setting.

Before we said goodbye, Rich told me that his company's main aim is to "eradicate human suffering in the world as it relates to technology by returning joy to what we believe is one of the most unique endeavors, the invention of software." And after twenty years of breakaway success, he appears to be achieving that vision…one experiment at a time.

Building Your Test Kitchen

Taco Bell's test kitchen consumes the entire second floor of the company's headquarters. The futuristic setup includes a sensory analysis lab, kitchens for both food and beverage tastings, and four different sophisticated cooking stations. In contrast to the taco chain's massive operation, Ferran Adrià, who is credited as the inventor of the test kitchen concept, had a far more modest approach. His award-winning restaurant elBulli was only open from mid-June through mid-December each year. Ferran would then travel to Barcelona for the remaining six months, toiling away in a small makeshift workshop to invent an entirely new menu for the following season. Rich Sheridan's test kitchen isn't a separate operation but rather a company-wide experimentation philosophy. The point is, no two test kitchens are identical, which provides you the creative freedom to craft yours to your own specific needs.

As you construct your own ideation factory, consider how you'll design each of the core elements required in any test kitchen environment: *gear*, *participants*, and *ingredients*.

Gear

Shake Shack tricked out its Innovation Kitchen with all the latest cooking equipment to ensure the staff had everything they needed to invent. They intentionally built the test kitchen under a working restaurant to have quick and easy access to real-life customers. Each design choice was purposeful to foster maximum results. Menlo Innovations made sure that its workspace was movable, allowing people to easily experiment with the physical environment. Mass Mutual used helium balloons to foster wide-scale experimentation.

Unlike the sterile labs of the past, your modern test kitchen doesn't require a permanent physical location. Taco Bell's version was a multimillion-dollar investment, but Simply Gum's Caron Proschan used the tiny stovetop in her apartment to conduct her experiments. If you don't have the budget or space for a permanent location, try converting a conference room one day a month. Dustin Garis, an innovation leader at P&G whom we'll meet in chapter 9, commandeered a working elevator to use as a temporary test kitchen when he wanted to get his team out of their normal routine. Or perhaps a field trip is in order...I've held ideation sessions inside the Detroit Institute of Arts, bobbing about in a boat in the Gulf of Mexico, at a working farm in Northern California, and in the storied halls of the New York City Public Library.

Whether permanent or temporary, equip your test kitchen with whatever gear will help you unlock fresh thinking. Fortunately, a laptop and Wi-Fi connection are all that's needed for millions of knowledge-based businesses. Additionally, consider what supplies might help stimulate creativity or help build crude prototypes. My shopping list includes giant-sized Post-it Notes, colorful markers, Play-Doh, construction paper, Nerf balls, duct tape, and squirt guns.

Participants

On the people front, I love Amazon's "two-pizza rule," which requires that you keep the group small enough to feed them dinner with only two pizzas. If two spicy pepperoni and mush-room pies won't feed the team, the gang may be too large. Mass

Mutual has thousands of employees, but experimental teams are purposefully kept small.

I'm also a big fan of teams that rotate to capture fresh ideas from a diverse set of minds. Pulling in people from seemingly unrelated backgrounds is a great way to spur creativity. When you think about who to invite, push to maximize diversity. A rock band with five guitar players and no other musicians would sound like a train wreck, and so does an ideation session where every participant is a mirror image of the organizer. Idea quality improves when capturing input from a wide array of perspectives. Consider the full spectrum of diversity, including race, gender, educational background, age, sexual preference, geographic origin, occupation, organization seniority, experience level, and even demeanor when assembling your test kitchen dream team.

Ingredients

In terms of ingredients, there are two approaches that yield outstanding results: the TV cooking show and the farmers market. Millions of cooking enthusiasts tune in each week to the Food Channel to see shows like *Chopped*, in which contestants are given a limited number of strange ingredients and are forced to create something edible. When you have to make a dish with dried fermented scallops, rose water syrup, and mashed potato candy, the odd and limited ingredient mix ensures that you'll invent a never-been-done-before concept. You can't follow your grandmother's recipe when combining rainbow chard, cactus pears, preserved duck eggs, and gummy bears. Here, a limited set of seemingly disconnected ingredients drives creative output.

In contrast to the limited set of ingredients from the TV cooking show strategy, the farmers market approach stocks the cupboards with abundant options. Imagine walking through a bustling outdoor market on an early Saturday morning, collecting ingredients based on what looks appealing rather than conforming to the requirements of a specific recipe. Returning to your kitchen with a smorgasbord of ingredients, you now have all the elements you could wish for when concocting a new dish. Shake Shack's Innovation Kitchen employs this strategy, keeping nearly every spice on the planet on hand for experimentation. Neither strategy is right or wrong. I've found success oscillating between both approaches when seeking to discover the next *Big Little Breakthrough*.

In terms of conducting actual experiments, there are more strategies than I can count, but I'd recommend starting with the simple approach of A/B testing. The goal here is to isolate a single variable to test in order to determine a causal relationship. For example, if you believed that sending a sales email with a funny subject line would improve response rates, you could easily test your hypothesis using a simple A/B test.

Instead of sending 50,000 marketing emails out with the same subject line, randomly split the group into two 25,000-person cohorts. Ideally, these groups should look as close to one another as possible. If you split the group by gender, for example, your test results would be inconclusive since the groups didn't mirror each other.

Once you have two equal groups, you'd send one group—your control group—the typical non-funny subject line, "Buy one, get one free." Concurrently, you'd send others—your test group—the sillier subject, "Screw it, let's just give everyone free stuff." You'd want to send on the same day, at the same time, and control for every other variable except the email subject line you're testing. With everything else identical, you can measure and gauge the impact of your idea, allowing you to reach a solid conclusion.

A/B testing isn't glamorous, but it's the easiest and most effective approach in many cases and is a great starting point as you embrace the test kitchen mindset.

For more insights on experimentation, including tools and worksheets, don't forget to check out BigLittleBreakthroughs.com/toolkit.

Experiments Lead to Results

At first, the idea got lost in the shuffle. A Microsoft employee working in the company's Bing division had the idea to change the way headlines were displayed in a search result. It was just a small tweak that added a slightly longer description when a paid search ad was displayed to a user. Since Microsoft earns revenue when a user clicks on one of these ads, the idea was that a slightly longer description would be more enticing, thereby generating more clicks and more revenue. The concept seemed unremarkable, and it languished on a long list of similar ideas to be tested at a later date.

Realizing how simple the code would be to change, the software engineer who had the idea decided to try a simple experiment. Embracing a "let's run the experiment" mindset, she tweaked the code herself and measured the impact of this tiny change in a controlled A/B test. After a single day of testing, the data showed a 12 percent increase in click-through rates. Thinking the enormous performance boost must have been an anomaly, she ran the experiment again. And again. And again.

The five-minute code tweak held up under further scrutiny, and it was eventually implemented on a system-wide basis, driving an additional $100 million in profits for Microsoft Bing. This simple *Big Little Breakthrough* turned out to be the division's best revenue-generating idea in its history, but it could have easily fallen on the shop floor. It came to life because Microsoft built a culture of experimentation, which gave the software engineer the courage to test out her hunch.

While the almost-lost innovation was remarkable, it wasn't an abnormality. According to Stefan Thomke, the Harvard professor and author mentioned earlier in this chapter, "Microsoft Bing's 'experiment with everything' approach has delivered surprisingly large payoffs. It has helped them identify dozens of revenue-related changes to make each month—improvements that have collectively increased revenue per search by 10 percent to 25 percent each year. These enhancements, along with hundreds of other small changes per month that increase user satisfaction, are the major reason that Bing is profitable and that its share of the US search market has risen to 23 percent, up from 8 percent in 2009, the year it was launched."

It makes sense that Microsoft's Bing would be able to test and adapt quickly in their digital environment, but can an experimentation mindset drive results in the physical world? This is the exact question that Doug Peterson asked himself as he moved halfway around the world to lead New Zealand's quest to capture the America's Cup.

The America's Cup is the oldest international sporting trophy, dating back to 1851 when the Royal Squadron of England offered a prize to the winner of a sailing race around the Isle of Wight. The first race was won by the New York schooner *America*, and the race became known as America's Cup ever since. Considering the United States has won twenty-nine of the thirty-five races over the last 150 years, the race's name is fitting. The competition has become a high-profile event, with huge sponsors and well-funded teams pushing the nautical boundaries for fame and glory.

Doug Peterson took the helm of Team New Zealand back in 1994 when the notion of his team winning the Cup was about as likely as my beloved Detroit Lions winning back-to-back Super Bowl championships. At the time, the mighty US had only lost once and was the favorite by a country mile. Doug was out-funded, outgunned, and facing what appeared to be insurmountable odds. Historically, the team with the biggest budget won the race, and compared to Team USA, Doug's war chest wouldn't even be considered lunch money. Team USA's lead helmsman was Dennis Conner, who was a four-time winner and was literally known around the world as "Mr. America's Cup." Experts at the time were sure that Team New Zealand would suffer a highly predictable routing, but that was just fine with Doug. While other teams and the media bantered about, Doug got down to experimentation.

Despite the overwhelming odds against him, Doug had conviction that his team could outsail the competition if they could out-experiment them. He instilled his rapid experimentation philosophy immediately upon his arrival in New Zealand, instructing the full fifty-person team that everyone's job was to run constant experiments. The multidisciplinary team included designers, naval architects, engineering researchers, analysts, and of course sailors, who each added "experimenter" to their job description.

As the team feverishly prepared for the race of their lives, they embraced the well-established four step experimentation approach of *design*, *build*, *test*, and *analyze*.

The *design phase* involved generating as many ideas as possible and then figuring out how to test them quickly and cheaply. The team generated ideas for new sailing techniques, new team communication strategies, and new training routines. They also set out to design the fastest boat in history by challenging conventional approaches. Instead of ideating on the sails, mast, and hull, which had been optimized by others over the years, Team New Zealand took the unorthodox approach of focusing on the keel. They hypothesized that it could be enhanced to deliver big gains in speed. In addition to generating new ideas, they had to figure out how to run successful tests. Could computer simulation work to deliver fast and inexpensive trials, or would they need to build physical models to conduct a particular experiment?

Once ideas were generated and experiments envisioned, the team entered the *build phase* to construct the actual tests. At first, they used cheap-and-dirty tests such as basic clay models, computer-simulated experiments, and even rough sketches. Crude experiments like these are referred to as *low-fidelity experiments* since they are not mimicking actual conditions. These rudimentary tests are ideal for the early stages of a big project, since they can disqualify unsuccessful ideas quickly and help identify which initial ideas merit further exploration. As the race toward the race continued, the team evolved into *high-fidelity experiments* that were closer representations to real-world conditions. The team build quarter-scale models of their ship, performing tests in wind tunnels and towing tanks. These experiments allowed the team to test out their ideas in a setting that closely reflected varying sea conditions, allowing them to simulate storms, high winds, and choppy waters.

Once experiments were constructed, the team proceeded to the *testing phase*. Here, the experiments were run again and again, isolating one variable at a time and comparing to a control group so that causality could be established (the classic A/B test in action). How did the flow of water on the yacht's surface change when a small tweak was made to the position of the mainsail?

With an elongated keel experiment, how did the ship respond when wind speed increased by three knots?

After experiments had been completed, the *analysis phase* began. Here, the team reviewed the test results, compared it to previous experiments, and then tried to fully understand the insights behind the data. At this point, the team would reach conclusions, form new hypotheses, and go right back to phase one of the experimentation cycle. Painstaking and meticulous, yet highly instructive. Rapid feedback loops drove rapid ideas, rapid changes, and rapid new experimentation.

"Instead of relying on a few big leaps, we had the ability to continually design, test, and refine our ideas," explains David Egan, one of the team's simulation experts. "The team would hold informal discussions on design issues, sketch some schematics on the back of a beer mat, and ask me to run the numbers. Using traditional design methods would have meant waiting months for results, and by that time, our thinking would have evolved so much that the reason for the experiment would long since have been forgotten."

In a Rocky Balboa–style victory on June 13, 1995, Team New Zealand swept all five of the competition's races. As the team made history, television commentator Peter Montgomery exclaimed, "The America's Cup is now New Zealand's Cup!" The phrase caught on quickly in New Zealand culture, becoming a national chant of pride.

When describing the unprecedented victory, the team's leader, Doug Peterson, remarked that it was rapid experimentation and a series of small improvements that won the race. "It is not a breakthrough boat," Peterson said. "It is a highly refined version of earlier designs. It has no gimmicks." Said differently, it wasn't a groundbreaking transformation that achieved the decisive victory but rather a large number of *Big Little Breakthroughs* that drove the team's remarkable success.

Rapid experimentation and *Big Little Breakthroughs* go together like peanut butter and jelly. Testing large volumes of tiny ideas is the new model for sustained growth and success. Whether you're leading a global team or just looking after yourself, *open a test kitchen* to boost your creative output. Your test kitchen may be tangible, or it may just be developing an experimentation mindset, but your testing obsession will surely lead to better results.

Now that we've enjoyed some goat cheese and maple-fennel pancakes in the test kitchen, we're ready to move on to the fourth obsession of everyday innovators, *break it to fix it*. We'll take a wrecking ball to the outdated maxim "if it ain't broke, don't fix it." From building the world's largest toy manufacturer to democratizing commercial real estate investing to reimagining education on a global scale all the way to reinventing how to eat a hot dog in record time, we'll explore how everyday innovators deconstruct and rebuild.

Chapter 8

Break It to Fix It

Like millions of other kids around the world, LEGOs were my absolute favorite toy growing up. The top of my birthday and holiday wish lists for years, I collected the modular pieces with an unhinged determination. Until my younger brother Ethan was born, I commandeered a spare bedroom that became known simply as the "LEGO Room" until my colorful pieces were evicted to make way for my younger sibling. I've never forgiven him.

For hours on end, I toiled away building rocket ships and cities, only to demolish them and start anew. Years later as a dad, I built complex LEGO Death Star sets with my oldest son, Noah. Nowadays with my four-year-old twins, building towers that stretch toward the ceiling is almost a daily occurrence. I confess...I'm a hard-core LEGO-head.

As a kid, I didn't build a LEGO castle in order to exhibit the finished work on a permanent display shelf. One of the greatest joys for me was dismantling something I built to quickly rebuild a better version. When my skyscraper toppled over, my next version included a steadier base to increase structural integrity.

And there was great delight in deconstructing a newly built race car to repurpose the bricks into a police boat. The fun wasn't finishing a project; it was the continuous process of creating and then rebuilding again. That's what LEGO-ing is all about, and that's exactly what the LEGO Group has been doing at the corporate level since its modest beginnings in rural Denmark.

Struggling to feed his family in the dire economic storms of 1932, a furniture craftsman named Ole Kirk Kristiansen started to make wooden toys to pay the bills. He named his one-man company LEGO, which is an abbreviation of the two Danish words "leg" and "godt," meaning "play well." The fledgling business produced wooden toy ducks and yo-yos, items that Kristiansen could craft with the same equipment he previously used to build furniture. But a 1942 fire that burned his small factory to the ground triggered the company's first of many reinventions.

The fire forced Kristiansen to reevaluate his business and ponder the changing world of play. Since he had to rebuild anyway, he wondered if he should equip the factory to produce the same wooden toys or explore something entirely new. Rather than rushing back to the routine, he explored new trends in the toy industry, manufacturing, and childhood development.

Kristiansen decided to boldly reinvent his business, allowing kids the opportunity to build their own toys instead of buying his finished products. In 1946, the company was the first in Denmark to purchase a newfangled contraption known as a plastic injection-molding machine to pursue a brand-new model. By the end of the decade, LEGO had transformed from a wooden toy business into a producer of interchangeable plastic blocks, known the world over as LEGO bricks.

While the factory fire wasn't by design, LEGO's transformation came by embracing the fourth obsession of everyday innovators, *break it to fix it*. Had the fire not occurred, it's quite possible that LEGO would be an unknown yo-yo maker rather than the largest toy company in the world. In fact, the LEGO Group's greatest innovation may not be their modular plastic bricks but rather the company's ability to reinvent itself on a continual basis.

As children fell in love with the modular construction sets, the LEGO system of play spread around the world. Growth and profits soared, but complacency never took root. Rather than gliding on autopilot, the company expanded into new territory in 1968 when it opened LEGOLAND, a LEGO-themed amusement park in its home of Billund, Denmark. To this day, the tiny town of Billund has population of only 6,662 people, but LEGOLAND had welcomed its five millionth visitor by 1974. Going from wooden ducks to plastic building blocks to becoming a holiday destination required a willingness to rethink their existing business identity. Today, there are nine LEGOLAND theme parks around the world in destinations including Germany, Malaysia, Japan, Dubai, England, Italy, and the United States. Not only is it a profitable stand-alone venture, visiting a LEGOLAND park deepens customer loyalty to the iconic toy maker.

Leaders at the LEGO Group have the characteristic of being perennially dissatisfied, viewing the status quo as their most nefarious enemy. In the same way I loved to bust apart my own LEGO creations to build new ones, the *break it to fix it* ethos permeates LEGO's corporate culture.

In 1969, the company expanded into the toddler market with larger blocks called DUPLOs. Easier for little kids to manage, the big blocks for small hands were an instant hit. The same thinking applied when the company launched LEGO Technic with gears and intricate parts to fascinate teenagers and young adults. Most companies would have rejected either new concept for fear of cannibalizing their business. Thankfully, platitudes such as "don't kill the golden goose" are forbidden in Billund, Denmark.

By 1999, the LEGO brick was named Product of the Century by *Fortune* magazine, and the company was a model of success. At this very point, many companies would start to coast and rely on previous success. In contrast, LEGO was just getting warmed up. From 1998 through 2002, LEGO's company tagline was "Just Imagine..." and that's exactly what they did. Refusing to be seduced into a protectionism mindset, leaders continued to *break it to fix it*.

From moon rovers to fortresses, the company had only produced sets that were designed internally. This only-created-here belief was tightly held, despite many offers from outsiders for licensed partnerships. Yet in 2000, LEGO broke the rule and signed a deal with Warner Bros. for a Harry Potter LEGO series. By 2007, licensing deals expanded with Lucasfilm to create *Star Wars* and Indiana Jones–themed sets. By the end of the decade, a licensing deal was struck with Disney Consumer Products for sets around the entire portfolio of Disney and Pixar properties. Licensing deals were new to LEGO and required the company to reimagine its core beliefs, yet the company was willing to replace old traditions with new ones.

By 2013, things were really clicking (sorry, I had to) for LEGO. In less than a decade, the company had quadrupled revenue and was expanding into a wide array of new opportunities, from LEGO robotics to video games. In a bold *break it to fix it* move, LEGO strayed from the toy business and got into the movie business. Teaming up with Warner Bros., *The LEGO Movie* was an international hit, raking in $468 million at the box office. The film's success led to three more movies, *The LEGO Batman Movie*, *The LEGO Ninjago Movie*, and *The LEGO Movie 2*, which generated a combined $1.1 billion at the box office.

Core to LEGO's ability to pioneer new ground is the LEGO Future Lab, a team dedicated to inventing the company's future. "It's a small area of the company that operates a little outside the rules," says former CEO Jørgen Vig Knudstorp. Following the *open a test kitchen* principle, the team has a dedicated building on the LEGO campus to tinker, experiment, and nurture new ideas outside of any operational demands. "Experimentation is something we can't afford *not* to do," explained Knudstorp.

With the help of the Future Lab, LEGO's *break it to fix it* advances seem unending. When an AFOL (adult friend of LEGO, the official acronym for diehards like me) suggested the idea of large, complex kits for adults, the Future Lab worked to bring it to life. Grown-ups now get to play with the LEGO Architecture Series, which includes kits to build intricate replicas of the Empire State Building, the Taj Mahal, the Eifel Tower, and London's Trafalgar Square. The sets sell for up to $400 and are designed to delight nostalgic adults rather than younger minds.

And there's LEGO Ideas, a crowdsourcing platform where customers can submit ideas for future sets. The site has become a massive hit as LEGO lovers around the world vote for their favorite user-generated ideas, many of which have become instant bestsellers. There's LEGO Mindstorms, an educational program in which students build working robots out of LEGO parts and compete for prizes and recognition. We can't forget the company's effort to help children and caregivers learn braille through a specialized set for the visually impaired. Or LEGO Life, the online app that is a safe, LEGO-based social network for kids too young for Instagram or Snapchat. Naturally, there's the LEGO "Bricksy" Series, which include sets that bring the street artist Banksy's works to LEGO life. There's even a business consultancy called LEGO Serious Play, which helps foster organizational creativity.

LEGO *broke it to fix it* over and over again as the company transformed from one type of business to the next. Start as a wooden toy company, break that notion and morph into a plastic brick company. Break that view to expand into theme parks. Break it again to enter the movie business. Break. And video games. Break. And robotics. Break. And adult toys. Break. And a social media network.

One brick at a time, LEGO continues to build and rebuild, deconstruct and reinvent. With $6.1 billion in annual revenue, $1.3 billion in profits, and nineteen thousand employees, the world's largest and most successful toy company is still privately held by the original Kristiansen family and still headquartered in the tiny town of Billund. But nearly everything else has changed. The company's epic success is directly tied to its ability to discover fresh opportunities rather than cling to old ones. Never afraid to challenge conventional approaches or defy their own traditions, LEGO continues to reach new heights by embracing the *break it to fix it* philosophy.

Video Killed the Radio Star

No matter how hard you try, it's one of those songs you just can't get out of your head. The Buggles, a British new-wave pop group, launched the catchy tune in 1979, and it's been an earworm ever since. The premise of the song is that a new innovation (music videos) renders the old approach (radio) obsolete. Most of us can remember the hypnotic refrain, repeated ad nauseum during the now-dated video that was uncoincidentally the first music video ever played on MTV. The station also made sure it was their one-millionth aired video during a star-studded celebration in 2000.

The song was a gigantic commercial success, reaching the number one spot on sixteen different national charts and named one of the Top 100 Songs That Changed History. Far beyond the musicality, the aptly named title aligns with the need to focus on what's next rather than what was.

The maxim "if it ain't broke, don't fix it" is cringeworthy. In the category of horrible advice, it's right up there with "don't rock the apple cart" and "don't speak unless you're spoken to." *Break it to fix it* is the antithesis of those outdated idioms, challenging us to confront products, systems, approaches, and processes that are working just fine. Instead of waiting for outside forces to render the current state obsolete, this obsession is the proactive approach of getting there first. Why wait to take action until your current system has been displaced?

In the same way that the milk in your fridge has an expiration date, I've often wondered why a mandatory refresh date doesn't exist on most things in the business world. When a new system or process is enacted, why is it assumed that the approach should be everlasting? Back to the *Frogger* principle from chapter 3, it doesn't make sense to ascribe permanence in a world that's changing so rapidly. I wholeheartedly believe that it's our responsibility to seek new versions, to deconstruct and rebuild, to reimagine and pursue a better way. It's up to each of us to discover our own "video killed the radio star" approaches.

Everyday innovators are constantly examining current conditions, looking for opportunities to break and then create new ones. Upgrades can pay significant dividends when applied to products, teams, production practices, safety standards, sales efforts, training, and nearly every other system, big or small. The same method used to reinvent an industry can apply all the way down to retooling how you run your Monday morning team meeting. Here's a simple yet highly effective *break it to fix it* methodology:

Step 1: Deconstruct

The first order of business is to carefully disassemble the current approach into its individual components. This is the equivalent of taking apart my LEGO pirate ship all the way down to singular pieces. If you offer a food product, you'd deconstruct it down to your initial shopping list (one cup flour, a quarter cup olive oil, two garlic cloves) or if you are attacking a process, you'd look at each of the mini steps that come together to form the broader approach. Physical or metaphorical, deconstruct your target into the smallest possible fragments in the same way you reduced fractions in Mr. Hoffman's seventh-grade math class...'til you could subdivide no more.

Step 2: Examine

Now that the components are isolated, it's time to examine them with the diligence of a fastidious scientific researcher. To that end, I recommend using a playlist. In Dan and Chip Heath's 2013 book *Decisive*, they differentiate between a *checklist* and a *playlist*. They characterize a checklist as a list of things that must all be done, whereas a playlist is an organized list of possibilities. When I'm working to solve a problem, I run a playlist of questions that helps me fully understand the deconstructed components at the root level:

1. What is this thing made of?
2. What's missing?
3. What was the thinking and context that led to its initial creation?

4. Why did this work in the past?
5. What's different today?
6. How has the customer's need changed since this was originally conceived?
7. What are the core rules, truisms, traditions, or beliefs that are currently holding this together but could possibly be challenged?
8. Where else in the world does a similar problem or pattern exist?
9. What technical advances have emerged since this version's construction that could be implemented for improvement?
10. How durable is it, and where are the likely fault lines or soft spots?

Just like a good detective, we want to gather as much evidence as possible before reaching any conclusions.

Step 3: Rebuild

With insights from Step 2, we now begin to reassemble the pieces with the goal of upgrading the end result. Give yourself permission to tinker a bit. At this stage, I like to run another playlist of questions:

1. What is one new component I could add?
2. What's one thing I could subtract? Or substitute?
3. If I could wave my magic wand to make this better, what would the end result look like?
4. How can this be reassembled or rearranged to save time or money? Improve quality? Solve a new problem?
5. How do other people solve a similar problem in my field? Outside my field?

6. What ideas could I could borrow from nature or art that could inspire an upgrade?
7. How might I make it bigger, such as adding more horse-power or computing capacity? Smaller, such as with a leaner footprint, less waste, and faster delivery?
8. If I have several possibilities, how can I build a prototype to quickly test them before proceeding?

Looking back to some of the innovators we've met together, we can see that this methodology was the underpinning of their eventual success. Some were *insiders*, who examined their existing business and found a fresh path forward. Mat Ishbia, for example, broke his small retail mortgage company in order to rebuild it into the largest wholesale mortgage provider in the country. Team New Zealand was already racing boats when they reinvented their approach to snag the America's Cup.

The insider approach centers on building a better version—an upgrade—of what you're already doing. The innovators at Shake Shack, for example, focus on improving their existing restaurant business rather than starting an industrial supply company or a commercial litigation law firm.

We've also examined *outsiders*, who used the approach to enter a new field altogether. Jenny Du wasn't a fresh produce veteran prior to cofounding Apeel Sciences, just like Chad Price wasn't in the health-care field when he launched Mako Medical. In fact, major industry shifts often occur when outsiders find a better way. The Jolliffe brothers used the *break it to fix it* approach to reinvent the game of golf, while Heather Hasson and Trina Spear took on medical scrubs from an outsider's perspective. (You'll hear more about them in chapter 11.)

The common thread is a refusal to accept things as they are, a disdain for the status quo. Which is exactly what propelled twenty-six-year-old Ryan Williams on a mission to fight against inequities while revolutionizing the stodgy real estate industry.

Deconstructing Inequality

Ryan Williams knows a thing or two about inequality. His great-great-grandmother, Addie Lynch, would have been a slave just like her parents had she been born just a couple of years earlier. Throughout the 1800s, Ryan's ancestors were forced into slavery, endlessly working the plantation fields in the broiling Louisiana sun to enrich the elite slaveholders to whom they were bound. Raised in a working-class family in Baton Rouge, Ryan experienced inequities firsthand in the form of segregation, crime, and persistent poverty. In his community, one out of every three African American men ended up in the criminal justice system. Seeing the toll that an unfair system took on his family, Ryan vowed early on to help make a change.

In addition to racial inequality, the wealth gap in the United States is a pervasive problem, creating more opportunity for those at the top and increasingly less for those toward the bottom. The gap between America's richest and poorest more than doubled between 1989 and 2016, and income inequality in the US is the highest of all the G7 nations. Meanwhile, middle-class incomes have grown at a slower rate than the upper tiers for each of the last five decades. By the time Ryan reached early adulthood, he couldn't stand by and let the cycle continue. Shortly after graduating college, he decided to *break it to fix it*.

One particular factor that helps the rich get richer is having access to the wildly profitable world of commercial real estate investing. Backroom deals over cigars and bourbon in wood-paneled libraries are by invitation only, after all. While all investors have access to publicly traded real estate investment trusts (REITs), the private deals are the ones that allow investors to afford their new yachts. Unless you have a membership to this secretive club, you just don't have access to these juicy opportunities. That is, until Ryan Williams came along.

With a mission to create fairness and equality in the highbrow arena of commercial real estate, Ryan founded Cadre, an online investment platform that brings transparency and access to all. It allows those of us outside the billionaire class to invest in high-quality, highly profitable real estate deals, even if we have a modest bankroll. For the first time ever, we get to feast at the same table as those who eat lobster and caviar, even if we have a beer and taco budget.

"Real estate is a Jurassic industry. It's antiquated," Ryan explains. Using the *break it to fix it* methodology, Ryan first deconstructed the situation. He studied how capital flowed from deal to deal, how money was made, and who had access. Next, he carefully examined the various elements. He learned that most real estate deals required minimum investment sizes that were far beyond the reach of the average person. He also learned that once an investment is made, there was no way to get your money out until another big transaction occurred, which could take a decade or more. If you're a zillionaire, it's no big deal to have your funds tied up for a long time, but the lack of liquidity created too big a barrier for most people. Finally, the best deals never made it to the public markets, which meant that regular investors could only access the leftover table scraps.

Once Ryan had broken things down and examined them carefully, it was time to rebuild. Cadre offers access to previously inaccessible real estate deals with lower minimum investment sizes and lower fees. Further, the platform allows investors to sell their individual investments anytime they want, thereby avoiding the liquidity problem. "The secondary market gives them the power to buy and sell their interests, which hasn't existed for direct investors until now," Ryan explains.

Back to his fight against inequality, Ryan's mission is to create access for everyone. "Previously, it went to the top 1 percent of the top 1 percent. With Cadre, we're giving people direct deal-by-deal access to commercial real estate, as easily as you would buy and sell something on Amazon."

In just six years, the company is valued at over $800 million and has completed over $2 billion in transactions on its platform. Now just thirty-two years old, Ryan plans to extend his *break it to fix it* approach to other asset classes beyond real estate. He hopes that one day, Cadre will be the place to buy and sell a wide array of investments that were previously inaccessible and illiquid. "With a laser focus on our mission, we're creating a platform that allows people to expand their financial futures," Ryan concludes. In the hypercompetitive world of commercial real estate, this young outsider is shaking things up while staying true to his commitment to fight inequality. The company's slogan, "real estate investing, reimagined," perfectly sums up Ryan's strategy, which he's applying toward his vision of a fair and just society.

History Reclaimed

From the birth of the auto industry in the early 1900s to the explosive race riots in the late 1960s, Detroit's downtown firehouse located at 250 West Larned Street has seen plenty of action. The site served the Detroit Fire Department since 1840, eventually transitioning from a working firehouse to the department's head-quarters, until it was sold to developers in 2013 to convert it into a boutique hotel. When the timeworn wood from its floors and walls was carted away to make room for the new digs, Mark Wallace saw something far more valuable than scrap timber.

Ryan Williams deconstructed commercial real estate investing in order to reassemble it a better way. But Mark Wallace saw reclaimed wood as an opportunity to make something entirely different from its original use. Mark took the salvaged pine and maple floorboards from Detroit's firehouse and lovingly transformed them into...a brand-new guitar. "I'm trying to take something that was once great but has been cast aside and trans-form it into something new and vital," Mark explained as we began our conversation.

Mark is the founder and CEO of Wallace Detroit Guitars, a company that takes reclaimed wood from landmark Detroit build-ings and turns it into beautiful handcrafted guitars. "Some of the structures in Detroit have incredible history," Mark tells me. "One of my favorites is the Brewster-Wheeler Recreation Center, which was in the Brewster-Wheeler Housing Project. For music buffs, this is a place where Diana Ross and all of the Supremes grew up. It's one of the most notorious old-school housing projects anywhere in the country. And it's a place where amazing talent and amazing music came from. It's quite possible that those folks were sitting there, watching basketball games in the rec center, and now I'm using those old benches to make guitars."

Wallace Detroit Guitars are as much a work of art as a func-tional instrument. The architecturally significant wood is restored, polished, and then handcrafted into striking guitars. Unlike mass-manufactured gear, these instruments have a soul, a rich history that now lives on. Whether the reclaimed wood comes from the old Cadillac Motors plant, the once-bustling city court-house, or a long-forgotten church, each guitar is stamped with a serial number that begins with 313 (Detroit's area code) and a number that specifies its origins and story.

The company also makes custom guitars for discerning clients. "We built a guitar for an auto executive out of wood from an old sawmill on Belle Isle in the Detroit River," Mark shares. "One of the special things we did for him is that we built the dots on the fingerboard out of a material called 'Fordite.' It's an imagi-nary name for a mineral, which actually comes from the old spray booths in the Ford paint factories. The booths would get covered with different layers of that year's paint colors. When you cut into the side of them, you see these little striations, little stripes of actual Ford model colors. Talk about a one-of-a-kind guitar!

"Our goal with these guitars is to preserve the history of the city we love while honoring its tradition of superior craftsmanship," Mark explains. "Detroit is a community of people who know how to make stuff, and our company is cut from that same cloth." After the buildings were deconstructed (Step 1 of the *break it to fix it* methodology), his examination (Step 2) led to something entirely new when he rebuilt (Step 3) the wood into one-of-a kind guitars with historical significance. And as a result, Detroit's proud tradi-tions of bespoke craftsmanship and great music live on.

How to Eat a Hot Dog

Every Fourth of July, contestants take the stage at the Nathan's Hot Dog Eating Contest to compete for the gluttonous cham-pionship title. Over the years, the spectacle has grown to epic proportions, with prize money and notoriety approaching that of the British Open. Typically, broad-shouldered contestants would shove down their dogs the same way they would at a picnic, only faster. Until a strange new competitor entered the field.

At 5'8" and just 128 pounds, Takeru "Kobi" Kobayashi looked nothing like the other contestants. In fact, he doesn't even like hot dogs. What seemed delicious to Kobi, however, was winning the prize money and becoming a competitive-eating champion. So, when he decided to pursue hot dog glory, he used the *break it to fix it* approach. Kobi deconstructed the task at hand, separating the meat from the bun. He was eating for sport, not for culinary pleasure, so he examined the components with the eye of an athlete instead of a hungry diner. To rebuild, he experimented with a variety of tactics to optimize speed and efficiency.

First isolating the dog from the bun, he discovered that he could fold the meat in half and then down it in one big gulp. The bun, on the other hand, was giving him a hard time since it required a lot of chewing. That is, until he tried the creative approach of dipping the bun into a glass of water, squeezing out the excess liquid, and then gobbling the doughy ball in one bite. Disgusting, to be sure, but also highly efficient.

Kobi trained for the competition, expanding his stomach capacity by drinking huge amounts of water and also lifting weights to build lean muscle mass to ensure peak performance. He's also known for the "Kobayashi Shake," his trademark full-body wiggle that helps food quickly clear his esophagus en route to his stomach.

After ninety years of competition, the world record for hot dogs consumed in twelve minutes was 25.1. On Kobayashi's first attempt...he ate 50! Kobi's *break it to fix it* tactics allowed him to double the world record, making him an instant celebrity. His creative approach to speed-eating helped him win fifteen other world records, including 337 buffalo wings in 30 minutes, 159 tacos in 10 minutes, 93 hamburgers in 8 minutes, 62 slices of pizza in 12 minutes, and 41 lobster rolls in 10 minutes. In each of his feats, he deconstructed, examined, and rebuilt the traditional approach, which has landed Kobi over $6 million in lifetime winnings.

Too often when we try to achieve more, we rely on outdated methods. But doing the same thing faster is no way to win a championship. Instead, let's follow Kobi's lead to discover a new and better plan of attack when we're attempting our next challenge. It's the creative *break it to fix it* strategies that deliver maximum results rather than the try-harder-go-faster approach that leads to underperformance and burnout. So, when you're ready to gobble up your most important opportunities, reinvent the process rather than just chewing faster.

I'd Like to Teach the World

Struggling in her high school math classes, Nadia turned to her cousin for help. Sal Khan was a mathematics whiz who worked as a hedge fund analyst in Boston, so he'd be a perfect tutor. The problem, however, was that Nadia lived thousands of miles away in New Orleans. Wanting to help despite the distance, Sal began to make very simple training videos that he thought might help explain some of the more complex concepts. It turned out, his cousin preferred these videos to a live session, since she could start and stop at any time, repeat sections when necessary, and not feel ashamed if she couldn't keep up. Sal didn't know it at the time, but helping his cousin Nadia with algebra would lead to a global revolution in education.

To his surprise, other people stumbled on the videos Sal posted on YouTube for his cousin. Before long, viewership skyrocketed and people started posting comments like this one Sal received early on: "My twelve-year-old son has autism and has had a terrible time with math. We have tried everything, viewed everything, bought everything. We stumbled on your video on decimals, and it got through. Then we went on to the dreaded fractions. Again, he got it. We could not believe it. He is so excited."

In addition to the feedback from students and parents, teachers started reaching out with gratitude. Some progressive teachers began using Sal's videos to augment their in-classroom lessons and experienced significant boosts in student performance as a result. Sal began to put the pieces together and realized he had the opportunity to really make a difference in education.

After a lot of reflection, Sal decided it was his mission to reimagine education altogether, making it accessible and free to all. With such a big vision, Sal had to embrace the *break it to fix it* approach. First, he deconstructed the various components of the learning process. There were in-person activities, which most often involved a group of students listening quietly to a teacher's lecture. Then there was the hands-on learning, which oddly was done at home in solitude. Sal broke down curriculums, educational theory, testing, grading, and, of course, results. To reinvent global education, the first step was deconstructing the current systems into their individual parts in order to explore new and better approaches.

Next, Sal's examination yielded some fascinating insights. It became obvious to him that the traditional educational approach was backwards. Lectures would be much more effective at home, he thought, since students could watch at their own pace. They could start, stop, or repeat as they wished, allowing them to fully grasp the content. While at school, professional teachers could actively participate in a hands-on learning experience rather than delivering a monotonous soliloquy.

It made so much more sense for the classroom experience to be active, collaborative, and participatory. Sal explains, "A teacher, no matter how good, had to give this one-size-fits-all lecture to thirty students—blank faces, slightly antagonistic—and now it's a human experience, now they're actually interacting with each other."

The other insight that Sal discovered is that students often advance without fully grasping core concepts, creating a downstream problem later on in their education. If a student learns 80 percent of an important concept, they're given a B grade and advance to the next level. But there's no system in place to later close the 20 percent gap, which unfortunately can compound to the detriment of the student's overall education. Sal likens this to learning to ride a bike. If you didn't master making right turns, you'd keep working on it until you got it. But in a school setting, they send you forward despite the risk of a future crash.

While some insights were surprising, others were more obvious. According to a United Nations report on global education, 617 million children worldwide are not achieving minimum proficiency levels in reading and mathematics, which the report describes as a "learning crisis." Minority and low-income areas are especially affected, as we learned from the story of Khali Sweeney's Downtown Boxing Gym in poverty-stricken Detroit. The challenges are even worse on a global basis. In Brazil, for example, only 7 percent of high school students reach grade-level proficiency in math, while just 15 percent of eighth graders in Peru manage to achieve basic reading and writing standards.

With a clear sense of the problems in education, Sal Khan left his cushy job in 2008 to launch Khan Academy, a nonprofit with a big mission: "To provide a free, world-class education for anyone, anywhere." After first deconstructing the situation and then evaluating to gain insights and ideas for change, Sal rebuilt education from the ground up. The Khan program consists of a massive library of free video courses in thirty-six languages, presented by experts who are fun and engaging in their delivery. This allows students to learn at their own pace, repeating lectures as they wish. It also enables teachers to flip the learning model, spending in-person time working closely with students rather than delivering generic lectures.

Sal explains, "In a traditional model, most of the teacher's time is spent doing lectures and grading and whatnot. Maybe 5 or 10 percent of their time is sitting next to students and working with them. Now, 100 percent of their time is. We are humanizing the classroom, I'd argue, by a factor of ten."

The Khan system also provides advanced technology for students and teachers based on the principle of "mastery learning," originally proposed by educational psychologist Benjamin Bloom in 1968. The philosophy is that students must demonstrate mastery in a subject before moving to the next, thereby eliminating persistent knowledge gaps. Sal calls the traditional learning holes "Swiss cheese" and strongly believes that students benefit tremendously if these holes can be pinpointed and filled.

In the Khan system, students are given online quizzes after learning a certain concept and are only allowed to advance once they get ten out ten correct answers in a row. It may sound arduous but it's actually very kind, ensuring that students don't miss core principles which can make future learning difficult or impossible. As such, activity is tracked and reported to teachers through colorful online dashboards, allowing them to zero in on the specific areas of need for each student.

Today, Khan Academy is delivering stunning results. In a recent study of more than one thousand fourth-grade students in Philadelphia using the Khan system for an average of thirty minutes per week, students were more than 2.5 times as likely to meet state standards compared to students who were not in the program.

In Long Beach, California, 5,348 middle school students integrated the Khan Academy mathematics program for one class per week, which delivered a twenty-two-point increase on the Smarter Balanced mathematics assessment scale score. This learning translated into two times the district target versus those who did not use Khan Academy. In 2019, 2.7 million students used the Khan Academy SAT prep course, which delivered an average score increase of 115 points with just twenty hours of participation.

These days, over 17 million students use Khan Academy each month. In 2019 alone, the platform delivered 8.7 billion minutes of free learning to curious minds around the world.

Because Sal pursued such an important problem (the global education crisis) in a highly innovative break it to fix it fashion, he was able to secure the requisite funding to bring his vision to life. The academy got off the ground through grants from the Bill & Melinda Gates Foundation, the Google Foundation, and other philanthropic donors. Today, the organization has an $85 million endowment and continues to reimagine education, helping to better equip the next generation of productive citizens.

Khan Academy is tackling one of the world's biggest issues, but the same break it to fix it mindset can work for even your smallest challenges. You can deconstruct, examine, and rebuild the way you interview a new job candidate, prepare a customer's invoice, or pack a grocery bag at the local market. Whether you're inventing a new video game, reconfiguring your office space to boost employee engagement, or load-balancing a long-haul truck full of building supplies, *Big Little Breakthroughs* come to life when you discard traditional approaches.

In the next chapter, we'll explore the fifth obsession of everyday innovators—*reach for weird*. On our peculiar adventure, we'll meet Olga Khazan, a researcher of misfits and outsiders; Dustin Garis, P&G's Chief Troublemaker (yes, that's his actual title); and Johnny Cupcakes, a prankster, successful entrepreneur, and T-shirt "baker."

Get ready to get a little funky and make some trouble.

Chapter 9

Reach for Weird

The uninterrupted line of eager fans stretched past two city blocks. Camping out in tents for up to thirty-six hours, many of the diehards compared tattoos of their glorious hero. The scene was electric as the crowd counted down the minutes until the gates opened and the limited-edition offering was finally available for purchase.

In the heart of Los Angeles, you might imagine this swarm of fanatics was waiting to buy Taylor Swift concert tickets or snag front-row seats to Ellen's daytime talk show. Or maybe it was some incredible new tech gadget from Apple, or a limited-edition Harley-Davidson motorcycle. Instead, hundreds upon hundreds of ravenous devotees were waiting in line to buy a $40 T-shirt.

Welcome to the world of Johnny Cupcakes, the prankster behind one of the most iconic apparel brands on the planet. His logo, a rotund caricature of himself as a rosy-cheeked, suspender-wearing, cupcake-chasing prepubescent boy, is proudly tattooed on the bodies of over two thousand fanatical customers around the globe. He was named the Top Retail Innovator by the *Boston Globe* and the number one young entrepreneur by *Bloomberg Businessweek*. The most revered business schools write case studies about the irreverent visionary, and his stores in Boston, LA, London, and Martha's Vineyard routinely draw crowds that require police intervention. With all the hoopla, you'd think he's a tech guru or rock legend, but instead...Johnny is in the T-shirt business.

Johnny looks like a young and fit Super Mario. With the same dreamlike wonder as Willy Wonka, he speaks quickly but thoughtfully. He wears a permanent grin, and he smells like vanilla from across the room. "I trick people for a living," Johnny beams as we begin our conversation. "I own a T-shirt brand and T-shirt stores that look and smell like an actual bakery. You enter through a giant oven that's a secret entrance to the store, but we do not sell food whatsoever. Instead, we display graphic T-shirts inside of industrial refrigerators. We use pastry boxes instead of shopping bags, and the store smells like frosting. We make people feel like a kid again through the art of storytelling, packaging, and creating unique experiences."

Boston's Newbury Street is sprinkled with dozens of upscale restaurants, art galleries, and specialty gelato shops. Unsuspecting customers often wait in line to enter Johnny's "bakery" looking for a sweet dessert. As steam rises from the "baking ovens" and throngs of people gather around the refrigerated display cases, it takes a while to realize it's all a prank. Half the new visitors smile, snap a selfie, and buy a $40 T-shirt, while the other half get angry and storm out. But 100 percent of them leave with a story to share. "It's actually the upset customers that do most of the talking for my brand," Johnny tells me. "Someone will say, 'Hey, that's that shop Uncle Frank hates. Let's go check it out.' And they leave with a shirt."

In a highly commoditized industry, Johnny Cupcakes enjoys a cultlike following and leads a fast-growing, wildly popular brand. His remarkable success in a crowded field is a direct result of the fifth obsession of everyday innovators: *reach for weird.*

Most of us make decisions—big and small—within a generally accepted range of possibilities. We've established left and right guardrails to ensure we don't drift too far afield, largely to protect ourselves from unfavorable consequences. Yet counterintuitively, the very act of playing it safe has become the riskiest move of all. We may not get laughed out of the room, but we run the far more frightening risk of mediocrity and irrelevance. To fight back, everyday innovators push themselves to explore the unexpected. They discard obvious ideas in favor of unorthodox ones. They realize that those oddball, peculiar, bizarre ideas are the ones that stand out and make history. Just like Johnny, everyday innovators *reach for weird.*

Johnny Cupcakes is a tangled spiral of contradictions. In his early twenties, he was in a heavy metal rock band but to this day he's never had a sip of alcohol or puff of a cigarette. In the digital age, he collects vintage typewriters. When a friend invited him to join his marijuana-dealing business in high school, Johnny instead started a candy business to serve his buddy's customers who all had the munchies. His cupcake stores only sell real cupcakes on April Fool's Day. "While my friends were hanging out with cute girls at parties, I was hanging out with cute old ladies at craft fairs," he laughs. Naturally, when it came time to start a creative business, he chose the dull, competitive, and commoditized field of T-shirts.

Rationally speaking, you don't want to go into the T-shirt business. On the high end, you're competing with billion-dollar brands like Ralph Lauren, Lululemon, and Gucci. On the low end, you're in a race-to-the-bottom price war, competing with sweatshop labor and a disturbingly corrupt supply chain. To stand out, you'd need an ad budget that rivals the GDP of Paraguay. But Johnny realized that he could win if he pushed the boundaries of weird. To this end, he and his team use "Cupcake Vision" (their playful term for in-your-face creative exploration) to stand out so boldly that they simply can't be ignored. From T-shirt design to store layout to marketing stunts, every decision must pass the oddball test.

During the Halloween season, stores are closed all day and only sell shirts in the dead of night. Retail locations are converted into haunted houses, complete with scary music, fog machines, and popcorn. Leading up to the holiday, the team will make movie trailers for films that don't exist, such as *Count Spatula* or *Rise of the Two-Headed Zombie Chefs*. These themes then become limited-edition T-shirts, packaged inside collectable VHS tape boxes.

Johnny continues, "I found a creepy guy on Craigslist to rent me a real hearse and a real coffin for $220. I was able to get hundreds of thousands of dollars of free publicity when the national news media showed up wanting to find out why there's a hearse at a bakery that doesn't sell food. There was a line of people across the street, waiting to come inside."

A couple years back, Johnny created the "World Ice Cream Tour," renting an ice cream truck and driving it around the country as a mobile T-shirt shop. Shirts were packaged in giant ice cream push-pops, making the experiment fun and memorable. Another time, he dressed up like a leprechaun and hid in the bushes of people's backyards in the Boston area. Johnny would post his whereabouts on social media and then quickly update his posting each time he was discovered. "If you got a graphic T-shirt from a little dude with a beard, hiding in someone's yard, there's no way on earth you would not share that story," Johnny chuckles with a feigned Irish accent.

Using the elements of humor and surprise, Johnny's business results are as noteworthy as his pranks. According to industry sources, the average cost to manufacture a T-shirt is $3.15. In contrast, Johnny Cupcakes sells shirts in the $35 to $60 range, with special-edition Ts selling for more than $400.

With his cute mobster name and his childlike playfulness, this provocateur is always using his Cupcake Vision to find new ways to inject weird. "My business cards smell like vanilla frosting. I let them marinate in a Ziploc bag with car fresheners. I was buying so many from Bed Bath & Beyond that we now manufacture and sell Johnny Cupcakes car fresheners."

When you open the box from your online order, you may find something strange and unexpected. "I love doing this; we will put random items in orders," Johnny tells me with a devious chuckle. "You might get a free sticker. You might get a $20 bill with your T-shirt. You might get a doll's head. You might get a pack of batteries. You might get a handwritten note. Sometimes you'll get a vintage New Kids on the Block or Ninja Turtles trading card."

The quirky prankster who started with no capital, formal training, or industry experience has built a powerhouse business by being weird. And that same unexpected approach can drive confetti-frosted results for us all.

Depending on your profession or personality, goofy pranks may not be your go-to move, but we can all push the boundaries of weird in our own authentic ways. If you run a car dealership, weird for you would be to have your sales staff dress in NASCAR racing jumpsuits instead of mustard-stained polyester plaid suits. If you own a neighborhood Italian restaurant, you could hand out biscotti-flavored fortune cookies after every meal. (Who says

Chinese restaurants get to have all the fun?) If you run a doctor's office, weird could be an on-time appointment guarantee where patients get to choose a mystery surprise from a colorful treasure chest if the doctor is running late. Weird looks different for each of us, which makes the notion even more alluring.

If you've ever felt like an oddball, misfit, outlier, or trouble-maker, this is the obsession for you.

The Perks of Weird

For as long as she can remember, Olga Khazan has felt like an outsider. Participating in a resettlement program for refugee Soviet Jews, her family moved from St. Petersburg, Russia, to Midland, Texas, when she was three years old. A Russian immigrant Jew living in the heart of the Evangelical Christian, overwhelming conservative Bible Belt is about as fish out of water as you can get. When she was four, a teacher punished her for not praying to Jesus before she ate her raisins. She remembers being confused, wondering, "Who is this Jesus person everyone keeps talking about?"

"I always felt like an outsider; on the periphery of everything," Olga explained to me as we began our conversation about being weird. Her focus on being a misfit led her on a five-year research exploration, culminating in her award-winning book, *Weird: The Power of Being an Outsider in an Insider's World*. She set out to study the effect of weirdness on creativity, relationships, careers, health, and happiness.

In addition to voluminous academic research, Olga interviewed people who were members of the same fish-out-of-water club she joined when landing in rural Texas. She spoke with a female NASCAR driver and a male kindergarten teacher. She interviewed a former cult member who was the rare bird that had the wherewithal to break free and a black female Muslim who grew up in nearly all-white Alabama. Olga became an expert in weird.

Olga concludes that being a little weird is a real advantage. "Those who feel like outsiders develop a stronger sense of empathy and are willing to see multiple sides of an issue. In fact, there's a body of social-science research suggesting that being an oddball or a social reject can spark remarkable creativity," she explains. "People who don't fit neatly into a particular group have been found, over and over, to perform better at outside-the-box thinking."

Johns Hopkins University professor Sharon Kim conducted a series of experiments to test this theory. She invited students to participate in an experiment but randomly rejected half of them upon their arrival. Professor Kim made them feel left out, explaining that they didn't qualify and didn't belong in the group.

After being ostracized, they were asked to complete a handful of creativity tests since they were already there. Scores were tabulated and compared to the control group that hadn't been rejected. In the end, the snubbed participants outperformed their warmly welcomed counterparts by a significant margin, indicating that those who were made to feel left out were more likely to take creative risks and push the boundaries of their imagination. It turns out, rejection and creativity are related.

It made me wonder, what percentage of people *don't* feel like an outcast, at least some of the time? Our minds trick us to think we are the only outsiders when truly there are far more misfits than fit-ins. It might seem that everyone else has it all figured out, displaying a deep sense of belonging while lacking any doubt. All the while, the person who feels like they fit in most of the time is about as rare as a T-shirt-gifting leprechaun hiding in the Boston bushes. Instead of feeling bad about what makes us different, let's celebrate it. Let's rejoice in the fact that we're all a little weird, at least some of the time. When we recognize this, we move a giant step closer to cultivating *Big Little Breakthroughs*.

Olga points to another study led by Professor Rodica Damian at the University of Houston. Professor Damian believed that unusual experiences can boost creativity, so she ran a simple experiment. Randomly dividing a group of subjects, she had half the participants wear virtual reality googles to experience a bizarre world where gravity pulled things up instead of down. The control group had no such fun. After the VR experience, both groups were given standard creativity tests, and as you might imagine, the group who experienced an upside-down world scored markedly higher. Key to this example, all the participants had a generous supply of strangeness going into the experiment. Helping subjects connect with their inner weirdo is what boosted creative results.

Putting aside my belief that we're all a little odd, you don't even have to *be* weird to *think* weird. "Creativity boosts can also happen for people who live in unusual frames of mind rather than exotic locales," Olga explains. In the simplest sense, *reach for weird* is all about challenging yourself to explore oddball solutions instead of quickly accepting obvious answers. To cultivate weirdness, Olga advises us to question perceived wisdom and challenge established norms. "It's good to be weird," she explains as we end our conversation, giving me great comfort that my own strangeness could actually be an asset rather than a liability.

Now that we know why unusual thinking makes sense, let's shift our focus to practical techniques. It's time to get weird!

Harvesting Strange

Whether you call it unruly, peculiar, or unconventional, creative approaches violate norms, rules, and expectations. Now that we're ready to start generating fresh ideas, I'm excited to share some of my favorite unorthodox yet highly effective ideation techniques. Knowing that you have hundreds of strange and beautiful ideas inside you right now, here are some fun extraction techniques to bring them to the surface:

The Bad Idea Brainstorm

With so much pressure to discover the perfect idea, we can easily get stuck. To break free, try a brainstorming round looking for the *worst ideas* to your problem instead of the best. Make a list of every horrible, illegal, immoral, unethical, or just plain lousy idea you can think of. After you've exhausted all your bad ideas, do a second round where you examine the depraved concepts to see if there's a little something inside each bad idea that could be flipped into a good one. The horrible ideas will push your creativity into uncharted territory. Then, it's just a matter of tweaking and adjusting the bad ones until they're ready for primetime.

As StockX's Greg Schwartz told us, his initial idea was ridiculed and thought to be preposterous. But his irregular approach of taking physical possession of every shoe transaction to validate each product's authenticity became their most powerful competitive advantage after enough refinement.

The World's First

In this exercise, you're only allowed to brainstorm ideas that begin with the phrase "the world's first." Perhaps you invent the world's first insurance policy for drones. Or the world's first 3D-printed burger joint. What about the world's first hotel that offers guests a mandatory warm chocolate chip cookie upon arrival? That's exactly what the DoubleTree hotel chain did, and that simple idea is credited for much of their competitive differentiation in the highly commoditized hotel industry. Brainstorming "the world's first" will push your creativity to new heights and help you unlock bold possibilities.

Coss Marte opened the world's first prison-themed gym. Caron Proschan created the world's first all-natural chewing gum. Lin-Manuel Miranda created the world's first Broadway musical scored to rap music. Even when tackling small challenges, the world's first can deliver a potent breakthrough.

Role-Storming

Instead of brainstorming as yourself (and being solely responsible for any ideas generated), here you get to brainstorm as if you are someone else. In other words, you're generating ideas *in character*. First, select a persona—from movie star to mad scientist; from villain to sports hero—and brainstorm as if you were that person. This technique helps you look at the problem or opportunity from an entirely new perspective. How would Steve Jobs tackle the issue at hand? Or Jay-Z? Or Ursula the Sea Witch? Role-storming is one of the most productive (and fun) approaches to generating amazing ideas while eradicating the fear factor.

David Burd's alter ego of Lil Dicky allows him to make his creative mark while in character. The unnamed artist known as Banksy creates his subversive works while playing a mysterious role. Lady Gaga thought of herself as a superstar long before she actually was one, so she started playing the part. She role-stormed herself into the star she wanted to become.

The Judo Flip

First, list out all the traditional ways you would ordinarily tackle the challenge you're facing. How have you always done it before? What's the preferred approach of industry veterans? What's the prevailing conventional wisdom? Next, draw a line down the page and write out the polar opposite approach to each of the traditional ones. If you sell cars and want to maximize profits, for example, you might *judo flip* painful customer negotiations to no-haggle pricing. If everyone else charges for haircuts one at a time, your salon could judo flip into a monthly subscription for unlimited cuts. Pushing yourself to explore the exact opposite of traditional approaches will awaken your creative intuition. Judo flip your challenges, opportunities, and threats into audacious new inventions.

Since everyone else in the industry was busy offering consumer mortgages, Mat Ishbia judo flipped his strategy to focus solely on the wholesale channel. The Jolliffe brothers invented Topgolf by studying the game of golf and then judo flipping the sport's norms to their advantage.

Option X

When we make decisions, big or small, we quickly narrow the field of choice. Our minds shift from an unlimited set of possibilities to an extremely short list: A, B, or C. Nearly every decision becomes a three-part multiple choice, with the options emerging from a reference point in the past. Instead of impulsively selecting A, B, or C, ask yourself, "Is there a D? Is there an E? Better yet, is there an Option X?" *Option X* is that bold, provocative, unexpected, bizarre idea that can be the game changer you seek. For this exercise, brainstorm a list of the strangest ideas, not the safest ones.

Johnny Cupcakes created his wildly successful T-shirt business with the option X approach of creating a faux bakery. Khali Sweeney used the Option X lure of a boxing gym to help at-risk kids become stronger students. Shake Shack invents Option X menu items in their test kitchen to delight millions of hungry customers.

For more brainstorming tactics, worksheets, and additional tools, don't forget to visit BigLittleBreakthroughs.com/toolkit.

Worldly Weird

Let's take a quick zip around the globe to see how *reaching for weird* has proven to be a winning strategy for everyday innovators. Check out these quirky option X approaches:

Location	Isafjordur, Iceland
Problem	Traffic accidents involving pedestrians had increased 41 percent over the last decade, many of which were caused by reckless drivers ignoring crosswalks.
Obvious Answers	Increase fines, add expensive lighting, hire more police.
Weird Solution	Repaint the crosswalks as a 3D optical illusion, making it appear as if the cement crosswalk is floating three feet in the air, thereby grabbing the attention of motorists and significantly reducing pedestrian collisions. Plus, it makes for great selfies!
Location	Amsterdam, Netherlands
Problem	Bicycle manufacturer VanMoof was experiencing a very high rate of damage when shipping its bikes to customers. As the problem worsened, costs skyrocketed and customer satisfaction plummeted.
Obvious Answers	More expensive and protective packaging. Or hire some fancy white-glove shipping carrier.
Weird Solution	Realizing that a packaged bike was approximately the same size and weight as an LED TV (which rarely suffered shipping damage), the VanMoof team disguised its packages to appear as if they contained an LED TV instead of a bike. With just a little extra ink on the box, damage rates were reduced by 65 percent.

Location	Kyoto, Japan
Problem	Flies have long been a pesky problem for the cattle industry, since cows can't swat away the annoying insects the way horses do. Flies interfere with feeding, grazing, and sleeping, taking a significant economic toll on cattle ranchers.
Obvious Answers	Expensive high-tech bug zappers, potentially toxic pesticides.
Weird Solution	Realizing that zebras don't get fly bites since their black-and-white stripes interfere with a fly's depth perception, researchers painted the cows like zebras using harmless organic paint. Fly bites dropped by over 50 percent, which would create a $2.2 billion savings if the solution were embraced by the worldwide cattle industry. Be on the lookout for a striped cow coming soon to a town near you.
Location	Singapore, Singapore
Problem	At crowded gas stations in this busy metropolis, time delays often occur when drivers incorrectly park their cars on the opposite side of the pump from their gas tank, requiring the frustrated driver to reposition the vehicle.
Obvious Answers	Add more pumps, hire attendants to route drivers correctly.
Weird Solution	Install overhead pumps with a flexible hanging hose that can reach either side of a parked car, thereby eliminating the problem entirely.
Location	Seoul, South Korea
Problem	Buying bananas in a grocery store creates a dilemma. A ripe bunch of yellow bananas are delicious today but will spoil quickly. Green bananas are great next week, but you can't eat them for days.
Obvious Answers	Buy two bunches of bananas, realizing many will go to waste.
Weird Solution	South Korean retail giant E-Mart created a package of seven bananas, organized by ripeness. The "banana a day" packaging delighted shoppers and reduced waste while boosting sales volume and profits dramatically.

Location	Kansas City, Missouri, USA
Problem	Frank Serano was frustrated by the big pothole on the road just outside his house. Despite his numerous complaints, the pothole wasn't getting repaired. Frank was worried that someone would get hurt or suffer vehicle damage.
Obvious Answers	Keep complaining, organize a neighborhood petition drive.
Weird Solution	Frank threw a three-month-old birthday party for the pothole, placing a colorful slice of cake on the crater, lighting candles, and singing "Happy Birthday" to the busted road. Frank posted a funny video of the festivities, which spread quickly to thousands of viewers and got the city road commission's attention. The pothole was repaired within twenty-four hours.
Location	Frankfurt, Germany
Problem	Dating website NEU wanted to reach single men and women to grow its business but only had a puny marketing budget to get the job done.
Obvious Answers	Overspend the budget, host an expensive dance party, or grow slowly.
Weird Solution	Produce hundreds of single unpaired white socks imprinted with the words "Auch single?" (translation: "Also single?") and the company's website address in a bold red font. Have an intern visit local public laundromats, sneaking individual socks into washing machines, to later be discovered by potential single customers.

As the research from chapter 1 clearly shows, we each have an abundance of creative, unexpected ideas waiting to be released. Being creative is who we are; it's our natural state. Now that we've learned some fresh extraction techniques, we're well equipped to harvest an abundance of *Big Little Breakthroughs*.

The Troublemaker

> To: Mr. Dustin Garis
> From: Procter & Gamble Human Resources
> Subject: Infraction
>
> *Dear Mr. Garis:*
>
> *You must immediately cease and desist riding a Segway inside any P&G office building, manufacturing facility, or distribution center. We do not have a policy governing Segway riding in the office, therefore, don't do it.*

Dustin was incensed. "Wait, what? Since we've never done something before and have no policy, the default position is that we shouldn't do it? I should never try anything new?!?" These are the words of Dustin Garis, P&G's former Global Innovation Leader and Chief Troublemaker. Dressed in all black, both his words and his beard are neatly trimmed. He speaks quickly, spouting pithy sayings such as, "If we want to disrupt the status quo, we can't spend our time just solving problems, we must be causing them." His gestures are refined and purposeful, reminding me of a finalist at the World Series of Poker competition.

Dustin beams with pride as he points to the many letters of admonishment that he's collected from the HR department over the years. Upon receipt, each letter was promptly framed and prominently displayed on his office walls. He's been scolded for beginning a meeting with a troupe of opera singers, moving his office into a working elevator, and riding a 1,800-pound bull during work hours. From eating blindfolded in Singapore to bucket-bathing in India, Dustin isn't afraid to make some trouble. At first, the "troublemaker" title was just how colleagues referred to him. Eventually, the 183-year-old corporate giant officially named Dustin Garis the company's first Chief Troublemaker.

After a couple of years in senior marketing roles, Dustin joined the newly formed renegade innovation team called P&G Future-Works, which he'd eventually go on to lead. Their mandate went far beyond traditional product-focused R&D. Instead, FutureWorks was tasked with reimagining the company's future altogether, pursuing new businesses, market segments, and customers.

Dustin explains, "FutureWorks was the entrepreneurial engine for the company. It was the hub for troublemakers to thrive, stretching the norms and expectations of business models and new products. This was my license to unleash creativity and explore all different avenues; to look at the company from a fresh perspective, outside the customary approaches of P&G, and unrestricted from any preconceived notions."

In the context of a large, conservative, $68 billion corporation, Dustin and his team got weird. They reviewed each of the P&G brands, looking for unexpected ways to innovate. Realizing that millions of consumers wash their clothes at home with Tide detergent, FutureWorks invented and launched Tide Dry Cleaners, which was P&G's first freestanding consumer business. Completely reimagining the typical mom-and-pop operation, Tide Dry Cleaners offers 24/7 pickup through a technology that's best described as an ATM for clean clothes. The high-tech, professional experience was transcendent, quickly gaining wide-scale customer adoption to the horror of deeply entrenched competitors. Today, there are 125 locations in twenty-two states, making it a wildly successful extension of the seventy-four-year-old Tide brand.

Building on the Tide win, Dustin and the team launched a chain of car wash locations under the Mr. Clean brand name. In Asia, they opened spas under P&G's high-end skin care brand name, SK-II. They even worked on a project developing clean water and telemedicine centers throughout India. The common theme was pushing the creative boundaries and doing what initially seemed rather weird. "Too often, people unnecessarily and automatically shut down their imagination in this kind of cognitive autopilot. Turning that in the opposite direction is the key to unleashing brilliant ideas," Dustin explained to me.

Dustin was a troublemaker long before he joined Procter & Gamble. He recalls a moment at his first postcollege job at the Coca-Cola Company: "I remember when I was just a peon at Coke, I got invited to a meeting where the CEO of the company was presenting. After his session, I chased him down in the hallway and introduced myself as his replacement. I was this twentysomething kid, but I had the audacity to say something that caught his attention. After that, we stayed in touch. As we got to know each other, I proposed a new position that I dreamed up, a global innovation role where I would travel the world to explore different innovation projects. He signed off on it, and away I went!

"Too often we shy away from instead of raising our hands to pursue a particular project that seems completely unrealistic," Dustin continues. "But when you put yourself in that situation, you figure it out." To that end, Dustin makes it a point to put himself in uncertain, messy situations that require him to adopt unorthodox strategies. For Dustin, weird wins.

Dustin was ecstatic to have the opportunity to express his creativity for such a legendary innovator. P&G is known for prolific innovation, with a long list of groundbreaking inventions such as the first disposable diaper (Pampers), first fluoride toothpaste (Crest), and the first synthetic laundry detergent (Tide). After all, these are the same mad scientists who invented the Swiffer. Frankly, I'm not sure how Tia and I would get through the day without following our twins around with a Swiffer.

But when Dustin joined the FutureWorks team in 2010, P&G was in desperate need of a creativity reboot. Back in the early 2000s, only 15 percent of the company's innovation projects were meeting their success targets. Under the leadership of then CEO A. G. Lafley, the company committed to turning around its fate by essentially building an innovation factory. More than its large financial investment, Lafley focused on creating a company-wide culture of creativity. He wanted every one of their 127,000 employees to *reach for weird*.

P&G leaders knew that they could no longer rely on the models of the past, so they shifted their approach to cultivate a vast number of *Big Little Breakthroughs*. The Tide brand, for example, grew revenues from $12 billion to $24 billion in less than a decade through a series of small wins instead of a single gigantic transformation. In addition to the dry-cleaning operation mentioned earlier, consumers now enjoy Tide to Go Instant Stain Remover, Tide Wipes, Tide Antibacterial Fabric Spray, and Tide Pods. Each new product offering was weird at the time, yet none of them were a radical departure from the brand's core focus on fabric cleaning. Instead, these weird little ideas coalesced into a massive growth story for this storied brand.

"We know from our history that while promotions may win quarters, innovation wins decades," said Bob McDonald, the CEO who replaced Lafley in 2009. Building on the innovation efforts of his predecessor, McDonald continued to invest in FutureWorks and other R&D programs. The intense focus led to remarkable results, as the company was able triple its innovation success rate from the meager 15 percent mentioned earlier all the way up to 50 percent, an unheard-of success ratio in the industry. In the span of a decade, P&G's revenue doubled, and its profits quintupled.

Building on its heritage of innovation, P&G still continues to forge new ground. For example, the new Lumi by Pampers baby monitoring system not only provides parents with reliable video and sleep monitoring, it also uses sensors to track room temperature, humidity, and even the wet/dry status of a baby's diaper. The new Oral-B iO electric toothbrush communicates with your mobile phone to alert you if you're brushing too hard and to provide guidance on optimizing your clean. And the Gillette TREO is the first razor designed for caregivers to shave someone else, containing built-in shave gel, a blade with a safety comb, and a handle designed for the shaver, not the person being shaved.

Long before Dustin was making trouble at P&G, the company pioneered weird concepts beyond its products. It was the first consumer packaged goods company to introduce a profit-sharing program to its factory workers. It was the first company to offer product sampling and the first to create its own in-house market research department. The company was even among the first to sponsor daytime television dramas, which is why the sultry shows have been known as "soap operas" ever since. Today, these strategies appear commonplace, but at the time they were as strange as one of Dustin's stunts.

The German philosopher Arthur Schopenhauer famously said, "Truth passes through three stages. First, it is ridiculed. Second, it is violently opposed. Third, it is accepted as being self-evident." Our key takeaway is that those who have the courage to pursue weird—early and often—are the ones who make history.

Think for a moment about the things we can't live without today through the lens of someone from a decade before each invention. Imagine how crazy the description of an iPhone would sound to somebody in 1997. If you tried to explain Google to someone in 1989, they'd suggest you seek immediate medical care. Describing Netflix to someone in 1930, before TVs were around, would sound utterly preposterous.

Weird moves society forward. Weird drives success. Weird creates needed change. Weird unlocks innovation. Weird works.

As we disembark from the Starship Weird, let's cruise ahead at warp speed to our next obsession of everyday innovators, use *every drop of toothpaste*. We'll explore how an electric motorcycle startup, a major research university, a robot artist, and a Kenyan distance runner were each able to get scrappy, do more with less, and achieve breathtaking outcomes despite being resource constrained.

Chapter 10

Use Every Drop of Toothpaste

In an electric show of musical wizardry, the punk metal band performed for thousands of screaming fans at an outdoor festival in Berlin. The bass player hunched over his instrument, bobbing his head rhythmically as his fingers fired with precision onto his instrument's thick strings. The drummer opened his eyes and mouth widely as he crashed his cymbals in lockstep with the thumping bass drum that kept the pulsating beat driving forward. The unexpected sound of an electric flute pierced through the crowd as its player raised the musical stakes by ripping an exhilarating solo. The music was good, but that alone wasn't what fascinated the adoring listeners. No, the mind-blowing aspect of this performance was the fact that the lively musicians were actually robot sculptures...all built from junkyard parts.

These musical metal sculptures are the brainchild of Berlin-based artist Kolja Kugler, who has been making art out of junk for twenty-five years. "I'm not trained in anything. Everything I make is very crude," Kolja modestly explains. He started working with scrap metal in the early nineties when he joined the Mutoid

Waste Company, a faction of artists that converted decommissioned army machinery into sculptures. He learned how to weld and fasten, but more importantly, he learned to see beauty in objects that others believed were worthless. Most people would look at a pile of scrap metal and see waste, but Kolja started to see birds, then dogs, and eventually humanoid sculptures to form his rock band.

"I found these pliers that helped me form a really scary-looking skull," he says. "Since the pliers were the bottom jaw, you could open and close the mouth. I was making sculptures out of junk and I started to use moving mechanical parts to make them come alive." Wanting to imbue motion into his creations, he began to study pneumatics—an engineering system using compressed air to create mechanical movements. This allowed Kolja to open and close the pliers mouth with a switch, widening the possibilities for his creative expression.

When Kolja's scrapyard parts and his new fascination with pneumatics collided, a love child was born. His name: Sir Elton Junk. Kolja spent the next decade working on Elton's limbs, hands, and head to make his robotic pal especially lifelike. He became obsessed with transforming worthless junk into art, and eventually into music. Could he create a touring robotic metal band using nothing but discarded scrap materials? The quest was on.

As Kolja forged ahead, the movable sculptures developed their own personalities. Today, Sir Elton Junk is the band's manager, sitting on stage in a broken shopping cart to oversee the musical act. After Elton was just right, Kolja got to work on the band's first playing member. "My sculpture was going to play bass and it had to look good," Kolja explains. "I was learning to get the balance between the mechanics and the sculpture's character. It took me four years, and I freaked out multiple times." In tribute to his numerous freak-outs, Kolja named the sculpture "Afreakin' Bass Player."

Afreakin's body is largely built from moped parts that Kolja found in the junkyard. The robot's chiseled chin was once attached to a VW Golf, while his shoes are made from unwanted BMW valve cover gaskets. His legs are made of discarded coal tongs and streetlight covers that Kolja found in a Copenhagen alley. A broken TV antenna serves as the sculpture's midsection, perfectly exhibiting the bass player's hard-core vibe.

On the drums is Rubble Eindhoven, who recently replaced his predecessor, Boom Tschak. "He's now my most sophisticated robot," Kolja says with pride. Naturally, the flock of flute-playing mechanical birds that are perched on a half-rusted TV antenna are known as the "Flute Flock." Despite a lack of funding, equipment, and new materials, I don't get the sense that Kolja has a shortage of creative ideas.

During concerts, Kolja controls the madness with a series of rigged switches, dials, and an old electric keyboard that he uses to orchestrate the music. Performances often include a technical malfunction, which forces the maestro himself to take the stage and make live repairs in front of his adoring fans.

Kolja Kugler is a now cult celebrity and has captured the hearts of both art connoisseurs and engineering aficionados around the world. His creations have been featured by the international media, and his One Love Machine Band has more groupies than most professional musical acts. Kolja's creative expression and remarkable success are a direct result of the sixth obsession of everyday innovations, *use every drop of toothpaste.*

When most of us think of innovation, we quickly create a mental checklist of all the resources we lack. There never seems to be enough time, money, raw materials, support, bandwidth, computing power, training, or staff. We allow the apparent lack of resources to trick us into thinking we can't forge ahead, but in fact, doing more with less is a hallmark of creativity. Everyday innovators recognize the need to get scrappy, using their internal resource of imagination to compensate for any lack of external resources. They realize that constraints drive breakthroughs far more often than abundance. They outpunch their satiated rivals by remaining hungry, squeezing every last drop out of their proverbial toothpaste tubes.

Kolja Kugler's robotic punk metal band wouldn't be special if he had a defense contractor–sized budget and unlimited materials from NASA. In fact, it's unlikely that he would have created musical sculptures at all if he had bountiful resources. Time and time again, the most notable innovations are born from scarcity. Which is comforting to those of us without a trust fund, safety net, or boss with an abundance mindset. From *Big Little Breakthroughs* to world-changing innovations, creators and makers achieve results by *using every drop of toothpaste*.

Somehow, your mom and dad were able to connect without a dating app. While it took me an extra year, I ended up graduating from college absent a cell phone, laptop, or even email. Hemingway managed to write decent books without Microsoft Word. *The Lion King* grossed more than $1 billion in theaters, yet the Disney animators drew most of the film by hand. JP Morgan became a banking legend without Excel, and Rockefeller Center was built with no computer-aided design (CAD) tools. Amazingly, Lewis and Clark had a successful expedition without Google Maps.

Using every drop of toothpaste is about making do with the resources you have rather than allowing those that you lack to impede your progress. The adage of necessity being the mother of invention is as true today as it was when the phrase was born back in the late fifteenth century. In fact, having to invent solutions with limited resources has been the bedrock of innovation since two sticks were rubbed together to unleash the first controlled flame. Caron Proschan squeezed every drop of limited resources to launch Simply Gum in the same way Khali Sweeney built Detroit's Downtown Boxing Gym on a shoestring budget.

Duct Tape and a Paperclip

From the time I saw MacGyver use candlesticks, an extension cord, and a rubber mat to create an improvised defibrillator to save a man's life, I was hooked on the show. Whether it was creating a makeshift bazooka out of a muffler, gear shift knob, seat cushion stuffing, and a cigarette lighter to escape a car chase or the time he used a magnifying lens, watch crystal, and a newspaper to craft a telescope, MacGyver has long been one of my all-time heroes.

Unlike Sylvester Stallone's aggrieved soldier in *Rambo* or Bruce Willis's tough guy in *Die Hard*, MacGyver relied on inventiveness rather than brute strength to save the day. Who needs military explosives when you can get the job done with chewing gum, a rubber band, and a flashlight? Instead of carrying a gun, he never left home without his trusty Swiss Army knife and a folded roll of duct tape. "Any problem can be solved with a little ingenuity," the TV character famously said. No matter how tough the bind, he always figured a way out with the limited resources at hand.

In tribute to his resourcefulness, the *Oxford English Dictionary* now includes the word "MacGyver" as a verb: "to '*MacGyver*' is to make or repair something in an improvised or inventive way, making use of whatever items are at hand," e.g., "He MacGyvered a makeshift jack with a log." The Urban Dictionary, my personal favorite, defines a MacGyver as a noun: "someone who can jump-start a truck with a cactus."

MacGyvering speaks directly to the heart of being scrappy. Everyday innovators MacGyver their challenges, threats, and opportunities. They figure out how to do more with less, wielding inventiveness as their weapon of choice. The next time we're facing a tough situation, let's MacGyver our way out of the jam. Let's *use every drop of toothpaste*—and perhaps a paperclip or two—to claim victory.

For me, having to MacGyver situations over the years has boosted my creativity rather than restricted it. Studying jazz guitar in college, I had a professor who would force me to remove strings from the instrument. One, two, sometimes three strings had to be removed before I attempted a musical performance. You might guess that gutting half of my available resources would crush my ability to play at all. To be clear, this made me wildly uncomfortable and even a little queasy. I studied hard to gain command over the instrument, but apparently it also made me a little lazy. Why stretch the creative boundaries when I already had a plentiful bounty?

When the strings were removed, I felt confused and off balance. My playing was awkward at first as I stumbled through musical potholes. But then a counterintuitive thing occurred...my creativity actually expanded. Since I could no longer rely on the patterns I knew, I was forced to solve musical problems in totally different ways. I had to make do with what I had and improvise my way through the music. I had to MacGyver it.

I started seeing new combinations that were previously hidden from view. I had to invent new scale patterns and chord fingerings since the ones I'd practiced for years were no longer viable. As the pace increased and my fingers resembled stubby hammers bearing down on my worn fretboard, both my dexterity and creativity were stretched. New shapes, fresh ideas, different approaches.

By the time I completed the exercise, I was visibly shaken. Sweating and out of breath, I felt exhilarated knowing that I'd expanded my creative boundaries. It also fortified my musical confidence, realizing that despite my many mistakes and misfires, I was still standing on the other end of the challenge. The MacGyver strategy not only helped me discover new creative ideas, it also boosted my musical courage.

Whether you work for a multinational conglomerate or you're a solo entrepreneur, resources are likely scarce. No matter how many dollars, social media followers, square footage, inventory, or raw materials you have, you probably wish you had more. But when we find ourselves in the inevitable resource-constrained situation, let's rock on with only three strings on our guitars.

If more resources equated to more creativity, the federal government would be the most imaginative organization on the planet while startups would be the most rigid and bureaucratic. Of course, just the opposite occurs as constricted resources serve as a creative catalyst. "More companies die of indigestion than starvation" is a common saying in the venture capital world for good reason. Accordingly, let's *use every drop of toothpaste* to break previous patterns and uncover an abundance of *Big Little Breakthroughs*.

Better Make a Run for It

Mexico City, 1968. Just like millions of others around the world, champion distance runner Jim Ryun couldn't believe what just happened. Ryun was the overwhelming favorite to win Olympic gold, considering he'd been unbeaten for three years, winning forty-seven consecutive victories. The 1,500-meter race was his favorite distance, and he had recently broken the world record in the category. Another victory was within sight...until the unimaginable happened.

The complete opposite of golden boy Jim Ryun, Kipchoge "Kip" Keino grew up in a small village in Kenya. He had no formalized training, no sophisticated equipment, and no expert coaching. Kip had a day job as police officer but always dreamed of bringing home a medal to his native country. Nevertheless, things were looking bleak for Kip when he collapsed in the middle of a race just two days earlier.

Kip was running a 10,000-meter race when the pain became unbearable. He was leading the race when an excruciating sting in his abdomen caused him to buckle, crashing to the ground. Doctors rushed in and demanded he quit, but Kip insisted on running the remaining laps to complete the race, still placing second despite his fall.

Even considering the diagnosis, Kip wasn't satisfied with his silver medal. After a battery of tests, doctors informed Kip that he had a severe gall bladder condition and was advised to withdraw from all upcoming events to seek immediate treatment. They told him if he ran, he could die. Unsurprising to those who knew him, the moment the medical staff left his bedside, Kip ignored the serious warnings and quickly dressed to catch a bus to his previously scheduled Olympic race.

The bumpy bus ride sent waves of pain through his body. When the traffic congestion slowed the bus to a halt, Kip wasn't about to let gridlock stand in his way. "I realized I was late," Kip said later in an interview. "So, I jumped out of the bus and I ran all the way to the stadium, something like two kilometers."

Despite debilitating pain that would send any one of us into screaming convulsions, Kip remained stoic. Beginning the race at a blistering speed, onlookers were sure that the young runner would quickly burn out. But to the amazement of the international audience, and most acutely to world champion Jim Ryun, Kip's pace never wavered. He won the race by more than twenty meters, which is still the largest margin of victory in the event's history. Kip not only set the world record, but also his pace was so fast that Jim Ryun's time in the race would have been a new record had Kip not blasted past him.

How did Kip defeat the legendary champion by such a decisive margin while suffering a torturously painful medical condition? Before the international sports media could reach a definitive answer, Kip's countrymen and countrywomen started winning race after race. Over the next three decades, Kenyan runners dominated the sport, winning nearly 70 percent of professional races while only representing 0.06 percent of the world's population. Six of the top ten fastest men's marathon times on record are held by Kenyans, along with four of the ten fastest women's times in history. At a recent Berlin marathon, Kenyan men won all five of the top five places, while Kenyan women came in first, second, and fourth.

Sports Illustrated senior editor David Epstein set out to discover how Kenya captured "the greatest concentration of elite athletic talent ever in any sport, anywhere in the world," which he researched extensively for his 2014 book, *The Sports Gene: Inside the Science of Extraordinary Athletic Performance*. As Epstein reviewed the background of hundreds of champion distance runners from Kenya, he noticed that the vast majority came from a specific tribe called the Kalenjin.

In the entire history of distance running, only seventeen American men have run the marathon in under 2:10. Meanwhile, thirty-two Kalenjin beat that time in just one month (October 2011). The oddity is so pronounced, it would be as perplexing as learning that 98 percent of the greatest American chess players all came from one specific neighborhood in Wichita, Kansas. Epstein became fixated on discovering what the heck was going on in the Kalenjin tribe.

First, he examined genetics. While it was true that the indigenous people had long limbs, thin ankles, and expansive lung capacity, so did millions of other nearby Africans who had never won a single race. He then explored environmental conditions as a possible explanation for the tribe's disproportionate number of victories. Kids ran long distances to school at an early age and spent time running after animals for sustenance. But again, these characteristics were not unique to the Kalenjin.

Eventually, Epstein uncovered the answer. It turns out, the secret of Kalenjin running success is their ability to forge ahead through adversity. To run fast on an empty tank. To achieve victory despite pain. To *use every drop of toothpaste*.

The Kalenjin are taught to withstand suffering from an early age. Their culture reveres unflinching courage, while demonizing those that succumb to difficulty. As children, they are raised to be fiercely tough and to tolerate extremely hostile conditions.

Their toughness is put to the test during a ritualistic rite-of-passage ceremony whereby teenage boys and girls are put through a series of endurance trials. They're forced to crawl naked through a tunnel of African stinging nettles. They're beaten, burned, and cut. During the ceremonies, the teenagers are "obliged to remain absolutely stoical, still, and unflinching," according to Epstein. "Mud is caked on the face and then it's allowed to dry. And if a single crack appears in the mud—your cheek may twitch; your forehead may crinkle—you get labeled a coward." Those who are unable to withstand the strange ritual are ostracized, stigmatized by the whole community, and never able to regain social status.

Epstein argues that the Kalenjin's ability to endure pain is the driving force behind their incredible athletic victories. Any endurance runner knows the pain of a long run, but the Kalenjin are able to forge ahead despite it. They view the adversity as a blessing, not a curse. To be clear, I'm certainly not endorsing any ritualistic pain ceremonies and don't believe we need to suffer to achieve great feats. But the Kalenjin's ability to dig deep through times of adversity can inspire us all, especially when we feel overwhelmed, shortchanged, or deficient.

Kip Keino made history by *using every drop of toothpaste*. It wasn't an abundance of comfort, but rather the lack of it, that enabled his success. At the moment when most competitors would collapse from pain and exhaustion, Kip broke the world record. He drew on his internal set of resources—grit, tenacity, persistence—instead of requiring external accoutrements such as high-tech gear, expert coaching, or even just a pain-free body. Kip and the other Kalenjin runners achieve more while having less. They override signals of distress and use whatever they have on hand to get the job done.

What's Missing?

Too often, scarcity impedes our willingness to see our innovations through. We might be lacking training, time, materials, money, talent, inventory, technology, land, warehouse space, desks, equipment, regulatory freedom, permission, or a whole host of other shortfalls that can discourage even the best of us.

But could scarcity be the very key we're looking for, disguised as an impediment?

Jeff Citty sure thinks so. Jeff is the director of the Innovation Academy at the University of Florida and the rare academic who's willing to vigorously challenge traditions. That's not an easy thing to do in any educational setting, but it's especially difficult in a prestigious, conservative university environment. When people hear the word "Florida" attached to any school of higher learning, they imagine tanned bodies spending more time at the beach than the library. But UF is a major research institution, ranked the seventh best public university in the United States by *U.S. News and World Report*. The school is considered a "Public Ivy," one of a small number of universities that offers a comparable education to the private Ivy League schools for a fraction of the cost. As a UF graduate myself, I can attest to the quality and rigor of the curriculum. With a campus that spans 2,000 acres and a $2.1 billion annual budget, the school is home to 56,000 students hailing from 140 countries. But even with the university's massive footprint and endowment, Jeff became acutely aware of several things missing.

Like all universities, UF has a utilization problem. It receives too many applications in the fall semester and too few in the spring and summer terms. Two thousand students graduate each December, leaving plenty of room for new learners, but the application numbers dramatically slump after the fall semester. The traditional school year strains faculty, facilities, and resources in some months but produces a surplus at other times of the year. This mismatch is very difficult to manage, considering costs remain consistent year-round. Further, the university only accepts 39 percent of applicants, largely due to resource constraints in the fall semester. Accordingly, many well-qualified students are unable to attend because of this timing mismatch.

Even in the large university setting, Jeff noticed a number of other things that were missing. While UF scored higher than the national average on diversity rankings, it was still only #473 out of 2,718 on this critical metric. Compared to its #7 spot of public universities, there was a gap that needed to be filled. Additionally, for graduates to succeed in the workforce, the need for creative problem solving, abstract thinking, and complex decision-making has become paramount, yet the traditional university curriculum lacked these critical skills. He also realized that the university's home of Gainesville, Florida, loses nearly all of the UF talent upon graduation. He envisioned the local impact that could be created if students had a compelling reason to stay in town.

Despite the university's overall success, Jeff concluded there were just a lot of things missing. There wasn't enough room for fall applicants and not enough students for the winter term. There was a shortfall in student diversity, too few graduates staying in Gainesville upon graduation, and a shortage of twenty-first-century job skills to make graduates attractive to employers. That's a whole bunch of scarcity.

Instead of hiding in the ivory tower, Jeff got to work. He convinced the school's president and provost to invest in a ground-breaking new program, which Jeff launched in 2013 as the UF Innovation Academy. The program offers a minor in "innovation" to students who are pursuing more than thirty different majors. Crucially, the program begins each winter term with a learning/living experience that lasts through the summer, thereby counter-balancing the seasonality conundrum.

The program is designed to attract diversity, so the ethnic and gender makeup of the students is substantially more diverse than the overall undergraduate population. The academy partners with local tech incubators and offers real-world entrepreneurial projects, bridging the gap from academia to the local business community in order to encourage students to launch businesses and stay in Gainesville upon graduation. And students learn critical skills such as how to pitch an idea, how to invent new solutions, and how to use creativity to tackle difficult problems.

The curriculum includes courses such as Creativity in Action, Principles of Entrepreneurship, and Fostering Innovation through Leadership. Focusing on hands-on learning and practice over theory, the program culminates in a senior project where students have to create their own startup idea and then present the opportunity to a panel of would-be investors. Students develop collaboration and presentation skills in addition to their immersion in an environment that cherishes creative expression.

The only program of its kind, the Innovation Academy has become a monstrous success. With 1,038 active students, the program represents 3 percent of the entire university's under-graduate population. Keep in mind, UF was founded in 1853, so 3 percent is a huge figure considering the broader university's 160-year head start. The Innovation Academy is also boasting better job placement upon graduation compared to the broader undergraduate population. Hiring companies such as Google, Citi, and NBC Universal actively recruit students from the program. "Employers embrace the entrepreneurial thinking that we help develop at the academy," Jeff explains.

When you examine the program today, it is an amalgamation of ideas rooted in the open-ended question, "What's missing?" Elements of scarcity, not the university's abundance, led to the Innovation Academy's creation, which now teaches the next generation of students to discover opportunities by asking themselves what's missing. Jeff *used every drop of toothpaste* to launch his leading-edge program, while making sure every new graduate embraces the same scrappy mindset.

Time's Up

Time is the constraint that's most often cited as creativity's rival. Ironically, it is the lack of time (also known as a deadline) that has inspired some of the greatest creative works in history. Lin-Manuel Miranda explains, "I always write with a deadline, or I'll get nothing done. When you have to be somewhere every night at eight, it forces you to organize your time." Lin-Manuel has plenty of money and support at this stage in his career, yet he's still subject to the same twenty-four-hour constraint that plagues us all. Yet he *uses every drop of toothpaste*, in the form of maximizing his limited number of hours, to create his best work.

Like it or hate it, the satirical and raunchy animated TV show *South Park* has been a massive hit since it launched in 1997. Now in its twenty-fourth season with more than three hundred aired episodes, it's one of the longest running and most economically successful shows in television history. Key to the show's success is the way creators Trey Parker and Matt Stone manage the clock. While most animated shows are designed and planned up to ten months in advance, Parker and Stone write and complete every episode in only six days, submitting the final version to the network just hours before airtime.

The looming deadline would send most writers into cardiac arrest, but the creative duo behind *South Park* cuts it close on purpose. Not only does it allow them to include extremely recent and topical references in the show, the deadline prevents the creators from overthinking and potentially diluting their best ideas. In the Netflix documentary *Six Days to Air*, Parker explains that the short deadline pushes their creativity and doesn't give them time to second-guess every decision. In the end, they believe that being time-constrained is the best way to push their creative boundaries.

To combat the looming clock, focus on the "little" in *Big Little Breakthroughs*. You don't have to write an episode for an award-winning TV show in six days to do more with less. Instead, think about small blocks of time as opportunities to micro-dose on imagination. The extra eleven minutes of rush hour traffic could be a mini creative session instead of an annoyance. The downtime between meetings may provide just enough space for a teensy-weensy idea. The mindset of everyday innovators is to make the most of scarcity.

When you lack resources, it's time to become resourceful.

Racing Ahead on an Empty Tank

Suited up in a jet-black, slim-fitted all-leather outfit, he looked like he belonged on the set of an *Iron Man* film. The blackout eye shield on his racing helmet made it appear like he was a villainous stormtrooper trying to conceal his mysterious identity. The sleek figure hopped aboard his two-wheeled rocket and instantly lurched forward on the private racetrack. Before long, he was whipping around hairpin turns, whizzing past onlookers, and accelerating to nearly 100 mph on the course's short straightaways. Taras, the stealthy driver, blasted forward on the hot June day. But something crucial was missing.

A high-performance motorcycle on a closed loop isn't an unusual sight, but this ride was groundbreakingly new. In a typical outing of this nature, you'd hear the roar of the cycle's combustion engine while inhaling the distinctive smell of oil, gasoline, and exhaust fumes. But today's event was whisper quiet and downright odorless. It was as if someone had completely disabled the bewildered onlookers' sense of smell and sound. All that could be heard on that hot day was the loud thumping of exhilarated hearts.

The engineering marvel that stunned both track rats and the international motorcycle community was the 100 percent electric, zero-emissions Tarform Luna. And its origins are as fascinating as the bike itself.

The Luna wasn't designed by motorcycle giants Harley-Davidson, Ducati, Yamaha, or Kawasaki. It's not a special project from BMW nor an offshoot of Suzuki. In fact, the revolutionary bike is from a Brooklyn-based startup, whose founder *used every drop of toothpaste* to best his billion-dollar rivals.

Taras Kravtchouk was born in Russia but grew up in Sweden. He studied visual communications, interface design, 3D modeling, and computer programming before beginning his career as web designer. With a wide range of interests, from design to protecting the environment, the last place you'd expect to find Taras is in a dimly lit motorcycle garage, repairing rusted-out hogs for tattoo-covered customers. But at age twenty, he fell in love with the two-wheeled beast. There was something about the experience of sitting on a motorcycle that represented freedom and beauty.

"My first bike was a Yamaha XS400 that I bought in Sweden, and I had no idea what the hell this thing was," Taras tells me as we begin our conversation. His words are refined, his clothes are bespoke, and his frame is thin. Now out of his Tony Stark leather riding outfit, I think to myself that he resembles the kind of guy that hard-core motorcycle fanatics beat up for fun rather than the person who is changing the field altogether. He appears as if he belongs in an Italian café, sipping a double espresso while discussing literature and philosophy. Instead, he sits in his cramped Brooklyn garage littered with spare parts, a smattering of wrenches and bolts, and a moat of computer cables to connect his various devices.

Just before moving to the US, Taras ran a design studio in Sweden by day and moonlighted as a motorcycle mechanic in the evenings. As these two worlds collided, he began dreaming of an entirely new kind of bike. Inspired by the success of electric car maker Tesla, he was drawn to the notion of a high-performance electric motorcycle. What if it could be both affordable and high quality? What if it could be both high-tech and high design? The Tesla of motorcycles, he thought.

In October 2017, Taras officially began work on his startup. While most wide-eyed entrepreneurs begin by raising a bunch of venture capital, Taras took a far scrappier approach. "I have a tiny shop with very basic tools. I said to myself...well, okay, let me just do it. Let me build a prototype and see where we end up. No resources, no money, no team."

"A key principle of design is that you are most creative within constraints," Taras continues. "If you don't have constraints, it's so easy to just drift in the universe. But if you have limited resources, then it forces you to truly push the boundaries." Taras set out to see how far he could get by using every globule from his very small tube of toothpaste.

Over the first few months, Taras refined his vision. He was uncompromising in his ideas but frugal in his approach. To this end, he shared his concept with engineering firms, advanced manufacturing companies, materials experts, and high-end design specialists to seek their help. Realizing the sexiness of his project, which could serve as an elegant case study for others, he asked for support from a wide variety of suppliers and specialists. From 3D printing firms to a company specializing in round LED displays, partners agreed to contribute expertise, equipment, and parts—for free.

"We got assistance not just in terms of pure materials but also their engineering and research," Taras explains. "We had three engineers at one partner company helping us prototype software for the motor because they thought it was a cool thing. It's every designer's dream to work on a project like this. We were able to build a community of people who were like, 'Yeah, awesome. How can I help? I want to be part of this.' And so, that was a huge help and a massive cost savings."

In less than eighteen months, Taras was able to build two working prototypes. This was accomplished for under $50,000 in a cramped garage with one mechanical engineer and one electrical engineer that Taras found on Craigslist.

In contrast, Harley-Davidson announced its pursuit of an electric motorcycle in early 2010 and has reportedly invested more than $100 million on the project. After nine years, the company started producing the Harley LiveWire, only to shut down production a month later due to mechanical failures. At the risk of taking the metaphor too far, Taras was able to accomplish more in a far faster time frame with his half-empty travel-size toothpaste tube than Harley-Davidson was able to deliver with a whole warehouse of toothpaste and a team of dental experts on hand.

In addition to conserving capital and scoring inexpensive materials, Taras was masterfully efficient with the clock. One time, he found a machine-learning specialist with knowledge in automotive visual recognition in two hours and had him working on the project forty-five minutes later. Somehow, Taras dug up a sustainability expert with a background in biomimicry in less than forty-eight hours to help incorporate high-performance biomaterials to improve environmental factors. The prototypes were modified and upgraded with the speed of a NASCAR pit crew, pushing closer and closer to Tarform's commercial launch.

Over the next year, Taras raised a modest amount of capital to hire additional staff, buy low-cost equipment, and drive the company toward a full-scale production launch. During this intense period, it was a series of *Big Little Breakthroughs* that coalesced into what is now a compelling brand.

With sustainability a priority to Taras, he designed his bike in a modular fashion so that core elements like the frame can last fifty years while aspects such as a battery pack can be easily replaced or upgraded as needed. In contrast, most vehicles outlast their factory warranty by merely a month or two and are discarded (probably to end up as one of Kolja Kugler's robot musicians). The drivetrain in a normal combustion-engine motorcycle contains more than two thousand moving parts, so the Tarform team designed theirs to have fewer than twenty.

The bike has zero emissions, never requires an oil change, and uses materials that are safe for the environment. "Components are made from flax fibers, recycled aluminum, and biodegradable leather. Our mission is to build sustainable vehicles without compromise," Taras explains.

On the design front, the bikes are stunningly beautiful. In contrast to early electric cars that looked like a toaster on wheels, Tarform blends modern and retro elements to create a visually exquisite motorcycle.

Advanced technology including sensors, cameras, and artificial intelligence generates both performance and safety. For example, if you are riding your Tarform Luna and another vehicle approaches too quickly from behind, you're instantly alerted through a small vibration in the seat while the rear camera view automatically appears on your round high-definition screen. To charge, plug the bike into a normal electrical socket and you'll be at 80 percent capacity in only fifty minutes. With no gearbox or clutch, your Tarform rockets to 60 mph in 3.8 seconds and boasts a 120-mile range.

When Taras officially launched the company to the public, the motorcycle world was stunned. After an onslaught of press interviews, Taras was invited to display the Tarform Luna at the prestigious Petersen Automotive Museum in Los Angeles. He explains, "That was a trippy thing because the world's most reputable automotive museum wants your bike that was built in the back of a shop in Brooklyn with a bunch of 3D printing. Being next to a Shelby Cobra was incredible, realizing that just two months earlier I was still gluing this thing together."

By the time of the June 2020 track day mentioned earlier, Tarform had received more than 1,100 orders. Incredibly, Taras had only raised a remarkably small $1.3 million of investment since the company's formation three years earlier. For comparison, it took Tesla six years and $187 million to reach the same point. Despite their massive resources, the world's top five largest motorcycle companies have yet to launch a comparable electric motorcycle. Thirty-five-year-old Taras Kravtchouk's ability to stretch both money and time, filling in any resource gaps with his own ingenuity, helped him outpunch even the most formidable of foes.

As we continued our discussion, I wanted to...*needed* to... know more. How did Taras accomplish so much with so little? "Before I started, I read a book called *Power in Flux* about the pursuit of electric motorcycles," he explains. "It was the story of ten companies that each attempted, and totally failed, to build a production-quality electric bike. I studied each story carefully, learning where they went wrong, where they overspent, and how I could avoid the same traps." His predecessors focused on inventing every component themselves, which drove up costs and wasted time. Learning from their failures, Taras uses off-the-shelf components and materials wherever possible, which allowed him to bring his bike to market far faster and cheaper.

As our conversation concluded, I asked Taras if there was one big thing that drove his success. I was delighted to hear that he agrees with the *Big Little Breakthroughs* philosophy. "It wasn't one thing...it was lots and lots of little things. It was the rounded LED display. It was our tiny shop in Brooklyn. It was blending sustainability with design. It's hundreds or thousands of small advances that all come together to create the big win."

As we said goodbye, Taras reminisced, "I was originally terrified of motorcycles. My mom told me early on to do whatever I want in life, but please just never ride a motorcycle." Isn't it ironic that pursuing the very thing that scared him the most was the pathway to his success? Taras started out short on confidence, money, experience, training, contacts, and resources. But he artfully managed to *use every drop of toothpaste* to forge a remarkable business, life, and legacy.

Now that we're minty clean and well brushed from our recently emptied tube of toothpaste, it's time to explore our next obsession of everyday innovations, *don't forget the dinner mint*. Together, we'll explore how an elite Michelin-rated gourmet restaurant, a disruptive health-care supplier, and an athletic shoe startup used surprise and delight to stand out and win, despite being outgunned by fearsome competitors.

CHAPTER 11

Don't Forget the Dinner Mint

When snow began to fall outside the soaring fourteen-foot windows, the young children couldn't contain their excitement. Sitting with their parents at the world-renowned restaurant, it was the first time either child had ever seen snowfall. The family was visiting from Spain and had been eagerly anticipating their meal at New York's Eleven Madison Park, which is consistently ranked as one of the top restaurants in the world. After a server overheard the children's delight, the team got to work creating an unforgettable experience.

"Their excitement inspired us," explains Will Guidara, the restaurant's co-owner. "We asked ourselves, how can we treat them to the most magical experience and allow them to enjoy that snowfall? We decided to procure four shiny, brand-new sleds. A chauffeur-driven SUV greeted them after their meal was over and whisked them away for a night of revelry in Central Park. When we witnessed the look of joy on the children's faces, we knew that our spur-of-the-moment effort was worth it."

Eleven Madison Park's refined, modern décor welcomes discerning culinary aficionados to enjoy some of the most exquisite and expensive food. Featured in the prestigious S.Pellegrino World's 50 Best Restaurants for eight of the last nine years, Eleven Madison Park topped the list as the best restaurant in the world in 2017, only the second American restaurant ever to do so. The establishment has won four James Beard Foundation Awards, including the time they crowned head chef and co-owner Daniel Humm the best chef on the planet. Between the *New York Times*, the *Michelin Guide*, the *Forbes Travel Guide*, and *Zagat*, Eleven Madison Park has substantially more stars than the American flag. But it's neither the food nor the vibe that makes Eleven Madison Park truly remarkable.

In the highly competitive fine dining arena, Eleven Madison Park stands out by embracing the seventh obsession of everyday innovators: *don't forget the dinner mint.*

Perhaps you've been to a nice restaurant and enjoyed a small chocolate truffle or a special sip of handmade grappa at the end of a great meal, compliments of the chef. If you'd ordered the items from the menu, they would be nondescript. Instead, it's the unexpected surprise and delight that makes the "dinner mint" special. A dinner mint—culinary or otherwise—is over-delivering on a promise, providing more than was asked. For our purposes, a dinner mint represents a small, additional creative flourish that elevates work product from commonplace to transcendent.

Eleven Madison Park co-owners Will Guidara and Daniel Humm have institutionalized the dinner mint concept, which goes far beyond the edible. The restaurant staff includes a small team called "Dreamweavers" who neither serve the food nor scrub the kitchen. Instead, they are singularly focused on dinner mints—surprise-and-delight experiences that are unforgettable, just like the one for the Spanish family who enjoyed an evening of sledding. "We've turned the private dining room into a rock-and-roll theater for a music fan and have created a faux seaside scene with a kiddie pool and beach chairs for a couple whose flight to an island vacation was suddenly canceled," Will explains. "It's moments like these that people will remember for the rest of their lives and probably tell their friends about. And it's moments like these that inspire our team."

The Dreamweavers are responsible for finding clues, through advance research and real-time conversations, and then acting quickly to make fantasy come to life. After researching a couple who had made a reservation to celebrate their anniversary, the Dreamweavers learned the pair bonded on their first date over snow cones. Once the couple had enjoyed their anniversary meal at Eleven Madison Park, they were presented with handmade gourmet snow cones, crafted moments earlier by the elite chefs in the kitchen.

Will and Daniel formalized their *don't forget the dinner mint* approach into a central operating philosophy they refer to as their "95-5 Doctrine." Will explains, "It means that 95 percent of the time, we manage our business down to the penny. The other 5 percent, we spend foolishly." Will shares that the team manages operations and budgets with "Terminator-like efficiency" so that they can invest 5 percent of their expenditures into surprising creative add-ons.

Sometimes the dinner mints are in the form of food, like the time guests were overheard complaining that they didn't have time to enjoy a New York hot dog during their visit to the city. The Dreamweavers raced outside, purchased hot dogs from a street vendor, and then brought them to the gourmet kitchen for some haute garnishes before presenting them on shiny silver plates to the unsuspecting guests. At other times, the dinner mints have nothing to do with food. For example, the 95-5 Doctrine is embraced for internal team members, who have enjoyed over-the-top staff parties, team-building retreats, and plenty of other unexpected goodies.

"I'll tell you a secret about the 95-5 Doctrine," Will confesses. "When I say that we spend that last 5 percent foolishly, I don't really mean it. It might *look* foolish, but in reality, it's intentional. In fact, it's some of the smartest money we spend, because it delivers a substantial, if immeasurable, return on investment. It's the 5 percent that makes memories and inspires people to rave about us. It's the 5 percent that allows for spontaneity in the workplace. It's what makes our restaurants and our company such fun places to serve and be served."

The philosophy goes far beyond their culinary delights. Trying to create the most memorable experience possible, the staff offers guests the option of placing their mobile phones in specially crafted boxes during their meals, allowing them to be fully present for their feast rather than reading texts under the table.

Small, creative, thoughtful touches are present even when unnoticed. By design, each plate is delicately placed in front of guests rather than plopped down on the table. The volume of background music changes depending on the number of guests in the restaurant. At the beginning of an evening, the music is louder to create a lively vibe as the place is still filling up. After more hungry guests arrive, the music softens to ensure patrons don't have to shout as the room fills to capacity. Even though customers won't likely tell stories about the gentle presentation of each dish or the optimal background volume, each of these *Big Little Break-throughs* adds up to an outstanding overall experience.

Eleven Madison Park's tremendous success illustrates the power of the dinner mint in action. Just a small dose of unexpected creativity can generate a disproportionately large return on investment. Will and Daniel's 5 percent investment has yielded colossal gains in terms of restaurant growth, profits, awards, and recognition. The impact of their proportionally small surprise-and-delight activities played a crucial role in their ascent to culinary greatness.

For us, the concept can apply in myriad ways. A dinner mint can represent any unexpected addition, from extra ideas to time savings to physical goodies. If you're asked to deliver a report on your top five competitors, a dinner mint version would be to expand your efforts to produce your report on seven competitors instead. Or maybe you could format the report in a colorful, well-designed presentation instead of a dull black-and-white document. Remember, it was Dave Burd's management report in the form of a rap song that launched his musical career.

If a client is expecting your response by Thursday afternoon, a dinner mint might be to shave a day off the timeline to deliver on Wednesday morning. While a dinner mint could certainly be a physical gift, you embrace the concept every time you overdeliver. Upgrading your work product with 5 percent more creativity can be just the boost you're looking for.

Free Prize Inside

Since Cracker Jack began including a free prize in every box of caramel-coated popcorn over a century ago, we've been hypnotically drawn to that little something extra. As a kid, I couldn't wait to dump out a full box of cereal to find a secret decoder ring. I also ate far too many burgers and fries from McDonald's, first to snag the prize inside a Happy Meal and later to play the McDonald's Monopoly game that promised the chance to win more prizes. Now as an adult, visiting Costco to binge on free samples is one of my favorite recreational outings. This isn't only because I'm cheap...the draw toward something extra is irresistible.

Bestselling author Jay Baer examined the prize-inside phenomena in his 2018 book, *Talk Triggers*. The premise of the book is that brands need to do something beyond their core offering in order to get people talking. He argues that small, creative investments can yield enormous word-of-mouth benefits. Jay makes the case for dinner mints of all shapes and sizes as the most effective and efficient marketing investment. Here are some examples he shares...

On the surface, the Magic Castle Hotel in Orlando, Florida, looks very similar to dozens of other area hotels. But unlike even the swankiest alternatives, the Magic Castle has a "Popsicle hotline" out by the pool. Guests are encouraged to walk up to the bright red wall-mounted phone to request their favorite flavor of Popsicle. Within minutes, a well-appointed team member presents the requested frozen treat to the guest on a silver platter. It isn't just that they give out free Popsicles but rather they've crafted a unique and compelling experience, differentiating the property from other similarly priced options. One delighted customer posts on Yelp, "ONE MILLION STARS. My eight-year-old daughter said this place deserves a 'one-million-star rating.' All businesses could learn about making a customer's experience beyond their expectations."

The Mike Diamond Plumbing Company provides plumbing, AC, and electrical service in Southern California just like countless other firms. Since plumbing repair is a fairly generic service, Mike differentiates by promoting his company as "the good smelling plumber." The firm guarantees every one of their plumbers and electricians will smell good, which cleverly implies that their competitors smell like the inside of a gym bag. Here, the dinner mint is the promise of a clean service provider, which gets people laughing and, more importantly, paying attention to the company.

If you've ever been to an amusement park like Disney World or Six Flags, you probably still remember how painfully the costs add up. Overpriced parking, soft drinks, and suntan lotion may or may not have prompted me to convince my kids that a free state park would be much more fun next year. But Indiana-based Holiday World takes a different approach. Their dinner mint is offering free parking, unlimited free sodas, and free suntan lotion stations throughout the park. In the competitive fight for entertainment dollars, the company outperforms even its biggest rivals. Instead of a huge ad budget, the company lets its dinner mints do the talking.

On the seventy-first floor of the Intercontinental Hotel in downtown Los Angeles, the La Boucherie steakhouse has great food and a nice atmosphere. But so do dozens of other restaurants in LA. What makes La Boucherie noteworthy is that every guest gets to choose his or her steak knife from an elegant briefcase, presented tableside with regalia by a knife sommelier. Keep in mind, guests don't keep the knives, so this isn't a gigantic cost to the restaurant. But the dinner mint of an extensive knife-selection prompts customers to spread the word and come back for more.

And let's not forget the Sip 'N Dip Lounge in Great Falls, Montana. The glass-sided swimming pool sits just behind the basement bar, allowing the staff to pull back a movie theater–style curtain each night from 9:00 p.m. until midnight to display a live mermaid show. The swimming staff, dressed in mermaid and merman costumes, are trained to splash around during their evening swim to the delight of bar patrons. This odd dinner mint got the attention of *GQ* magazine, which ranks the establishment the #1 Bar in America Worth Flying to Visit. Without this creative extra, I'm pretty sure the good folks at *GQ* would have never made it to Great Falls, Montana.

These examples show how dinner mints can come in many forms. In each case, it's a surprise-and-delight experience that gets people talking and helps creative companies win in their highly competitive fields. Whether you run an industrial chemical manufacturer, a personal injury law firm, or a podcast production company, think about what creative ideas you could add to get your customers talking. Regardless of your field or profession, never underestimate the power of a dinner mint.

Isolate and Attack

There are as many metaphorical flavors of dinner mints as there are actual ones. In the same way you can choose to devour an Andes Crème de Menthe chocolate and peppermint thin, a Werther's Original butterscotch caramel, or Caron Proschan's Simply Mints (ginger is my favorite), there is no shortage of options. The same applies to each of us as we leverage the *don't forget the dinner mint* ethos. The trick is to isolate a single point of focus at a time and then explore how you can add dinner mints to boost performance.

When you think of your own profession, there are dozens of individual elements that can be isolated. A building materials supplier could isolate recruiting, field sales, internal communication, procurement, logistics, marketing, or customer service.

When I played guitar for a living, factors such as genre, practice routines, marketing efforts, gear, and musical collaborators could each be isolated for a possible dinner mint upgrade. In many cases, a single dinner mint applied to just one focus area can yield monumental gains. In other words, you don't need to dinner mint every single aspect of your business, career, or life.

Many of us dream of flying our own planes, but a mistake for an amateur pilot could be the difference between life and death. After all, an aircraft mishap isn't the same as a fender bender at the grocery store parking lot. Commercial and military pilots with advanced training and extensive experience rarely make a blunder, but a hobbyist has a far higher probability of a catastrophic error. According to the National Transportation Safety Board, 97 percent of all aviation fatalities occur in private planes.

Improving the safety of small aircraft is what inspired Alan and Dale Klapmeier to start a company in the basement of their parents' barn in rural Baraboo, Wisconsin. It was 1984, and the duo named their new enterprise Cirrus Aircraft. Their dream was to build a plane that was as safe to fly as driving a car. But how could they possibly win against aviation giants like Boeing, Raytheon, and Cessna? The brothers started out offering a kit plane that owners could assemble and fly themselves but struggled to compete, floundering in the early days of their venture.

Staying true to their dream of providing pilots a safer flight, Alan and Dale devoured all the latest research on aviation safety. They studied academic reports, read every trade journal, and tracked the latest technology advances. Interviewing owner-operator pilots validated that safety was the single biggest deciding factor when making a purchase decision. The brothers isolated just one factor—safety—as the only chance for their company, and eventually their customers, to take flight.

Diving deep into emerging trends, the duo learned about a brand-new aviation safety technology being developed in nearby St. Paul, Minnesota. Ballistic Recovery Systems, located just 215 miles away, had been founded four years prior by Boris Popov, who survived a hang-gliding accident and became fixated on improving the safety of air travel. Boris was working on a new kind of parachute system to protect an entire aircraft, not just an individual wearing a backpack. Alan and Dale made the three-hour drive to visit Boris and the rest, as they say, is history.

Perhaps one of the greatest mash-ups since chocolate and peanut butter were fused into a Reese's, Cirrus Aircraft teamed up with Ballistic Recovery Systems to develop the first-ever full aircraft parachute system. Over the next decade, the two companies worked together on the revolutionary concept while they were both struggling to keep the lights on and grow their respective businesses. To stay afloat, Cirrus abandoned airplane kits to offer a fully built single-engine propeller plane while Ballistic licensed their patent to the military.

By 1998, testing and certification had been completed and the Cirrus Aircraft Parachute System (CAPS) became standard equipment on every new Cirrus plane. According to the Cirrus website, "The CAPS system was the industry's first general aviation parachute system produced in an FAA certified aircraft. And to date, Cirrus continues to be the only company to include a whole airframe parachute as standard equipment on all certified aircraft models."

Aircraft sales climbed faster than the planes themselves, with amateur pilots clambering for the only airplane with a parachute. The pip-squeak company from the middle of Wisconsin was winning a disproportionate share of the market, even against competitors that were geometrically larger. Today, the company's

SR22 line of aircraft is among the most popular planes on the market and have even been used to set a solo pilot world record when my friend from Australia, Ryan Campbell, used his Cirrus to circumnavigate the globe. Since its introduction, the CAPS system is credited with saving more than 150 lives.

While the CAPS system is far more complex than a bowl of peppermints, it still represents less than 5 percent of the plane's overall manufacturing costs. It was the dinner mint of a parachute, not traditional comparison factors such as speed, range, or cargo space, that allowed Cirrus to lift off as a company and eventually fly. What began as a dinner mint differentiator—an airplane with a parachute—continued to evolve into the basis of the company's competitive strategy.

Later deciding to offer a jet in addition to their bread-and-butter propeller planes, Alan and Dale continued to innovate around their vision of safety when launching the Cirrus Vision Jet. The plane, also known as the SF50, uses a single engine, which makes it the world's most fuel-efficient jet. Just like other Cirrus aircraft, it comes standard with a full-airframe parachute. But a couple decades of technology advancements allow the company to take its safety dinner mint to a whole new level.

In addition to the parachute, Cirrus developed a self-landing mechanism that can automatically land the plane if a pilot becomes incapacitated. With the press of a big red button that either of my four-year-old twins could easily operate, the plane's high-tech systems take over. Once deployed, the navigation system automatically locates the closest airport while the communication system notifies air traffic control, the FAA, and local authorities. Advanced software, sensors, and controls guide the flight to a smooth and safe landing, so gentle that the drink in your hand won't even spill.

Ask yourself, if you were in the market for a small jet that you planned to fly yourself, is there even a chance of you buying the plane without a parachute and self-landing technology? It's no wonder there's a seven-year waiting list to purchase a new Vision Jet.

The key takeaway is that Cirrus isolated a single aspect of the aviation business—safety—and then put all their creativity into that specific point of differentiation. People line up to buy Cirrus aircraft because of their highly coveted dinner mints around safety, not because of other factors that normally impact a purchase decision. The Klapmeier brothers teach us success comes from isolating a single area for creative expression and then maniacally focusing to create irresistible dinner mints in this category.

If the Shoe Fits

The hot and dry city of Okara, Pakistan, had primarily been known for its sugar mill and dairy farms until Sidra Qasim and Waqas Ali did something that no one could have predicted. With limited economic options, the married couple dreamt of starting their own company together, but the two lacked formal training and resources. Many people dream, but Sidra and Waqas's pursuit began to take shape when they *fell in love with a specific problem*— the problem of ill-fitting shoes.

It turns out that most of us have feet that are slightly different sizes. In fact, 70 percent of people have at least a one-quarter size difference between their two feet. Maybe your left shoe always feels tighter than the right one, or you tend to get soreness in one foot but not the other. If people's feet are different proportions, the couple wondered why pairs of shoes are only sold in a single size.

Sidra and Waqas had a big little idea. What if they started a shoe company that was completely focused on fit? But starting a shoe company in their Pakistani hometown seemed as impossible as swimming across the Arabian Sea. Trying to compete against entrenched behemoths Nike, Reebok, and Adidas would be a high-risk proposition, even if Sidra and Waqas had a $50 million bankroll and matching Harvard MBAs. But a husband and wife from Okara, Pakistan, with no resources, experience, or training taking a shot at the big boys appeared to have about the same odds of success as my tiny Yorkie getting appointed to oversee the Department of Homeland Security.

Yet once again, creativity becomes the great equalizer. It allows everyday people like you and me—and Sidra and Waqas—to level the playing field and gain an edge when we apply the principles of everyday innovators. The couple honed their idea and bet their life savings to pursue their vision.

Following the approach of concept isolation, they centered the entire business on fit. The company only offers one shoe—the Model 000—which only comes in a few monochromatic colors with no visible logos. There are no celebrity endorsements, no fancy graphics, no neon-yellow laces. The shoes are sold direct to consumers, so no channel distribution strategy exists. In fact, the shoes are curiously basic except for one crucial thing: they come in quarter sizes. The name of the company—Atoms—pays tribute to their belief that small adjustments improve fit. They are like the *Big Little Breakthroughs* of feet.

Here's how it works: I normally wear a size 8 shoe. Buying from Atoms, I'd select my color preference and the company would ship me *six* shoes. I'd get a 7¾, an 8, and an 8¼ for each foot. At home, I'd test out the fit of various combinations and then select my favorite two. I may end up with a 7¾ on my right foot and an 8¼ on my left. The rejected four shoes are then returned to the company (shipping is free both ways), and I end up with a pair of shoes that fits perfectly.

Atoms uses the dinner mint strategy of perfect fit as their primary point of differentiation. It's the only company to offer one-quarter sizes and the only company that will sell you a left shoe that's different from the right. In the highly competitive shoe market, Atoms now has over one thousand five-star reviews and has enjoyed an unrelenting sales surge since the company launched in 2018. Today, they struggle to keep up with demand as the startup savors against-the-odds success. The isolation of fit, combined with the dinner mint of independent quarter-size shoes, has rocketed this unlikely couple into the big leagues.

Edge-Storming

At this point, you might be wondering how to invent compelling dinner mints in your business, career, or community. To that end, here's a simple brainstorming technique that's designed to help you develop your own minty solutions. Normal brainstorming sessions, as previously noted, tend to yield incremental and rather dull ideas. *Edge-storming*, on the other hand, takes your imagination to a whole new level.

Start by isolating a single opportunity point. For Cirrus Aircraft, it was safety. For Atoms, it was shoe fit. Yours could be any broad company factor such as manufacturing efficiency, client service, or data mining. You can also apply edge-storming to any specific problem or opportunity, such as "How can we reduce our employee turnover rate?" or "What can we do to increase sales of our corn tortillas in the Milwaukee area?"

Once your target is set, try an ideation sprint whereby the only ideas that can be shared take the concept to the edge. In an edge-storm session, you're simultaneously pushing your creativity to the far edges while setting aside all execution, cost, or risk factors. Simply put, you're not allowed to share an idea unless it is extreme.

Edge-storm ideas to reduce employee turnover might include doubling everyone's salary, bringing in gourmet chefs to provide free food, or building a sand volleyball court inside the finance department. Increasing tortilla sales in Milwaukee edge-stormed ideas could include launching a summer concert series where famous Latin bands perform their hits dressed as giant tortillas, holding a contest to give away eleven million tortillas to the lucky winner, or offering free weekly cooking lessons from celebrity chefs.

To be clear, none of these ideas are remotely practical. They're all too expensive and too outrageous. But it's far easier to push your creativity to the edge and then later ratchet those expansive ideas back to reality than to start with puny concepts that would be difficult to elevate.

The sand volleyball court could be modified down to an annual company mock Olympic event where employees compete for prizes and bragging rights. Instead of celebrities dressed like tortillas, the summer music series idea could be abridged to a single musician recording a series of songs and then releasing them on social media instead of a concert hall. It's much more productive to start crazy-big and then sand off any rough edges than to start small and succumb to the gravitational force of practicality. Even if you're seeking a small innovation rather than a big one, use edge-storming to unleash extreme imagination and then lasso the far-out ideas back to reality for later deployment.

Dinner Mint Roundup

Still searching for your favorite dinner mint flavor? Consider how these organizations used the dinner mint approach to stand out in their crowded fields:

Variety

Coromoto, the legendary ice cream parlor in Merida, Venezuela, holds the world record for offering the most flavors of ice cream. It has 860, to be exact. Flavors include chili, tomato, gherkin, garlic, red wine, and cream of crab. The shop has decent ice cream to be sure, but so do hundreds of others. It's the dinner mint of enormous variety that makes Coromoto world famous (pretty sure they offer dinner mint–flavored ice cream, too).

Offering a massive selection is a proven dinner mint strategy. Thomas Publishing, for example, catalogs six million industrial products, ten million CAD drawings, and over five hundred thousand detailed supplier profiles. If you're on the hunt for these things, there's no other company that's even close in offering such a vast number of options.

Speed

You can snag a turkey sub from just about anywhere, but you likely turn to Jimmy John's if you need it fast. This company's commitment to "freaky fast" sandwich delivery is the dinner mint that sets it apart from hundreds of other shops. In our hurried society, being the fastest can become a massive differentiator in any field. Think how you could be the fastest gunslinger in your own industry.

Humor

Moosejaw, a retailer that offers outdoor gear such as clothing, tents, and hiking boots, competes with industry giants such as REI, Bass Pro Shops, and even Amazon. The product mix is the same, and it certainly can't win on price. Instead, Moosejaw uses snarky humor as its preferred dinner mint. Funny lines scroll on the company's home page instead of special offers. "Did you ever wonder if 'boo' is just ghost language for 'hello' and we're all over-reacting?" Or one of my favorites, "Let's get serious here...how do you throw away a trash can?" Customers are invited to follow the company on social media: "Follow us. Or don't. Check out our Instagram for cool pics, gear giveaways, dogs, and captions that my mom brags to her friends about." On the feedback page: "Moosejaw is the only company aside from Hokey's Stuffed Dragons that sends personal responses even though you have to fill out this stupid form. Love the madness!"

Moosejaw stands out in a crowded field by being whimsical. If you're looking for a waterproof hoodie, why would you patronize a dull supplier when you can have a laugh-out-loud shopping experience at Moosejaw? Instead of a generic sale, Moosejaw says things like, "You'll save so much money, you can start making origami out of it." Keep in mind, the humor dinner mint adds zero dollars to the company's cost structure.

Functionality

Is there a little something you could add to your product or service to create a functional benefit? Back to ice cream, my oldest daughter, Chloe, just turned twenty-one. For her birthday, Tia and I sent her four pints of Tipsy Scoop Boozy Ice Cream. The alcohol-infused dessert comes in flavors such as Dark Chocolate

Whisky Salted Caramel, Raspberry Limoncello Sorbet, and Cake Batter Vodka Martini. It was the addition of booze that sealed the deal when we purchased the birthday gift. And I'm quite sure Chloe enjoyed her very first taste of alcohol on her big birthday.

The consideration here isn't developing an entirely new product or service but rather using your imagination to plus-up your offering with a little something extra. Proportionately, the splash of tequila in Mango Margarita Sorbet is a small fraction of the overall cost, but that little infusion makes all the difference in the world.

Impact

The secret of Tom's Shoes' raging success had absolutely nothing to do with their product. The company pioneered the buy one-give-one model in which Tom's donates a pair of shoes to someone in need for every pair you buy. Since the company was founded thirteen years ago, it has given away more than one hundred million pairs of shoes to children in developing countries, which also means the company has sold more than one hundred million pairs. Obviously, Tom's included the costs for the donated shoes into its retail pricing, so it really was a clever way to get customers to fund the company's philanthropic mission. All the while, this plan helps Tom's Shoes stand out from every other alternative.

The dinner mint strategy is all about building a habitual instinct. Before you deliver the proposal, send an email, give a presentation, ship a product, launch a new website, or make your case to the jury, pause and ask yourself, "What dinner mint can I add here that will really boost this up?" Shoot for just 5 percent extra effort, time, or cost. That little something extra, the added creative flourish, can help you score a disproportionately over-sized benefit.

Scrub That

The sound of clanking dishes and boisterous conversation filled the thick air in the crowded diner. Heather Hasson, a former med student, was catching up with an old friend who was on a break from her job as a nurse practitioner at the hospital across the street. As the two reminisced about old times, Heather was having difficulty staying focused on the conversation. It wasn't the smell of french fries, the sight of busy waitresses working the midday rush, or the feel of the chipped coffee cup in her hand that was distracting. Instead, Heather couldn't stop noticing how bad her friend looked.

Heather's friend wasn't sick or unkempt, but the dull, baggy hospital scrubs she was wearing simply looked awful. The ensemble didn't fit right and look horribly uncomfortable. Worse yet, the prominent label announced her friend's size for the world to see. Heather's mind raced as she wondered why scrubs were so dreadful. With brands like Lululemon and Nike creating fashionable athletic wear, why were scrubs still in the dark ages?

After catching up with her friend, Heather decided to investigate further. She quickly learned that medical apparel is a $60 billion industry, $10 billion in the United States alone. She also discovered that 90 percent of those purchases are made directly by the medical professionals themselves as opposed to the manufacturing sector where employers provide the required uniforms.

Heather also learned that the purchase experience is as bad as the unsightly outfits. Nurses like her friend generally shop at dimly lit medical supply stores where the baggy scrubs are displayed right next to canes, wheelchairs, and oxygen tanks. Online options weren't much better as health-care workers choose from drab, scratchy, unflattering generic scrubs or exaggerated, cartoon-like options such as obnoxious floral patterns or overstated ugly palm trees.

Heather realized she was onto something. With nearly twenty million horribly dressed health-care workers in the US as the target market, she and her good friend Trina Spear founded FIGS in 2013. The company was named after Heather's favorite fruit in an homage to other fruit-named brands such as Apple, Lululemon, Blackberry, and Kiwi Airlines. The pair set out to create highly fashionable scrubs that looked great and performed far better than current options.

Before ordering thread and fabric, the two *fell in love with the problem*, spending hours interviewing health-care professionals to better understand the problem with traditional scrubs. They learned that female doctors often tie their wedding ring to their bra strap, since there is no safe place to store their jewelry during procedures. One doctor they interviewed said he was on his fifth wedding band because he kept losing them at work. Besides a lack of functional pockets, the frumpy clothes fit so poorly that they'd sometimes come apart right in the middle of a patient visit, or even surgery. "How can you be focused on saving lives, curing diseases, and caring for patients when your pants are falling down?" quips cofounder Trina Spear. Further, the coarse fabric irritated nurses' skin so frequently, it had become a running joke among the staff at many hospitals.

Following the second obsession of everyday innovators, Heather and Trina *started before they were ready*. The two cashed in their 401(k) plans and maxed out their credit cards to create prototypes and eventually a small amount of inventory. Based on their research, they designed FIGS scrubs to be form-fitting, stylish, comfortable, and highly functional.

Being scrappy (*using every drop of toothpaste*), they set up coffee stands in hospital parking lots during shift changes. The two dressed up in their gorgeous FIGS scrubs and offered fresh java to the medical professionals. Lured by the cup of free joe, hospital staffers instantly noticed the stylish, well-tailored scrubs, which Heather and Trina happily sold from the trunks of their nearby cars. Within weeks, they ditched the free coffee since a line of eager customers was waiting for them each time they pulled up with a fresh trunk full of merchandise. Before long, demand exploded. The combination of design and functionality clicked with health-care workers as word spread like an infectious disease.

Heather and Trina formalized their business, refined their designs, and attracted startup capital to begin larger scale production. Even though they had initial customer demand, growth was neither smooth nor easy. "Early on, we had a huge issue with our production, where we swapped the inseams of our pants, so our men's pant had a women's inseam," recalls Trina. "That's the distance between the top of the pant and…well, you get it. We only realized it after getting a number of emails from our male customers with 'My Package' as the subject line. It's funny now, but at the time, it was devastating. It was our first production run. We'd put all of our money into this company. To have this happen during our first production run was demoralizing."

The two friends learned and persevered. "I'm almost happy in a way that it happened so early on because it ensured that nothing like that will ever happen again," Trina explains. "Plus, it's a great story to tell. It's about being able to push forward and not look back; being resilient and persistent."

With production hiccups behind them, the company started to grow at breakneck speed. The disruptive cofounders attracted media attention, which helped them secure $75 million in funding from high-profile investors, including actor Will Smith and the former CEO of Lululemon, Christine McCormick Day.

Heather and Trina continued to search for more dinner mints to make FIGS scrubs even better. How could they plus-up the look, function, durability, and comfort of their scrubs to make them the undeniably obvious choice for customers? Once they nailed the form-fitting style, they focused on usability with dinner mints such as zippered pockets and easy-access compartments for stethoscopes, phones, and IDs. They explored hundreds of textile options, ultimately creating their own fabric that is wrinkle-free, antimicrobial, and as comfortable as an old T-shirt.

Just seven years after hawking their wares from the trunk of a car, FIGS is forecasted to generate $250 million of revenue in 2020, up from $100 million in 2018, which itself was up 9,938 percent since 2014. Heather and Trina won the highly coveted EY Entrepreneur of the Year Award, and *Fast Company* named FIGS one of the Most Innovative Companies in the World.

Keep in mind, Heather and Trina's entrée into the medical apparel industry was rooted in a simple dinner mint concept: medical scrubs that looked good.

"We're transforming the health-care experience by creating innovative, comfortable, and supremely functional medical apparel for modern health-care professionals," Hasson explains. "We believe that what you wear affects how you feel and ultimately, how you perform. We designed FIGS so that you look good, feel good, and perform at your best no matter what your day throws at you."

Continuing to innovate forward, the company embraced the *open a test kitchen* principle. FIGS now has an innovation center in Taipei and a 2,000-square foot design lab in its Los Angeles headquarters. Today, the design team includes experienced fashion pros from Ralph Lauren and Lululemon along with materials experts from skiwear and sports apparel companies. FIGS releases a new color grouping each month, along with new weekly styles, playfully called "infusions." It also produces limited-edition collections based on popular trends. FIGS recently partnered with New Balance to co-create a line of fashionable, functional, comfortable shoes specifically designed for the needs of health-care professions who are on their feet for up to fourteen hours at a time.

Forty-seven manufacturing facilities strong and nearly one million customers who each buy eight to twelve sets of scrubs each year, FIGS appears unstoppable. Heather and Trina took the boring, utilitarian medical scrub to a whole new level by isolating fashion as their first dinner mint. Scrubs that were form-fitting and attractive, followed by the dinner mint of comfort, which led to the next mint of highly functional gear. Heather didn't have a solitary lightning bolt of inspiration to create the perfect scrubs. Instead, she began with a single plus-up (fashion) to an otherwise commodity offering. The company grew to become a market leader in health-care apparel, one fig-flavored dinner mint at a time.

Looking ahead to our eighth and final obsession of everyday innovators—*fall seven times, stand eight*—we'll explore how tenacity and resilience factor into the creative process. We'll uncover some hysterical flops, see how a blazing fire created a spectacular rebirth, and fly aboard racing drones to examine the intersection of creativity and persistence.

CHAPTER 12

Fall Seven Times, Stand Eight

The violent wall of flames rose so high into the night sky that it appeared to be a volcanic eruption. It took 115 firefighters more than seven hours to subdue the raging fire, which left a charred mountain of destruction in its wake. Nearly two million square feet of equipment, inventory, and warehouse space was reduced to smoldering ash during the 2016 blaze at the Gap distribution center in Fishkill, New York. Thankfully no lives were lost, but the damage put Gap's business on life support. The company's second-largest facility burned to the ground less than three months before the critical holiday shopping season, seriously jeopardizing its ability to fulfill orders and retain customers.

We've all had fires in our lives, metaphorical or real. While there is an endless string of clichés and platitudes around the glory of failure, pithy advice doesn't reduce the agony of a major setback. Let's face it: falling on your face is a painful experience that none of us crave. It's one thing for a plaid-jacketed motivational speaker to instruct us to love our failures, but those shallow chestnuts don't do much to help us actually overcome an agonizing defeat. I've personally failed many, many times, and believe me, in those moments the last thing we want to hear is a vapid, cheesy line. When I'm bleeding on the floor, I need a game plan, not a hug.

To get back in the fight, the Gap had to embrace the eighth obsession of everyday innovators: *fall seven times, stand eight.* Translated from the Japanese expression "nana korobi, ya oki," the phrase is a Zen proverb for resilience. It challenges us to bounce back from difficulty, refusing to concede defeat even when facing a bleak outlook. It teaches us to focus only on the next step ahead in a levelheaded, methodical way even when emotions run high and to have the fluidity to adapt to changing circumstances, adjusting our approach each time we dust ourselves off to move forward.

With steely determination, leaders at the Gap had to figure out how to get 1,300 displaced employees back to work and make sure that customers got their orders on time. "It was a very tough time," said Kevin Kuntz, Gap's senior vice president of global logistics operations. "We literally set up a remote command center in Nashville that night."

Kuntz and his team focused on pragmatic action, using their creativity to bounce back as quickly as possible. Within days, the team set up a "pop-up" distribution center in a nearby warehouse, allowing them to manually fulfill orders as a larger plan to rebuild took shape. The makeshift center wasn't efficient, but it got the job done so customers of the Gap, Old Navy, Banana Republic, and Athletica got their gear on time. The team dove into problem-solving mode, tackling one challenge after another to rebound and rebuild.

Once the immediate problems had been stabilized, the team began to see opportunity in the charred wreckage. Since they were forced to rebuild anyway, they decided to use the situation as a springboard for innovation. The old distribution center was working fine, so there was no impetus to reimagine operations. But with a blank slate, they could completely rethink everything from equipment to staffing to safety procedures. It became an opportunity to invent the operation of the future, driving productivity and efficiency to new heights. In fact, the team decided that they should create a standard-setting operations center, one so effective that it could serve as a model for the company's other locations around the world.

"Now that we have a clean sheet of paper, how are we going to build a facility for tomorrow, the next year, the next decade?" posited then CEO Art Peck. "It was a moment of innovation." Peck's clean sheet of paper led to the company embracing new technology such as robotic sorting, machine learning, and an extensive network of sensors to optimize operations. The team took the same blank-page approach to staffing, logistics, warehousing, and environmental impact. The fire's destruction forced the team to innovate every aspect of their work.

Nearly two years after the devastating fire, the distribution center in Fishkill, New York, became the most effective facility in the company's network with the capacity to process over one million units per day. According to a company statement, "The newly rebuilt facility is able to sort nearly twice the number of shipments per day than before the fire."

"A time of crisis is when you show your true colors. And this was Gap at its finest," said Shawn Curran, executive vice president of global supply chain and product operations. The company used the fire as an opportunity to rethink its entire approach, and a wave of innovation spread to other areas of the business. As a result of the catastrophe in Fishkill, New York, a new blaze was lit for the Gap, one that is still stoking the flames of creativity companywide.

The *fall seven, stand eight* philosophy is best described as the intersection of creativity and resilience. It's not a Pollyanna you-can-do-anything cliché but rather a deliberate response to adversity. Instead of dogged persistence, everyday innovators use setbacks as an opportunity to bounce back with a different approach each time, using inventive thinking to guide the way. Removing the judgment of right or wrong, they view stumbles as data that can inform subsequent creative attempts. Fusing tenacity with imagination, the fight is won through a series of creative tweaks and adaptations.

The Graveyard Doesn't Have to Be Scary

In the movies, creative breakthroughs are conceived and perfected instantaneously. The cunning leading character has her a-ha moment and the idea is flawlessly executed within seconds. Innovation in Hollywood, it turns out, is about as realistic as cop shows and daytime dramas. The problem is, we've become entranced by this mythology and hold ourselves to a ridiculously unrealistic standard. When our ideas pop out muddled, fragile, and unpolished, we view the invention as a total flop. Worse yet, we internalize the belief that we're just not very creative or that we can't measure up to others. In contrast to the fantasy, let's explore how innovation most often surfaces through a series of setbacks and mistakes.

First, new ideas are messy. In the same way we'd never expect a newborn baby to be self-sufficient, we shouldn't set such an unrealistic standard for newborn concepts. The truth is, early ideas are almost always flawed. While the artist's job is first to create, equally important is the cycle of testing, examining, and refining the work until it's just right. Artists—and let's not forget that we're *all* artists—realize that stumbles and missteps are indeed part of the creative process and that quitting after the first failed attempt is akin to forfeiting a game of chess after your opponent's opening move.

Another hard truth is that not all ideas will pan out. There's never been a successful inventor without a failure, no legendary poet without blustered prose, never a prolific musician without a misplaced note. If we're not stumbling at times, we're simply not trying hard enough. Everyday innovators neither seek nor relish failure, but they accept it as an important part of the creative process. The learnings and insights of our worst work becomes the kindling of our next masterpiece.

Not only do individual innovators recognize the *fall seven, stand eight* rhythm of creative discovery, so do the most successful organizations. Google, for example, has certainly enjoyed many extraordinary successes. But they've also failed as spectacularly as they've won. The website KilledByGoogle.com denotes 205 (and counting) failed products the tech giant sent to the graveyard. A tombstone icon next to each eulogized endeavor visually shows us the magnitude of Google's failures.

An epitaph is listed next to each headstone describing what the product was and how long it graced the earth. Google leaders are comfortable saying goodbye and taking the loss. Some efforts are killed within months, such as Google Related, which was supposed to be a navigation assistant to help people find useful and interesting info when surfing around the internet. Recognizing its flaws, company leaders had no problem killing the project after just eight months of life. And there was Google

Hotpot, a local recommendation and review system akin to Yelp that Google killed just five months after launch.

There are also long-range terminations that were undoubtedly difficult to authorize. Halting an offering that's been around for years requires writing off significant capital investment and displacing team members. Yet Google is willing to let go in order to move ahead. Google Directory, a categorized listing of various places of online interest, was laid to rest after eleven years in operation. Google Search Appliance, a rack-mounted device that provided search indexing for corporate clients, met its maker after nearly seventeen years of life.

From Picasa, a digital photo organizing and storage service, to Google Hangouts, a communication platform that included video chat and messaging, Google celebrates its failures instead of hiding them. The company recognizes the beauty and insight that a failure can generate, savoring the blank space left behind as a new canvas for creative expression.

P&G embraces a similar approach at its Cincinnati world headquarters. The company's "Wall of Failures" showcases many of the company's bombs since its 1837 inception. Lisa Mulvaney, the P&G historian responsible for the exhibit, explains, "The only thing worse than a wall of failures would be not having the display at all, forgetting why a product didn't work out and making the same mistake."

One of Lisa's favorite failures on display is Febreze Scentstories, which was a contraption resembling a CD-player that produced a playlist of scents. Every fifteen minutes, a new aroma was released to keep a room smelling fresh. Consumers were confused, wondered why it didn't play music, and quickly rejected the product. Another elegantly displayed failure is Charmin Space Maker, designed to consume less shelf space at grocery stores and in consumers' pantries. The company basically squished rolls of toilet paper flat and then tightly seal-wrapped them into a smaller package. However, the rolls didn't take shape properly once the package was opened, causing customers to hate their squashed toilet paper.

Like Google, P&G pays homage to its failures. The company has the confidence to openly share and learn from its setbacks, recognizing that every innovator's legacy has both creative hits and misses. Think about the messages that the Wall of Failures sends to the thousands of would-be innovators employed at the company: it is okay to take responsible risks, and they work in a safe environment for creative expression. For anyone who feels this is a risky move, I'd respectfully ask in response, what's the risk of *not* doing something like this? Irrelevance? Mediocrity?

Having interviewed some of the most successful people in the world—from billionaires to celebrity entrepreneurs to Grammy Award–winning musicians—the best of the best not only win more, but they also fail more. They look at their setbacks as a badge of honor, not a scarlet letter. They endure the momentary pain of defeat in order to learn, adapt, and improve. More often than not, long-term victory is the direct result of a seemingly endless stream of short-term losses.

Dr. Samuel West, for one, loves failure. As an organizational psychologist who focuses on creating optimal conditions for innovation, he's researched the role that failures play in both encouraging and hampering organizational creativity. In an effort to inspire experimentation and exploration, he opened the Museum of Failure in Helsingborg, Sweden, in 2017. Exactly as the name suggests, the museum showcases hundreds of flops from some of the most successful organizations in the world.

There are well-intentioned ideas that the market rejected, such as the futuristic Ford Edsel. The company invested a fortune in design and marketing, but the overpriced car was a commercial bomb. The Barnes & Noble Nook was a copycat version of Amazon's Kindle that had a couple of cool new features, but it still couldn't overcome Amazon's head start. Coca-Cola spent two years developing Coke BlaK, but its high hopes were quickly dashed. The mix of cola and coffee stimulated few people beyond the testing lab, and the product was hurriedly cancelled.

And then there are the products that were so far off, they should've never been launched. Thirsty Dog and Thirsty Cat were designed to replace your pet's boring water with flavored, vitamin-fortified spring water. The ugly brown water came in crispy beef flavor for dogs and tangy fish flavor for cats. A surprise to no one other than its creator, the ill-conceived idea was gone in less than a year.

And who can forget the UroClub? The museum's description of the perfect companion for every golfer is as hilarious as the product itself:

> The UroClub looks like an ordinary golf club, but it is a cleverly disguised urinal. First unscrew the leak proof cap, then clip on the privacy towel to your belt, fumble around under there a bit, and then stand there and try to look like you're pondering your next move. The little towel-like piece of fabric that hangs down in front of your pants is called a "privacy shield". It ensures that nearby lady golfers are not offended. It is recommended that you practice at home in front of a mirror to boost confident use.

Apparently, the market size of golfers who are unable to hold it for nine holes wasn't a big enough target. In a strange twist, urologist Dr. Floyd Seskin didn't lose the $300,000 he invested to bring his dream to late-night informercials since the product is still available for sale as a gag gift.

The Museum of Failure's slogan "innovation needs failure" celebrates the creative attempts that didn't pan out. Dr. West explains, "Innovation and progress require an acceptance of failure. The museum aims to stimulate productive discussion about failure and inspire us to take meaningful risks." The museum recently opened a permanent location in Los Angeles and has also presented temporary exhibits in Shanghai and Paris.

Dr. West demonstrates that organizations seeking more innovation have to increase their tolerance of failure as a necessary step in the creative process. Ironically, the master of failure had his own blunder when getting the museum off the ground. Dr. West misspelled the word "museum" when he originally registered the domain name for the museum, thereby failing even before launching his tribute to failure. Despite his poor spelling, West is removing the stigma, showing us that failure is an important part of the process. He helps us realize that failure isn't a four-letter word—unless, of course, he misspells it that way by mistake.

Slip 'n Slide

Like me, Dr. Tom Rifai is a self-described "pizzaholic" (he also claims a "PhD in the anatomy of a KitKat"). In addition to being a fellow pizza and comfort food lover and dear friend, he's also the founder of wellness company Reality Meets Science. Dr. Tom developed a Harvard-recognized lifestyle system for optimal health, a program that helped me cut my "bad" cholesterol by almost half without drugs and drop twenty pounds, reducing my risk of heart attack by over 50 percent. In that journey, one of the many tools he shared with me—SLIP—is not only an effective cognitive behavioral therapy (think "mindset") technique for healthy eating but an approach that is equally productive when facing a setback of any kind.

SLIP is an acronym for Stop, Look, Investigate, and Plan. SLIP turns our mindset from crisis to opportunity. It's a simple, nonjudgmental technique that helps us regroup and bounce back after a setback of any magnitude. For instance, if I went nuts on a Friday night, washing down an entire sausage and pepperoni pizza with a bottle and a half of pinot noir, I could engage the SLIP technique to help me bounce back. Otherwise, it's all too easy for me to get caught up in the "blame game." Frustration and shame can quickly spiral into an extended streak of unhelpful behaviors and choices when we don't pause to realistically recalibrate.

So after an overly glutenous evening, my first step of the SLIP technique is to *stop* before taking the next action. I may wake up with a mid-grade hangover craving maple glazed doughnuts as a "quick fix" to numb the pain. But some of that pain is guilt. Stop is where you "get real" and honestly accept what happened as a learning moment and opportunity to improve. You might tell yourself, "*Stop*, it's okay—I'm human and didn't die, so there's no reason to keep pushing the envelope."

Next, I'd *look* at the situation in an objective, realistic, and balanced way. No more worshiping at the false altar of "all or nothing." Instead, I think, "Yes, I ate and drank more than ideal. But by no means am I a horrible person or totally out of control. It happened, I own it, but now I get to decide what happens next and I'll be better for it."

In the third step, I'd *investigate* the situation. Here, I'm evaluating what happened in a supportive, judgment-free way. Okay, I was with friends and I got carried away with food and booze.

Looking back (i.e., investigating), I could have still had a great time with some slight modifications. Next time, I'll have a glass of sparkling water between each glass of vino. That would slow down my consumption while not feeling deprived. And, while on a SLIP roll here, maybe—just maybe—I could also still indulge on the pizza but start with a healthy salad first—making it easier to not inhale the two extra slices.

I'd round out the intervention with the *plan* step, making a deliberate choice of what to do next. Here, I could decide to eat super healthy for the next three days or add in some extra cardio exercise to burn off the splurge. I'd also plan a thoughtful approach for the future so the next time I'm hanging with friends over pizza and wine, I could have a predetermined strategy so that I'm not derailed in the moment. Stop, Look, Investigate, Plan.

The simple SLIP methodology is an ideal approach after a stinging defeat. Whether you've botched a big presentation, suffered a negative job review, or lost funding from your lead investor, taking a moment to SLIP the problem helps you learn from failure rather than wallow in it. We don't want one bad situation to cascade into several more, so arresting a screwup quickly will help get things back on track. Dr. Rifai encourages us to embrace our SLIPs and not to think of them as a defeat, even if they feel like one in the moment. The SLIP technique is a powerful way to get back on your feet and stand tall, regardless of how many times you've been knocked to the ground.

A League of His Own

Tightly gripping the controls, you see another airship come within inches of crashing into your left wing as it whizzes past you into a fluorescent pink neon tunnel. As you fly at top speed, a different competitor smashes into a nearby wall. You barely have time to notice the fiery explosion since you're nearing the glowing purple obstacle that will require an upside-down flip to navigate. Heavy metal music blasts into your headphones, blocking out the high-pitched noises of highly tuned engines racing by. You feel like you're inside of the Space Battle of Naboo, the intense action seen in *Star Wars: Episode I—The Phantom Menace* in which a fleet of futuristic fighter pods engage in aeronautic acrobatics to protect the Rebel Alliance.

But this is no sci-fi flick.

"The Drone Racing League is the global professional circuit for drone racing," explains Nicholas Horbaczewski, the league's founder and CEO, as we begin our conversation. "We take this very new, high-speed, exciting, tech-enabled sport and we put on events around the world in front of audiences of thousands and then we broadcast the sport to tens of millions of fans in more than ninety countries."

Nicholas speaks with jarring precision, exhibiting the lyrical prose of a spoken-word poet. His clean-cut appearance suggests Ivy League, but his competitive tenacity reveals a streetfighter. Within minutes, I feel like I'm speaking to someone who is destined for the history books, as if I were interviewing Serena Williams before she reached the pros. His voice is both confident and humble, determined and curious.

Best described as Formula One racing for drones, the DRL is packed with speed, drama, competition, and technology. The sport is now flying high, but getting it off the ground was as challenging as the races themselves. In bringing his vision to life, Nicholas experienced triumphs and crash landings, victorious wins and crushing defeats. As we ride along with Nicholas, we see how his high-speed, high-stakes story embodies not just *fall seven, stand eight* but all eight obsessions of everyday innovators.

Drone racing got its start in 2010 when amateur pilots in Australia started tinkering with their unmanned aircraft. They installed cameras, which provided them the experience of flying inside the drones at their command. In turn, the hobbyists started to race one another, outmaneuvering their friends for bragging rights. Crude courses were built, grainy YouTube videos were created, and drone racing soon became an underground cult phenomenon.

By 2014, drone racing had spread around the world, and Nicholas was able to see his first live race. "It was on Long Island, outside of New York City, in a field behind a Home Depot," he tells me. "People had set up pool noodles as gates. They were racing these homemade drones, and it was so amateur, it was so backyard...and yet there were these moments of greatness. I thought it was coolest thing I'd ever seen."

At that moment, Nicholas *fell in love with the problem*. He envisioned drone racing becoming a high-quality, professional sport but quickly learned how many obstacles were standing in his way. Nicholas explains, "Lots of people were wondering how we could take this hobby that we loved and share it with the world. I think the difference for us was stepping back and asking, what is the underlying problem? If this is as cool as we feel it is, it should have gone more mainstream by now, so what's stopping it?"

There was a massive technology shortfall, considering no platform existed that could supply industrial-grade cameras, controls, onboard diagnostics, scoring, and sensors. Additionally, you need sponsors, investors, professional competitors, media contacts, venue owners, and adoring fans to build a sport. It turned out to be a multidimensional stalemate, since each constituent only wanted to join the fun once the others were already in place. Rather than locking his sights on a particular solution to any of his growing list of challenges, Nicholas remained open-minded, willing to adapt to changing conditions as they unfolded.

With no investment capital or detailed game plan, Nicholas started before he was ready. "We started off full speed in the wrong direction for a couple of months before we stepped back," Nicholas explains. In one of his first of many knockdowns, he didn't fully grasp the technology deficit until he'd begun his pursuit. The industrial-grade tech he needed simply didn't exist. "There was only the hobby version of it. When we charged forward to make the sport better, we discovered the foundation wasn't there. We had to stop, completely reset, and turn into a technology company. To this day, the core of DRL is really engineering. More than half our team are engineers."

Raising capital was another difficult struggle. Nicholas explains that investors would either laugh him out of the room thinking the idea was nuts or they'd immediately get it but had wildly unrealistic expectations. They could imagine the *Star Wars* pod fighter scene but would become disappointed that DRL wasn't there yet. "We bounced between the fact that some people thought it was too crazy and some people were already envisioning the most perfected version," Nicholas remembers.

Once he was able to score some limited startup capital, Nicholas *opened a test kitchen*. Through rapid experimentation, the team cobbled together the first version of their technology platform. Fast cycles of tinkering with the drones, operating mechanics, and the course itself were enacted to get the sport up and running. But just when things were starting to look promising, Nicholas found himself on the floor once again. "Our first test event was a complete disaster," he says with a pained voice.

"We'd invited all of our prospective investors and nothing worked. It was very sobering."

As the company took shape, Nicholas needed a reservoir of *fall seven times, stand eight* resilience. Two months before the ill-fated demonstration event, the technical performance was so bad they scrapped everything and rebuilt the drones from the ground up. Nicholas had overpromised to investors and partners, and his worst fears played out in real time during the disastrous event. Guests were expecting 120 drones, but DRL showed up with only 12, many with missing parts. It was a humbling experience, but it made him and the company stronger. Rather than wallowing in shame, the team got off the mat and got back into their test kitchen.

The continued experiments finally paid off in December 2015 when the DRL had its first real race at Dolphin Stadium in Miami. "We built the course, turned on our homemade radio system, and we flew the drones for the first time around the racetrack. It was a really special moment. I was standing there with our head of technology, and we looked at each other and realized that we were the first people in the world to ever see a drone fly that complex a course, at that speed. It was a reminder that we were breaking new ground." In less than one year, the video of the Miami event had been seen forty-three million times around the world.

When it comes time to *break it to fix it*, Nicholas might as well be carrying a sledgehammer to work instead of his laptop. While most sports haven't materially changed their rules of play since the Eisenhower administration, the DRL retools their entire scoring system *every year*. "Most people say we're crazy and no sport should reinvent their scoring system. I say we have to because the pilots get so much better, the technology gets so much better, and the possibilities get so much broader that we need to adjust the scoring to make the sport as compelling as possible. We can't get stuck in old ideas."

The team doesn't just tweak their previous approaches; they douse them with high-octane drone fuel and set them ablaze. "We blow it up entirely. We scrap it all and start from scratch," Nicholas beams. "You need to be able to wall off everything you've done in the past. Forget those experiences and start with a fresh piece of paper."

"One of the great things about our sport is that we don't have a legacy holding us back," Nicholas says excitedly as he continues to share his *break it to fix it* approach. "We keep evolving the sport as we go and as technology enables us to do new things. That's everything you can think of from letting people race against the pros remotely through VR drones to potentially giving the drones offensive and defensive capabilities to use in the air against each other. We want to bring everything that you've ever seen in a video game into the sport. It's a promise we make to our fans that every year the sport will evolve and get more exciting."

Reaching for weird, Nicholas and his team thought it would be cool if some drones were piloted by artificial intelligence technology rather than humans. The company formed a partnership with Lockheed Martin to create autonomous drone racing, which now performs as the undercard to the professionally piloted main event.

In another *reach for weird* strategy, Nicholas decided to recruit the next generation of professional competitors directly from his fan base. "We talk a lot about the fact that drone racing sits on this blurry line between the digital and the real because it's a sport of remote robotics. Because you're remotely controlling robots, you can have the experience of sitting and flying a simulated drone instead of a real one. We built a DRL Simulator, giving anyone the chance to learn how to fly a racing drone. Then once a year, we hold a tryout. Anyone who's playing with the simulator can start competing and, if they win, they get a contract to be a DRL pilot."

I'm pretty sure no fans ever left their nosebleed seats at an NFL or NBA game to suit up and play with the pros. "It's the only sport we know of in the world where you can learn it entirely through simulation, win a competitive simulation, and immediately go into the real-life professional league," Nicholas tells me with pride.

Though the company succeeded in raising startup capital, they didn't have a massive bankroll, which forced the team to use *every drop of toothpaste* in the wildly expensive arena of professional sports. The Buffalo Bills, the lowest-valued NFL team, is worth $1.9 billion, while the highbrow Dallas Cowboys are valued at $5.5 billion. If you think buying a single pro sports team is crazy expensive, imagine the costs of launching an entirely new sporting league.

Despite sounding like a multibillion-dollar affair, Nicholas figured out how to get it done for far less. To that end, he formed early media partnerships with NBC Sports and Sky Sports and worked to secure early major sponsors, including the insurance company Allianz. Even today, the entire league consists of just one hundred full-time employees as Nicholas stays true to his resourceful, scrappy roots.

Naturally, DRL embraces the *don't forget the dinner mint* strategy. When I explained the concept to him, Nicholas said, "There's always going to be surprise and delight. The dinner mint philosophy is critically important to driving down complacency. For example, every year in the championship race, we put something in the course that has never been seen before. Not by the pilots, not by the fans, not by the team. I think it's really a delight for both the fans and the pilots, and I think it makes our championships really exciting."

Another dinner mint is the way fans experience each race, since the DRL is the only sport where the audience enjoys the identical experience as the competitors. Cameras mounted in the drones feed video signals back to pilots, who are wearing VR goggles and feel as if they are sitting inside the drone as it flies. But the pilots aren't the only ones having fun, since the signal is also shared directly with the audience. "It lets us play with what it means to spectate a sporting event," Nicholas tells me. "You're not just watching, you're actually on the field of play; you're experiencing it yourself. It's like sitting inside a fast jet plane as it whizzes through the air. It's a unique, immersive experience for the audience."

As he built his implausible dream into reality, Nicholas crashed nearly as often as his drones. But his *fall seven, stand eight* mentality allowed him to persevere through funding crunches, tech failures, pilot drama, and now the COVID-19 crisis. There will inevitably be more failures as the sport evolves, and perhaps some of his flops will be featured one day at the Museum of Failures. "When you've got drones whizzing around, you'll see a lot of crashing. About half the drones crash in every race. There are these spectacular crashes where drones flying ninety miles an hour clip a wall and explode into a million pieces," Nicholas says.

Although he's talking about drones on the surface, I'm pretty sure he's internalized the concept as well. That some creative ideas will make the finish line while others will die trying. That speed and complexity lead to both successes and stumbles. And that creative resilience is needed to launch and sustain any noteworthy endeavor.

Nicholas is the personification of everyday innovation. He views creativity as a daily habit, a discipline that must be cultivated. His gigantic all-caps INNOVATION of a new pro sports league came to life through dozens of capital-I Innovations and thousands of lowercase innovations (a.k.a. *Big Little Breakthroughs*). By using each of the eight obsessions, he's built a juggernaut that has no meaningful competition and no limits to its growth potential.

But Nicholas doesn't want to talk metaphor or hypotheticals. Instead, he gets back to the amazing race. "When a fan shows up to one of our races, the first thing you're going to see is this elaborate, three-dimensional, brightly lit course weaving through whatever building we're in. We've done races everywhere from traditional sports stadiums to palaces outside of London to the BMW headquarters in Munich. Wherever we're doing a race, you see these neon lights and it feels like something out of a science fiction movie."

Nicholas smiles as we end our conversation. "It's three-dimensional racing. It's racing with robots instead of cars. The performance these athletes are putting out is really equivalent to a Formula One or NASCAR driver. It's all of these different pieces, but ultimately, it's about who gets to the finish line first."

Through Nicholas's creative leadership, DRL is indeed the company that has reached the finish line first. And as we weave through the complex and competitive racecourses of our own careers and lives, the same exciting ride is ours for the taking. There will likely be painful moments, when we slam into the wall at high speed. Our difficult course may change as we fly, and there will undoubtedly be others whizzing by, trying to knock us from the skies. Euphoric a-ha moments that drive glorious gains may be followed by stinging crashes that require us to rise from the ashes to persevere in our creative pursuits.

But now that we understand our true creative capacity, we're armed for battle with the latest gadgetry. Through cultivating the habit of daily creativity, we start to build our own proficiency in the same way the simulator-based amateur drone pilots morph into paid professionals. Just as their skills developed through rigorous training, our creative skills will expand as we embrace the mindsets and tactics we've learned together.

Innovation, just like drone racing, is not a members-only club. It's open and accessible to women and men of different backgrounds, physical attributes, and geographies; different perspectives and ideas. Innovation is a sport that is within the grasp of us all.

And now is the time to share our creativity with the world.

CHAPTER 13

Your Shot

We've come a long way together. We dove into the latest research on human creativity to reveal that every one of us has a deep reservoir of capacity, even if we need to awaken it from hibernation. We saw the importance of innovation in our careers and communities, exploring how even a small creative upgrade can amount to a massive competitive advantage. We studied the habits of creative people from many walks of life to reveal that our skills expand with small doses of daily practice. And we confirmed how the universal power of human creativity can provide a meaningful edge, regardless of our respective backgrounds.

The most notable song from Lin-Manuel Miranda's *Hamilton* is called "My Shot." The lyrics speak of young Hamilton's ambition and how he planned to use his hunger and scrappiness to make a name for himself and an impact on his country. It spoke to his resolute commitment to taking his shot, unwilling to waste it. The song is about rising up to his potential, relentlessly pursuing his calling, and refusing to throw away his shot. In addition to taking his own shot, he insists that others rise up and take their shots too. He argues that we all have a shot to take and that it's our responsibility to take it.

Hamilton refused to throw away his shot, and now that you have the requisite tools and mindsets, it's time to take your own shot. Like Alexander Hamilton, it will take courage and commitment. But even a shot that misses the mark is better than the shot not taken.

Author Nido Qubein put it beautifully when he acknowledged, "The price of discipline is always less than the pain of regret." While it takes an investment of discipline to fully cultivate our creative skills, our inventiveness becomes the key that unlocks the vault of our full potential.

Chad Price of Mako Medical showed us how *falling in love with the problem* helps us discover creative openings and fresh solutions. Just as Catherine Hoke's deep connection to the problem of criminal recidivism helped her break the cycle for hundreds of now reformed inmates.

In her effort to help women around the world lead better lives, Mallory Brown *started before she was ready*. She dove in quickly, figuring things out as she progressed. In the same way, Greg Schwartz's remarkable success with StockX is the result of his ability to launch fast and course-correct later.

Whether focused on inventing a new specialty burger or just improving the crispiness of the fries, the leaders at Shake Shack *opened a test kitchen* to drive both innovations and refinements. From insurance company Mass Mutual to software development firm Menlo Innovations to New Zealand's championship sailing team, rapid experimentation led to stunning results.

From Mark Wallace's guitars made of reclaimed wood to Sal Khan's reinvention of global education, those who embrace the *break it to fix it* strategy enjoy massive rewards. The LEGO Group's unlikely journey to becoming the world's largest toy manufacturer came as a direct result of its willingness to reimagine and reinvent on an ongoing basis.

Researcher Olga Khazan and prankster Johnny Cupcakes both demonstrated the strange yet powerful *reach for weird* mindset. P&G's Chief Troublemaker Dustin Garis showed us that oddball tactics can drive meaningful progress in organizations of any size.

Street artist Kolja Kugler helped us get scrappy, quite literally, as he crafted his robot band exclusively from scrap materials. Kenya's Kip Keino, the University of Florida's Jeff Citty, and electric motorcycle pioneer Taras Kravtchouk each showed us what can be accomplished when we *use every drop of toothpaste*, doing more with less.

The culinary wizards at Eleven Madison Park showed us how a small dose of extra creativity can have a disproportionately large impact when embracing the *don't forget the dinner mint* philosophy. Sidra Qasim and Waqas Ali used the strategy to craft the perfect-fitting Atoms shoe, while FIGS' Heather Hasson and Trina Spear used the unexpected approach of fashionable scrubs to reinvent a stale industry.

And who can forget how Nicholas Horbaczewski crashed again and again but eventually was able to launch his Drone Racing League to incredible heights through his *fall seven times, stand eight* resiliency. I'm also guessing that being featured at the Museum of Failure wasn't on your bucket list until now.

As you gear up to take your shot, remember that even the most world-changing innovations are nothing more than a collage of tiny creative acts. Your most successful path forward isn't taking gigantic, wild swings but rather to cultivate small, daily shots of creativity that coalesce into meaningful results. When we build the habit and develop our skills, our shots become less risky and more impactful.

How Far You'll Go

In the 2016 animated Disney hit *Moana*, the namesake character lived on a tranquil Hawaiian island. Her family had lived there for generations, and they encouraged Moana never to leave. Things were comfortable on the lush island and although she was safe, she yearned for more. The sea called to her, and she knew she was destined to leave her cozy island to make her mark. The challenges and opportunities beyond the horizon were unclear to her, and she wasn't completely sure how far she'd go. But in her heart, she knew she had to leave the safe shores of her isolated island to fulfill her destiny.

For us, I fully recognize how safe our islands may feel. I appreciate that it takes a little courage to get into our boats and sail into uncharted waters. However, the skills we've learned together will make your quest far safer, giving you all the needed tools to reach your destination. Armed with your newly developed skills, it's time to cast off and sail toward your full creative potential. It's time to see just how far you'll go.

Lin-Manuel Miranda wrote "How Far I'll Go," the song that Moana sang as she sailed away from safety in search of purpose and adventure. In the lyrics, Moana sings of her deep desire to explore the boundaries and go beyond what others expected of her. Every road seemed to lead her back to the water, where she could sail free and discover what's possible. Staring out into the distance, she wonders how far it goes, referring not only to the sea but also to how far she can go as a person. An inner voice calls her to travel to new places, reach new heights, and change the world around her. She realizes that she needs to sail into unknown waters to discover just how far she'll go. I can't think of a more fitting and inspiring scene to depict the calling we all share: to become everyday innovators and leave our own fingerprints on the world.

As we conclude our time together, I wish you success and fulfillment as you sail off into the horizon to explore your own creative abilities.

It's time to take your shot.

It's time to see just how far you'll go.

Acknowledgments

Writing a book may appear to be a solitary act, but the endeavor is truly a team sport. This work would not have been possible without the unyielding support of my crew, to whom I'm deeply grateful.

To my incredible partner in crime, soul mate, wife, and hero Tia Linkner…you inspire me and push me to be my best. Without your unconditional support, this book would have never come to life. Thank you for being my muse, my editor, my therapist, and my inspiration. I love you…and some.

A gigantic thank-you to my colleagues at Platypus Labs. My longtime business partner Jordan Broad, the hysterically funny Matt Ciccone, the extraordinary and dashing Connor Trombley, the mysterious Kaiser Yang, and Lina Ksar, the quiet assassin. It is a great honor to work with you, and I'm grateful for your commitment to making the world a more creative place. A big shout-out to Tori Anderman, whose research was instrumental in this effort.

As this book came to life, I enlisted the help of some of the smartest people I know to be test readers. These poor souls read the rough manuscript chapter by chapter. They then provided invaluable feedback that made the final product far better. Thank you to

Acknowledgments

Alex Banyan, Ben Nemtin, Mike Scott, Renita Linkner, Bill Wood, Suneel Gupta, Ryan Deisenroth, Ethan Linkner, Gabe Karp, John Tracy, Scott Schoeneberger, Robb Lippitt, Rich Gibbons, Lenny Cetner, Michael Farris, Nick Tasler, Peter Sheahan, and Barry Demp. I truly appreciate your contribution.

A big thanks to the team behind the launch and publication of this book: Anthony Ziccardi, Maddie Sturgeon, and Meredith Didier at Post Hill Press; Mark Fortier and Megan Posco at Fortier Public Relations; Shannon Marvin from Dupree Miller; and social media whiz Chris Field.

Thanks to the many innovators who permitted me to interview them for this book, including Mat Ishbia, CEO, United Shore Mortgage; Coss Marte, CEO/founder, CONBODY; Jesse Cole, CEO/owner, Savannah Bananas; Mark Wallace, Wallace Detroit Guitars; Johnny Cupcakes, CEO/founder, Johnny Cupcakes; Caron Proschan, CEO/founder, Simply Gum; Chad Price, CEO/founder, Mako Medical; Greg Schwartz, COO/cofounder, StockX; Jeff Citty, Director, Innovation Academy, University of Florida; Mallory Brown, activist, filmmaker, founder of Walk-a-Mile; Duncan Wardle, former head of innovation, Disney; Massoud Hassani, CEO/founder, Mine Kafon; Rich Sheridan, CEO/founder, Menlo Innovations; Dustin Garis, former Chief Troublemaker, P&G; Nicholas Horbaczewski, CEO/founder, Drone Racing League; Taras Kravtchouk, CEO/founder, Tarform; Olga Khazan, author of *Weird: The Power of Being an Outsider in an Insider's World*; Asaf Kehat and Ayal Lanternari, cofounders, nanobébé; and Trewin Restorick, CEO/founder, Hubbub.

I received so much professional guidance and support from industry colleagues and friends, including Nick Morgan, Peter Sheahan, Tim Sanders, Jon Reede, Marc Reede, Alec Melman, Daniel Ymar, Barrett Cordero, Ken Sterling, Nancy Vogl, Duane

Ward, Shawn Hanks, Brian Lord, Angela Schelp, Richard Schelp, Rich Gibbons, Kelly Eger, Christine Farrell, Martin Perlemuter, Mark Castel, Gordon Alles, Neil Pashricha, Johnny Cupcakes, John Foley, Jim Keppler, Warren Jones, Kelly Skibbe, Matt Jones, Kristin Downey, Victoria Labalme, Brittanny Kreutzer, and Jennifer Lier. Thank you x100!

A big shout-out to my strange and creative family. To my four kids: Noah, Chloe, Avi, and Tallia. I'm so proud of you and love you beyond all reason. A profound thank-you to Renita Linkner, Larry Warren, Constantin and Marcelle Kouchary, Ethan and Tara Linkner, Sara and Nick Zagar, Ryan and Carla Deisenroth, Michael Farris and Joe Wert, and all my crazy cousins, nieces, and nephews. A special salute to my four-pound Yorkie, DaVinci—the little-little dog with a big-big heart who kept me company throughout this writing. And to those we've lost who still played an important role in the ideas set forth: Leonard Linkner, Ronnie Linkner, Robert Linkner, Benjamin Farris, Mickey Farris, and Monica Farris Linkner.

Finally, thank *you* for devoting a few hours toward your own creativity. I hope you've learned and laughed, and I wish you tremendous creative success ahead. Go make some trouble!

Josh Linkner
Fall 2020
Detroit, Michigan